CUT
THE
CLUTTER

Cynthia Townley Ewer of OrganizedHome.com

CUT
THE
CLUTTER

A SIMPLE ORGANIZATION PLAN for a CLEAN and TIDY HOME

Penguin
Random
House

For Steve, who knows why

Writer Cynthia Townley Ewer
Project Editor Diana Craig
Project Editor, revised edition Anne Hildyard
Project Designer Saskia Janssen
Jacket Designer Nicola Powling
Pre-production Producer Andy Hilliard
Print Producer Che Creasey
Creative Technical Support Sonia Charbonnier
U.S. Managing Editor Lori Cates Hand
Managing Editor Lisa Dyer
Managing Art Editor Marianne Markham
Art Director Maxine Pedliham
Publishing Director Mary-Clare Jerram
U.S. Publisher Mike Sanders

First American Edition, 2006
This edition published in the United States in 2016 by
DK Publishing, 345 Hudson Street, New York, New York 10014

A catalog record for this book is available from the Library of Congress.
ISBN 978-1-4654-5305-1

DK books are available at special discounts when purchased in bulk for
sales promotions, premiums, fund-raising, or educational use. For details,
contact: DK Publishing Special Markets, 345 Hudson Street, New York,
New York 10014 SpecialSales@dk.com

Printed and bound in China

All images © Dorling Kindersley Limited
For further information see: www.dkimages.com

A WORLD OF IDEAS
SEE ALL THERE IS TO KNOW

www.dk.com

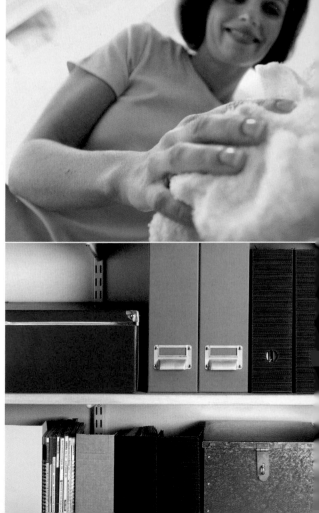

contents

6 My journey to an organized home

8 **A well-run home**
Solving the problems of clutter, disorder, and dirt

16 **Skills for a well-run home**

18 Decluttering your home
The STOP clutter method;
what's your clutter personality?
decluttering throughout the house

36 Organizing your home
How organized is your home?
Principles of organizing

48 Cleaning your home
Commercial cleaning products; "green" cleaners
from the pantry; choosing cleaning tools; tips
from the pros; teaching kids to clean

72 Planning your home
Daily do-its; weekly and monthly checklists;
time-saving tips; habit, the wonder worker;
the Household Notebook

88 **Cycles of an organized home**

90 Food
Plan, save, organize, store
Menu planning; shopping tips; food storage
guidelines; decluttering the kitchen; creating
activity centers; setting up a pantry

122 Clothing
Plan, shop, launder, store
Planning wardrobes; clothes buying guide;
decluttering and organizing closets and drawers;
clothes care; laundry basics

154 Surfaces & systems
Select, save, maintain, clean
Walls, floors, fine furniture, beds and mattresses;
plumbing and electrical systems; safety tips and
emergency checklist

178 Room to live
Cut clutter, organize, clean
Where does your clutter pinch?
Decluttering and organizing bathrooms, bedrooms,
linen closets, and family rooms; organizing books;
household storage

218 Paper and finances
Sort, save, organize, store
Setting up an information center; decluttering
paperwork; household filing systems

232 Resources
234 Index
240 Acknowledgments

My journey to an **organized home**

Folks who know me only through my writing imagine a lot of things: that I'm blonde (sorry, brunette here), that I'm tall and willowy (I wish!), and, most of all, that I am naturally organized, tidy, and frugal. That sound you hear is hearty laughter, and it comes from those who know me best: my husband, daughter, and son. They know the truth: that I was playing hooky the day that innate organization ability and financial skills were handed out.

I am not naturally organized, but I have learned how to be —the hard way. I know the exact day when my journey to an organized home began: December 25, 1983. That's when I realized that I had a problem with clutter and chaos, and that I needed to find a solution to create an orderly and happy home for my family and me.

It was the evening of Christmas Day. Recently divorced, I had sent my two young children to spend the day with their father, so I visited my parents' home for Christmas dinner. But when I returned to my little house late that night, broken glass littered the front porch. Someone had tried to break into my house while I was away!

I called the police and waited, shivering on the porch. An officer responded, approached the house cautiously, and slipped inside my front door. A few minutes later, he emerged, scratching his head. "Lady," he said, "I don't understand it. Your deadbolt held and the door wasn't opened—but somebody got in and ransacked your upstairs."

Guilty secret

Embarrassed warmth flooded my face. "No, no," I protested, "that's just the way I left it!"

The officer peered at me keenly. "Do you know what it looks like up there?"

To my immense shame, I did. The two rooms that served as my home office, bedroom, and sewing area were knee-deep in crumpled photocopies, legal pads, fabric scraps, piled

clothing, holiday wrap, stacked files, spilled coffee, and dirty dishes. Dust festooned the corners, and a narrow path wound through the mess to the islands of my desk and my bed.

New order

That night, I confronted the truth: I had a problem. I wanted to raise my children in a clean and comfortable home, but the place looked like a crime scene. I needed to learn what to do, how to do it, and when to do it to create the organized home my children and I deserved.

Next day, I began to search libraries and bookstores for guidance. I read books. I tried many different organizing methods. I learned about cleaning and began to plan and schedule housework in the same way as my business activities. Little by little, I learned how to conquer clutter, clean house, and run an organized home.

Did it work? Fast-forward five years to September 1988. I'd met a young doctor-in-training at the medical school library the week before, and this was to be our first date. My house was clean and orderly. My school-aged children were eating dinner at the kitchen table, as clean and orderly as it was in their nature to be. All was well as I opened the door.

My date followed me to the kitchen as I made coffee, and to my amazement, began to ask me about my calendar, my tickler file, and my family information center. I showed him my lists, my cleaning schedule, even the little note with the date and time of our date.

He seemed impressed, but I had a little sinking spell when the evening was over. How could I have shown this man my housekeeping system? What could he be thinking about my schedules and file cards and notebooks? They seemed a long way from the hip-mama image I wanted to project.

Homemaking skills

Later, I learned that he was impressed, indeed. On the night he proposed marriage, my husband Steve told me that he knew I was right for him from that very first evening. A fourth-generation physician, he understood that a doctor's wife has to be organized, self-reliant, and independent in order to deal with the demands of her spouse's profession. Nothing could have shown that capability more clearly, he felt, than the visible evidence of my skills as a homemaker that he saw when he came to my house on our first date.

Sharing the journey

Since 1998, I've taught those skills to the thousands of people who have visited my Web site, OrganizedHome.com—and more lately, to print readers who found the 2005 edition of this book. Along the way, I've learned much more than I've shared, traveling together with visitors and readers—male, female, older, younger—on the path to better home organization and management.

In this book, we'll take that same journey together. Our goal: a clean, organized, and cost-efficient home. The methods offered here worked for me, and they've worked for those who have found them on the Web or in the first edition of this book. Put them into practice and you'll find them working for you, too.

There's hope. There's help. Come join us!

Cynthia Townley Ewer

▶ **Need help** running a calm and cost-efficient household? Look to the Web! Clean your house, cut clutter, and save money with online tips and resources from OrganizedHome.com.

a well-run
home

The problem:
clutter, disorder, and dirt

How do you really feel about the state of the house? Here's a quick test: imagine that the doorbell rings. Is there panic in the pit of your stomach at the possibility of unexpected guests—or a bill collector? You're not alone. For many, clutter, disorganization, and dirt interfere with the day-to-day business of life at home.

Clean ... and green!

Taking aim on clutter is a great first step to more sustainable living. Tackle domestic chaos and live a greener life with these tips:

■ **Bag the bags.** Stow reusable shopping bags on a hook near the car keys. They'll be easy to grab on your way out the door—and will stop plastic supermarket sacks from invading your organized home.

■ **Junk the junk mail.** Removing your address from direct mail databases and calling catalog companies with stop requests takes time up-front, but saves the household—and Mother Earth!—from being buried in unwanted paper.

■ **Set free the surplus.** Recycling or repurposing unneeded appliances, clothing, tools, and craft supplies not only clears storage space, but also gives these items a new and useful life.

■ **Waste packaging waste.** Smart menu planning means less reliance on single-serve or convenience food items—and a corresponding reduction in needless food packaging. Build a pantry and buy in bulk to keep packaging waste to a minimum.

Sound far-fetched? Not for those of us who find it difficult to maintain a clean and organized home. Studies have shown that around 40% of American families find it difficult to keep their homes neat and organized.

For these families, keeping a clean house seems like an impossible dream. Working parents struggle to find time to clean. Disorganized spaces send the whole family into a tailspin on a regular basis. Clutter mounts up and puts the brakes on a streamlined, organized life.

Impossible standards

For all their numbers, they may as well be invisible. Modern media pummels people with misleading standards of perfection.

Even in real life, we seldom see the truth about our neighbors' clutter and chaos. At a friend's holiday open house, we admire the beautiful home, but don't realize that it was achieved only by tossing dirty clothes, surface clutter, and stacks of newspapers into a padlocked bathroom.

Perfect pitch: the haves and have-nots

Take heart: you are not lazy, crazy, or stupid. You just need to learn the skills necessary to create a clean and organized home.

Think of innate organizing ability as a kind of musical pitch. Some people have very little—they're the "tin ears" of the musical world. Others have perfect pitch: an inborn and accurate sense of which note is which and the relationships between them. The rest of us struggle at scales in-between.

In the same way, some folks naturally have an orderly relationship with their stuff. They keep things tidy without thinking, and they breeze through domestic life without turning a hair. They have the home management equivalent of perfect pitch hard-wired into their brains.

The rest of us have to work at learning organizational skills. But, just as we conquered musical scales and intervals, we can master planning and scheduling, cleaning, and clutter control. And, like a well-rehearsed recital piece, our organizing abilities strengthen and become part of us as we use them.

"Most of us are not born with organizing skills. They are something we must learn."

▲ **Children's toys** are one of the prime spawning grounds for clutter and disorder. Learning the necessary skills can help even the organizationally challenged to keep the problem under control.

Doing what doesn't come naturally

Problems arise when the two camps try to communicate. Tell someone who's been gifted with a big slug of organizational ability about your new menu plan, and you're apt to get a puzzled, "Huh? Doesn't everyone do that?" On the other hand, it's not always possible to benefit from the experience of a naturally organized person. For them, it comes easily, so they short-cut directions, assuming that the rest of us can follow.

Naturally organized people write way too many books about home organization. It's easy for them, so it should be easy for the reader, right?

Wrong. It takes one to know one—and to teach one.

The solution:
skill sets and cycles

How do you go from chaotic to controlled, cluttered to clean on the home front? Learn four simple skill sets, and apply them to the cycles of home keeping. In this book, we'll start with the basic skills needed to declutter, organize, clean, and plan a well-run home. Then we'll apply these skills to the cycles of life in every home: food, clothing, surroundings, paper, and finances.

Part One: Skills for a Well-run Home

In high school home economics classes, I learned to make bound buttonholes, set a pretty table, and bake a dozen cookies that were all the same size—but I wasn't taught the real skills needed to create a clean and organized home. How to keep clutter under control. How to organize and clean house. How to plan my time and family activities.

Think of Part One of this book as Home Ec 101 for the real world: an introduction to the four basic skill sets everyone needs—declutter, organize, clean, and plan.

Decluttering your home At bottom, the problem isn't about "stuff;" it's about the habits, personality traits, and thought processes that encourage the build-up of clutter.

In the declutter skill set, we learn a 20-minute method to banish clutter anywhere. We gain a deeper understanding of personality traits that encourage cluttering, and explore ways to fight the thought processes that tie us to our stuff. Finally, we share tips to deal with other people's clutter.

Organizing your home A well-organized home makes life flow smoothly, speeds cleaning, and means you'll never have to look for misplaced items again ... well, most of the time.

In the organize skill set, we focus on the three basic rules of home organization. We establish a place for everything, bring the family on board, and create activity centers to focus space and possessions. Finally, we look for storage solutions to contain clutter and make living spaces work.

declutter ▲ see pages 18–35   **organize** ▲ see pages 36–47

Cleaning your home It's not how long you clean. It's not how hard you clean. It's how efficiently you clean that makes the difference between grimy and gleaming.

In the clean skill set, we cover the basics of speed cleaning—cleaners, tools, and methods. We find out how to clean the way the pros do, fast and well. We stress teamwork, explore ways to bring children onboard, and share cleaning tips to get the family out the door and on to better things.

Planning your home It's an old saying: if you fail to plan, you plan to fail. Planning daily routines, housework schedules, and family activities is key to smooth sailing at home.

In the plan skill set, we explore the secrets of checklists, calendars, schedules and to-do lists. We share timesaving tips and point out time-traps to avoid. Finally, we discover the organized family's power tool: the Household Notebook.

Part Two: Cycles of an Organized Home

Around the house, the calendar turns—and so do the basic cycles of home life. Food and cooking. Clothing care. Dealing with clutter, cleaning, and organizing. Paper handling and bill paying. In Part Two, we apply our newfound skill sets to each of these major cycles.

Food In this first section, we tackle all aspects of food: menu and meal planning, grocery shopping, and food storage. We declutter, organize, and clean the kitchen, setting up activity centers to make it easy and quick to get the family fed. We also tackle bottom-dollar issues of energy efficiency, kitchen appliances, and setting up a pantry.

Clothing Section Two takes us into closets, dressers. and drawers as we organize all aspects of keeping ourselves clothed. We plan wardrobes, declutter, and organize the clothes closet, clean out clothing clutter, manage seasonal storage, and learn the best ways to launder and care for our clothing investment.

Surfaces and systems In Section Three, our surroundings start to shine. Here, we learn to care for walls, windows, floors, and furnishings, maintain bedding and mattresses, and get acquainted with household systems that keep us comfortable and safe. We focus on home safety and energy savings, too, as we make home a clean and comfortable place to be.

Room to live Section Four offers room-by-room help for clutter, cleaning, and organization issues. Whether it's the family room, children's areas, bedroom, or bath, we cut the clutter, get organized, and clean up quickly and well.

Paper and finances Section Five tackles information handling: sorting, organizing, and accessing paper and information. We learn which documents to keep--and how to keep them. Activity centers streamline bill-paying, filing, and paper handling.

clean ▲ see pages 48–71   **plan** ▲ see pages 72–87

The solution:
do it your way

Learning basic skills—how to declutter, how to clean—is only the first step on the road to better home management. To reach the goal of a clean and organized home, we must craft our own personal home management habits and routines. Any method we select must work with our unique personality, lifestyle, and strengths.

In home management, as with pantyhose, there is no such thing as "one size fits all." One person's list-based routine seems scattered and annoying to someone who prefers the tighter structure of a daily planner. Your neighbor swears by the scheduling advice she found online, but the tight blocks of time in her day don't work with your more casual approach. Your sister thinks it's essential to have all counters and surfaces bare of distractions; you can't work well unless you can see your tools and supplies.

Get personal

Knowledge is power—but self-knowledge is empowerment. Moving from disorder and chaos to effective, orderly living requires more than simple information or one person's example; it requires personally devised solutions that will work for you as an individual—not for your sister or your neighbor or anyone else.

Throughout this book, we'll help you tailor advice and recommendations to suit your own personality and family lifestyle. We'll identify your "clutter personality"—the habits and thinking that have caused you to become a clutterer (*see pages 30–31*)—and offer strategies to help you work in harmony with it.

"There is only one right way to get organized: yours."

Instead of establishing one level of "clean", we'll help you assess your own family's needs and constraints, so you can reach the right state of "clean enough" for your home.

Where do I start?

It's easy to pick up a book about home management, read along, laugh at the jokes, and put the book down again. Translating that experience into a cleaner, more organized home is another matter.

If you find yourself looking around your disorganized home and thinking: "Where do I start?" the simple answer is: you start where you are, then take a single step.

Getting organized isn't a race—it's a journey. On a journey, what matters is the trip, not where you start or how fast you make it, or where other people are along the way.

Too often, folks frustrated by the condition of their homes see getting organized as a hundred-yard dash: an activity with a beginning and an end and a lot of heated pounding in between. "I will clean things up," they vow, "and this time, it's going to stay that way!" A week later, they have little to show for all the effort, because they haven't effected the real change that will solve the problems of disorder and chaos.

To make that change, take a single step toward better organization, right where you are. Tomorrow, take another step toward better home life. And another. And another. Just as chaos and disorder didn't spring full-blown into your home in a single day, so it won't be conquered in one day, either. The important thing is to take the first step, make the first change—and just keep traveling.

▶ **Start small.** Developing good habits, like clearing up clutter that has accumulated at the end of each day, provides easy-to-see results that will help to keep you motivated.

Find fellow travelers

Anyone who's taken a walk with friends knows that sharing and friendship make even the roughest climb easier. It's no different in your journey to better home management. Look for like minds to walk with you and lighten the way.

There are a number of places where you might find potential fellow travelers. In your community, be alert for friends or neighbors who might form a support network for your get-organized efforts. Seek out a "declutter buddy": a friend who brings a detached view to decluttering sessions. Without the ties that bind, she'll help you see your stuff in

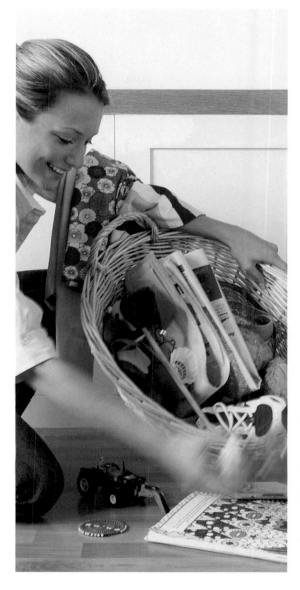

"The important thing is to take the first step—and just keep traveling."

a new light and help you release it; next week, it's your turn to help her clear out the closet. Check with church groups, clubs, or parents' associations to find other folks with whom to share your progress; their support will make all the difference and will help to keep you motivated and enthusiastic.

Dedicated support groups can be a wonderful source of accountability and motivation. In North America, Clutterers Anonymous (CLA) applies the Twelve Step program first modeled by Alcoholics Anonymous to issues of clutter and hoarding. Other clutter recovery support groups are offered by counseling centers or volunteer organizations. Community education services or church groups may offer classes and workshops on home management.

The Web offers a wealth of interactive support groups to help members inspire one another to get organized and run a sustainable, cost-efficient household. Friendly online communities share success stories, offer accountability, and cheer members on as they cut clutter and improve home management. Check the

Resources section (*see pages 248–249*) for Internet groups to help you cut clutter and save money at home.

Online or in real life, change is easier to come by when shared. Look for others to travel the road with you, to encourage you when you are flagging and to inspire you with their example, as you move toward your goal: better home and personal organization.

skills for a
well-run home

"Getting organized" means different things to different people, but in most disorganized homes, you'll find clutter.

Clutter gets between you and the things you want to do. Living in a cluttered home, nearly every action is handicapped and impeded. Either you're wasting time looking for something you need, pushing clutter out of the way to create a workspace, or you're simply distracted by the scatter of out-of-place items.

Problem is, attacking the clutter itself won't resolve the issue, because the "stuff" is just a symptom. What causes clutter is a cluster of personality traits, thinking, and behavior. To rein in clutter at home, you have to start with you: your thoughts, your habits, and your day-to-day behavior patterns.

Reversing the tide of clutter is a slow and steady job, but the rewards are great. In this section, we'll focus on basic methods to STOP clutter and retrain the family to a new, uncluttered outlook.

Clear clutter:
the STOP clutter method

Household clutter is made, not born. Its hidden cause? Deferred decision-making. Each item of clutter in your home represents a frozen decision or an incomplete action. Worse, the stale energy of piled clutter attracts more clutter, accreting together into an avalanche of pent-up "must-do, should-do, wanna-do" decisions that are tiring even to contemplate.

For example, bringing in the mail, you notice a catalog you'd like to browse, so you set it aside on the counter. Next day, three more catalogs, a stack of bills, and a page of pizza coupons land in the pile, and by the week's end, the lone catalog has mushroomed into an unwieldy stack of magazines, letters, bills, permission slips, and store receipts that will take an hour to sort, file, and finish—and you still haven't found time to peruse the new catalog. The STOP clutter method fights clutter at the heart by thawing the decision-making process. It's short,

◀ **Keep it brief.** To prevent flagging spirits, declutter in short sessions of between 15 and 20 minutes.

sweet, and powerful, and is designed to help you blast through all those frozen decisions quickly—no more sitting on the fence in the face of chaos! By forcing you to make decisions rapidly, you cut through the mass of clutter and regain your organized home. Using the STOP technique, you'll attack clutter in four easy steps: Sort, Toss, Organize, and Put away (see opposite).

STOP clutter tools

The tools you'll use for each STOP clutter session are simple. They're designed to set limits, encourage decision-making, and make it easy to wrap up each session of cutting clutter. You will need a kitchen timer, three large boxes, and a garbage bag.

sort ▲

toss ▲

4 **Put away.** When the timer bell rings, stop the session and put away the items in the Put Away box. Store the timer and boxes for the next STOP clutter session. Toss the garbage bag in the trash.

STOP clutter around the house:
declutter strategies

Just as clutter builds up gradually, reversing the flow takes sustained effort and there are limits to what you can achieve in a single STOP clutter session. You may make short work of the mess on a shelf, in a drawer, or on a countertop. But where do you start to tackle a whole house full of clutter? Answer: one step at a time. Use the following strategies to take your battle against disorder to a global level.

Where the shoe pinches

The process of cutting clutter can be psychologically uncomfortable, so bolster motivation by putting your first STOP clutter efforts where they'll bear the most fruit. Look for the places where the shoe pinches, and focus clutter-busting efforts where they'll count the most. If it's a challenge to get out of the house to work each day, for example, tackle the jumbled cosmetics on the bathroom counter, attack the clothes closet and clear clutter away from the key rack.

Front Door Forward

The most straightforward path through whole-house clutter? Use the Front Door Forward method. Start at the front door and move to the right around the house, decluttering as you go. Start each session next to the last area you cleared.

The advantages of Front Door Forward are that you always know which location is next in line for a clear-out. Better still, the house's public areas are decluttered first—no more wincing at the sound of a neighbor's knock at the door!

A Clean Sweep

Overwhelmed by a house full of clutter? Try doing a Clean Sweep. Once a day, grab a garbage can liner and circle the house, looking for trash which can be tossed without the need for decision-making. Grocery bags, unmated socks, broken kitchen tools, foods past their "use-by" dates, and makeup more than a year old are among the suitable candidates. When the garbage bag is full, toss it!

The Penicillin method

One day, you declutter the small table in the hallway. By the following week, a whole new species of clutter has infected the same area. One online declutterer, Ellen, likens it to a dish of mold, to which a lab researcher daily adds a single drop of penicillin. Next day, only the area around the drop is mold-free but, as the steady drop-drop-drop of the penicillin continues, the clean areas begin to grow together until the entire dish is cleared of mold.

To apply the Penicillin strategy, use the STOP clutter method to clear clutter from a small area each day. The following day, check to see that the first area is still clear, then move on to liberate another cache of clutter.

A Drawer-a-Day

Practitioners of Feng Shui believe that clutter and accumulated trash are traps for stale "chi," the energy that flows throughout home and life. Liberate the trapped chi step-by-step with the Drawer-a-Day method: fighting clutter by attacking it in small, daily nibbles.

Simply put, take 15 minutes to use the STOP clutter method (*see pages 20–23*) on a single drawer, shelf, countertop, or corner each day. Visualize restoring a free flow of life-giving energy as you declutter and clear each choked storage area or counter.

▶ **Clutter Costs!** Piled paperwork, misplaced bills, and hidden checkbooks get in the way of good financial management. Keep clutter at bay to keep the household bottom line healthy.

Short and sweet, a quick evening sweep makes for happy mornings. Before bed each night, patrol the house for out-of-place belongings. A records box or basket with handles makes it easy to gather up discarded shoes, magazines, plates and glasses, toys, television remotes, and schoolbooks. Circle the whole house and return items to their proper place.

Families with children do well to build family "put-away" time into the routines of daily life. Just as in any good preschool or kindergarten, returning playthings to their places at day's end trains children to habits of order—and keeps parents from stubbing toes on scattered toys in the middle of the night!

Keep clutter from
coming back

Getting to clutter-free is only half the job; you'll need to develop new attitudes and habits to keep clutter from coming back. Right-size household possessions with these strategies for sustainable clutter-free living.

Trash to **Cash**

Cut the clutter—and fatten your wallet—by selling unneeded items for ready cash:

- **Hold a yard, tag, or garage sale.** Take out ads, and be sure to note big-ticket items. Use group pricing—"Four for a dollar" or "$5 per bag"—to encourage sales. Arrange for a charity to pick up any unsold items at the end of the sale to make sure you sell out.
- **Sell online.** Online auction sites like eBay make it easy to find buyers for surplus books, craft supplies, collectibles, or electronics. Larger items find a new home when listed on www.craigslist.org for sale.
- **Consign it.** Consignment stores aren't just for clothing anymore. Fitness equipment, baby items, and children's clothing shops now offer an easy way to sell surplus items.
- **It pays to advertise.** Place low-cost classified ads when selling big-ticket items. Many newspapers and community centers offer free or low-cost classified ads for private sellers. Use this service for a quick way to find new homes—and a few extra dollars—for unneeded appliances, furniture, or fixtures.

Home, home on the range

A primary cause of clutter? It's the homeless ... mail, toys, or newspapers. Without a home, common household items wander, lose their way, meet bad companions, and make the transition to clutter.

Establish good homes for your stuff. Newspapers may be folded and stacked on a coffee table before being read, then given shelter in a box while they wait for recycling. Devote prime domestic real estate to use as a Launch Pad (*see pages 182–183*) for each family member: a location for purses, school papers, backpacks, and briefcases. Give paperwork proper files so it never has to huddle in lonely stacks on kitchen counters. With a home to go to, good stuff will never become bad clutter.

One-In, One-Out Promise

The simplest way to deny clutter houseroom? Make the One-In, One-Out Promise. For every new garment, video game, or magazine that enters your home, resolve that one older garment, video game, or magazine must leave. For example, when this month's issue of your favorite magazine arrives in the mail, set aside an older issue to share at the library. Pretty new towels may enter your home only if the older set is recycled for use as car-wash rags or put in the charity bag.

The No-Buy-It Diet

Go on a No-Buy-It Diet to build clutter-free habits and avoid buying more "stuff." The No-Buy-It Diet is simple: find ways to rent, borrow, or swap for items you need, rather than buy them. Try these No-Buy-It strategies to share the wealth and cut the clutter without buying new:

▲ Consume creatively to cut clutter—and lend a hand to Mother Earth! Repurpose or donate gently used clothing, or organize a wardrobe swap with friends to keep clothing in circulation—and out of the landfill.

■ **Video and computer games.** Stream or rent videos and computer games rather than buying them. Streaming media services bring movies to you without creating video clutter at home—and you'll have access to a large library of movies and TV shows. Borrow video games from the local library, or arrange a swap with friends and neighbors for a clutter-free alternative.

■ **Equipment for parties.** Throwing a party or reunion? Borrow special-use equipment like punch bowls or coffee urns from friends or community sources. Churches, community groups, and fast-food restaurants offer clutter-free access to specialty equipment for your celebration; at the end of the event, the items are returned for others to use.

■ **Youth sports equipment.** This can be costly and is often outgrown from season to season. Band with other parents to organize swaps of uniforms and equipment for children's sports activities. For example, ski swaps can outfit youngsters inexpensively before each season, and find new homes for outgrown ski boots at year's end.

"Organize a wardrobe swap with friends to keep clothing in circulation—and out of the landfill."

■ **Maternity and infant clothing.** Expecting a baby? Other moms are an excellent source of gently worn maternity and infant clothing, so swap and recycle instead of buying new. Circulate a "maternity box" of maternity clothing among a group of young-mom friends. After the child is born, remove worn-out items, and add any new clothing before handing the box on to the next expectant mother.

Observe oosouji

To hold the line against clutter, and start the New Year fresh, borrow a Japanese custom. To prepare for a happy and prosperous New Year, the Japanese perform *oosouji*, cleaning and organizing homes and offices in the run-up to New Year's Day. By this practice, they tie up the old year's loose ends and outstanding projects, and make room for the blessings and challenges of a new year.

Take a tip from the Japanese, and ring in the New Year from a clean and decluttered home. At year's end, create space in each shelf, cabinet, and closet for the new possessions that will come with a new year.

What's your
clutter personality?

It's silent. It's sneaky. It creeps about in corners: clutter. While it's tempting to launch an all-out battle in the war against clutter, it's best to know your enemy first. There are as many reasons for household clutter as there are clutterers. Target your household's clutter problem by going to the root of the problem: your own thinking.

The hoarder: "This might come in handy someday."

Know a hoarder by his or her collection ... of the most unlikely objects. Hoarders save everything, and I do mean everything: plastic shopping bags, newspaper flyers, and worn-out clothing. Hoarder creativity knows no bounds. Ask a hoarder why she's holding onto three years' worth of local newspapers, and she'll describe the papier-mâché angel figure she hopes to craft from them. Problem is, hoarding knows no limit, so our friend can't see that she has enough materials to create angels for each home in the subdivision ... and then some!

Hoarding is rooted in insecurity, financial or otherwise. Deep down, hoarders are afraid that they'll never have the resources they need if they let go of any possession, no matter how worn, useless, or superfluous. If cabinets and closets are crammed with cracked margarine containers, small kitchen appliances that haven't been used in decades, and old catalogs, there's likely hoarding behavior underlying the clutter.

Hoarders need to remind themselves that resources will always be available. Where can a hoarder look outside the home for a substitute hoard? Reassure yourself! Stuff will be with us always. Find magazines indexed at the library, kitchenware marked down at yard sales, and every small appliance known to man can be found (cheap!) at the thrift store. Think of these off-site treasure troves as attenuated household storage areas. Dare to dump it!

The deferrer: "I'll think about that tomorrow."

Those of the deferral mindset are guilty of the great set-aside. Bills, notices, old newspapers, items that need cleaning or repair, and household projects are all set aside to be dealt with another day. The deferrer will leave dinner dishes in the sink, wet laundry in the washer, and dropped fruit underneath the backyard apple tree.

Deferrers need to be reminded that tomorrow has no more time or energy than today—and that deferring decisions drags down each new day with yesterday's unfinished business. Since this behavior is grounded in procrastination, apply the best remedy: action. For deferrers, simply making a start creates the momentum needed to finish the job. Remember, it's easier to keep a rolling stone in motion, than it is to pick it up and start it rolling the first time!

How to push the inner deferrer off the dime? Force action with a cut-off date. For example, when you find an unfinished cross-stitch project, circle a date on the calendar, and make a note. If you haven't finished the project by that date, the item must go—but by making a start on the project, you're liable to keep going until you finish it. The jump-start of taking action is often enough to spark even the most confirmed deferrer's battery, so harness this effect to resume momentum on stalled clutter issues.

The rebel: "I don't wanna and you can't make me!"

Somehow, it's all Mom's fault. Rebels were forced to pick up after themselves as children; as adults, they're still expressing the mute and stubborn determination of a four-year-old who refuses to pick up his toys. Rebel clutter can be anything, but often centers on household activities. No, the rebel won't put his or her clothes in the hamper, cereal bowl in the dishwasher, or car in the garage—even when the clothing gets wrinkled, the cereal bowl hardens into yellow goop, and the car gets damaged by roadside traffic.

Rebels need to remind themselvwves that the war is over. They don't live at home with Mom and Pop anymore—and their own family deserves an adult on the job, not a sulky child. Tell that inner rebel, "It's okay—I'm the parent now, and I want a house that's nice to live in." By switching places with the old authority figure, it is possible for the Rebel to find a way out of the "I don't wanna!" mindset. By reminding yourself that you are in control of your decisions, you can defuse the inner rebel's imaginary power struggle.

The perfectionist: "Next week, I'll organize everything ... perfectly."

Perfectionists are wonderful people, but they live in an all-or-nothing world. They do wonderful things—when they do them! Perfectionism forms an inner barrier to cutting clutter because the perfectionist simply cannot abide doing a less-than-perfect job. Without the time to give 110 percent to the project, the perfectionist clutterer prefers to let matters—and the piles of stuff—slide.

For example, plastic food containers may be overflowing from their kitchen cabinet, but the perfectionist clutterer won't scrabble them to rights until he or she can purchase the perfect shelf paper, lid holder organizer, and color-coded folders and labels. As a result, the massed and crowded containers stay put, falling down onto the feet of anyone hapless enough to open the cupboard door.

Perfectionist clutterers need to remind themselves of the 20–80 rule: 20 percent of every job takes care of 80 percent of the problem, while fixing the remaining 20 percent will gobble 80 percent of the job. By giving themselves permission to do only 20 percent, perfectionist clutterers get off the dime and get going. It is perfectly fine to tell the inner perfectionist, "Today, I'll do the important 20 percent of that job: sorting, stacking, and organizing those food containers. Later, I'll do the other 80 percent, buying organizers and putting down shelf paper." If later never comes? Well, you've outwitted your inner perfectionist clutterer...congratulations!

The sentimentalist: "Oh, the little darling!"

Sentimentalists never met a memento they didn't like—or want to keep. Children's clothing and school papers, faded greeting cards, souvenirs from long-ago trips, and jumbled keepsakes crowd the environment of the sentimental clutterer. Problem is, there's so much to remember that the truly endearing items get lost in a flood. Who can find the first grade report card in an attic full of boxes of paper?

The sentimental clutterer needs to reduce the mass of mementos to a more portable state, changing his or her mindset from an indiscriminate "Awwww!" to a more selective stance. Remember, what's important to the sentimental heart are the memories and emotions. So, for example, a sentimental clutterer can corral each child's school papers into a single box by selecting one best drawing, theme, or project each month—everything else goes in the trash can.

Other ideas for reining in rampant sentimental clutter include scrapbooking the very best photos and papers, or photographing surplus sentimental clutter before letting it go. Sort it out, choose the best, keep the memories, and dump the rest!

Fighting clutter
from the inside out

It isn't just our homes that are clogged with useless stuff. Clutter takes hold of our minds, too. Psychological issues like fear or sentiment can prevent us from giving excess stuff the heave-ho. Solution: confront the inner forces that stand between your clutter and the trash can. Try these counter-measures to release your grip on clutter.

Scarcity thinking: "I might need it."

People with scarcity thinking refuse to part with clutter out of fear that they will not have—or will not have enough of—the goods and items they need at some future time. Result: drawers filled with folded aluminum foil and stacked egg cartons, garages drowning in bent nails and broken tools.

Deal with scarcity thinking by dragging your fear into the open and staring it down—then move past it to release the hold on your thinking. For example, confronted with a cabinet full of empty yogurt containers (no lids), ask yourself, "When was the last time that I ever used one?" An answer that ranges from "never" to "about 25 years ago" means that scarcity thinking is behind the clutter problem.

Face the fear! Remind yourself that the world is full of empty yogurt containers. Your belief that they might all disappear is just that—only a fear. Out they go, both the containers and the fear behind them.

Protecting an investment: "I paid good money for that."

Financial issues often bond us to clutter; a mental refrain of "But I paid $20 for that!" can keep us from releasing items we no longer need or want. Problem is, yesterday's purchase price no longer has much relationship to today's value. Prime example? Computer equipment. Three or four years after purchase, the actual value of a personal computer is only a fraction of the original price due to rapid advances in technology.

It's not what you paid for the item that matters; it's what it's worth today—and that is the value you must assess when considering whether to give the item houseroom or let it go as clutter. Online auction sites are wonderful allies in this process; they'll give you a quick, real-world value for any product. Knowing what something is worth today will shift your thinking and make it easier to part with the item and move on.

Thrill of the chase: "It's a collection."

Collecting can be fun, but it can also lead to immense clutter problems. In the thrall of pursuit and acquisition, little else matters—until you have to find homes for the new additions on already-crowded shelves. By the time a cherished collection must be stored in dusty attics or on high shelves, it's crossed the line and become clutter.

To break the bonds of collection clutter, assess your collection with an eye to finding the heart: those three or five or seven items with a true tie to your affection. Only those items with meaning, use, and value deserve a place in your home.

All in the family: "It was my grandfather's."

Family: it's the tie that binds—and binds you to unwanted stuff in the form of "heirloom clutter." Heirloom clutter is any item you don't want, don't need, don't use, and don't value, but which you keep because it once belonged to a family member.

We're not talking about true heirlooms. I have one: a beautiful quilt hand-made by my great-grandmother Kirchener. Each time I find the tiny squares of "ABC" fabric, salvaged from a childhood dress of my mother's, I feel the love of four generations in my hands. My quilt tells a story, and I will pass it—and its story—along to my own grandchildren.

Heirloom clutter is more like Grandpa's old sofa. It's tattered. It's ugly. You can't sit on it for fear that it will fall apart, but you can't get rid of it, either. Why not? "Because it's an heirloom!" Learn to distinguish between a true heirloom and heirloom clutter. To help, ask these questions:

- What do I know about this item?
- Do I have a memory related to this item?
- Does the item have use or value in my everyday life?

Identity crisis: "Those beer kegs were in my room in college."

Identity clutter is possessions we no longer use, but hold onto because they symbolize a younger, earlier identity. Identity clutter is easy to spot, because it's usually branded closely with

▲ **Be selective.** True family heirlooms deserve a place in an organized home, but not all inherited items qualify. Do keep your grandparents' love letters, but find a shredder for their utility bills.

its time and place. The macramé wall hanging you made at summer camp. Boxes of music CDs from your college years.

To cut the bonds of identity clutter, remind yourself that you are not your stuff. The memories and the growth are the true gift of these earlier identities. The leftover stuff no longer has a use, except to tie us down and hamper our current, richer life. To retain the memories, save a symbol of that stage of your life, and then release the identity clutter. Write a journal entry about your summer at camp and ditch the dusty macramé. Frame a selection of your favorite album art, and donate the music CD collection to the local thrift shop.

Dealing with
other people's clutter

Clutter issues, like red hair or blue eyes, tend to run in families. While an occasional brown-eyed, naturally organized joker does sometimes enter the pack, chances are that household clutter is a family problem. When you're taking the first steps down the road to order in your own life, other people's clutter can create major roadblocks. What can you do to deal with the clutter created by others?

Establish clutter preserves

There's no such thing as clutter-free living. Even the tidiest among us still tosses clothing on floors from time to time.

Accept reality by establishing dedicated clutter preserves. Like wildlife preserves, these are limited areas where clutter may live freely, so long as it stays within boundaries.

■ **In a bedroom,** one chair becomes the clutter preserve. Clothing may be thrown with abandon, so long as it's thrown on the chair.
■ **A kitchen junk drawer** can house vitamin bottles, rubber bands, clipped recipes, expired coupons, and shopping receipts that are unwelcome outside their clutter preserve.
■ **A large magazine bucket** in the living room is fair game for catalogs and magazines, so long as they can fit inside the bucket.
■ **Crafting, sewing,** or hobby projects create instant chaos—but too-rigid pick-up rules invade scarce crafting time. Dedicate a small folding table or outfit a spare closet for craftwork to keep inspiration flowing. To keep the hobby clutter in bounds, close the closet doors or screen the table between sessions.

Where to start? Change begins with you!

You've worked for weeks to declutter the family room and kitchen, and once again, you wake up to wall-to-wall mess. Other people's mess. Tempting as it may be to call a family meeting and lay down the no-clutter law, resist the urge. Any forced regime of clutter-free living will last only as long as you stand over family members and nag them to pick up their socks, newspapers, and toys.

Instead, recognize that change must begin with you. Only when you have met and mastered your own clutter challenges can you turn your attention to helping other family members along the path to order. Moreover, their progress will be just like yours: made in small steps. Just as you must make slow and steady progress toward building new habits, setting up activity centers, and cutting off new clutter at the source, so with other family members.

Tips for the family clutter consultant

Fighting over disorder and disorganization gets nobody anywhere—and it doesn't clear the clutter. Instead, adopt the role of clutter consultant to help other family members get a grip on clutter. Acting as a helper takes the heat off the dispute, and creates a sense of teamwork. Try these tips to inspire others to order in your household:

▶ **Storage areas** Create storage in a child's room: chests are good for tidying away toys, and baskets and containers can slide under the bed. A unit can hold files and books, and more baskets.

Work with the clutterer's personality "My-way-or-the-highway" clutter fixes are based on a faulty premise: that there's one right way to cut clutter and get organized. Wrong! Personality styles dictate the shape of successful clutter solutions. A clear-desk strategy that works for a visually oriented parent won't have meaning for a child who prefers his tools in view. Contain his colored markers in a cheerful mug on the desktop, rather than in a closed drawer, to respect his personality style.

Attack the problem, not the clutter Clutter is only a symptom; the true problem lies within the clutterer's relationship to stuff, space, and order. As a clutter consultant, your job is to attack the problem, not the stuff. Picking up a child's scattered papers after she returns home from school is a one-time symptom fix; setting up a Launch Pad for the child (*see pages 182–183*), and teaching her to visit it before and after school offers the true solution.

Be flexible Spouses, roommates, or housemates often disagree on what constitutes clutter. One person's trash is another one's treasure, and everyone has different tolerance levels, so why waste time defining your terms? A successful family clutter consultant is flexible, and reaches for solutions rather than confrontation.

In my home, husband Steve's poker materials had become an unwieldy collection of books, printouts, and scraps of paper that drifted from sofa to table to floor, depending on where Steve had been studying last. To my eyes, it was simply clutter, while to him, it was his poker library: an indispensable resource for a man who hopes to compete at a world-class level some day.

Solution: I designated a small shelf unit to accommodate his poker library. By making a home for the poker library, Steve has easy access to his reference materials—and I no longer have to see them piled across the breakfast table or heaped on the sofa.

Getting organized isn't about how the house looks: it's about how it works. How quickly can you wrap a gift, pay the bills, or change a sick child's bedding in the middle of the night? In an organized home, stuff and surroundings are arranged to make it easy to carry on the work of daily life.

Organization is more than simply stowing items neatly into boxes, cabinets, or drawers. It's about storing a household's supplies, tools, and materials in a meaningful, logical pattern—and in a way that makes it easy to return them after you're finished with them. Good organization speeds and simplifies every daily task.

In this section, we'll learn the basic principles of home organization, how to create activity centers to focus everyday tasks, and how to use containers to create an organized home. We'll also look at ways to involve all the family in organizing the home. Our goal: to create livable, workable space and storage that makes daily life flow smoothly.

How to
organize a home

Home. It's where the heart is, where you belong, come to recharge your batteries, and rest your head—and, for most of us, there's no place like it. Our homes are more than shelter from the elements; they are the stage on which we live our lives. Sentiment aside, however, just how well does your house work for you?

Think back to the last 24 hours. Were you out the door without delay ... or did you lose the car keys again this morning? At mealtimes, was it easy for family members to help set the table, or were the dishes stored too high, too low—or sitting, still unwashed, on the kitchen counter?

"Getting organized is not about how things look: it's about how things work."

When you went to bed, was it a relaxing transition from a busy day, or did you have to shove aside a pile of clothing and evict the dog from your pillow to rest your weary head? If daily life is getting you down, it's time to get organized.

Think function, not appearance

First, we need to get clear about what organizing is, and what it isn't. Organization is not a decorating style—it's about how well your home functions, not how it looks. A home organized with mismatched found-and-made containers can be far better organized than one fully outfitted with pricey built-in organizing "systems" that don't work. The paradox is that tidy houses are not always organized houses. Neat stacks of paper can hide

◄ **Getting organized** means having everything you need easily to hand so that you can perform the everyday tasks that keep home and life running smoothly.

unpaid bills and missed appointments. A clean and streamlined bedroom won't show the ripped and wadded clothing jammed into drawers or crammed into closets. By contrast, a busy desk may be the best evidence of an organized household: bills paid, papers filed, letters answered.

One can be tidy without being organized. Tidying is the process of returning out-of-place possessions to their homes. But what if those items don't have the right homes in the first place? Then you're back at Chaos Point One, still looking for the house keys, your wallet, or the dog's leash. "Put away" does not necessarily equal "organized." So don't fall for the organized look. Go for the organized function—it's what makes the difference between chaos and calm.

Think process, not product

Pick a yard sale, any yard sale. Chances are, some pretty pricey organizing products will be featured for sale: rotating plastic turntables; bathroom shelf units; specialty organizers like can holders; tie racks, and shelf extenders. All on sale for a tiny fraction of their retail price—and all mute witnesses to a would-be organizer who has confused "getting organized" with "buying stuff."

There's a difference between organization and the products you'll use to achieve that goal. Organization is a process, not a product. It involves time and thought, effort and motivation—and you can't buy these factors in any store. No tangible item, no matter how useful, can set you on the road to better organization all by itself. The moral is: nobody got organized by buying stuff. Instead, they ended up holding a yard sale.

The rules of
home organization

The bottom-line test for organization is function. Does your house work for you? Can you find things, carry out tasks, and live daily life without stress? To organize a home, follow the three rules of home organization: a place for everything, bring the family on board, and create centers for household activities.

1 A place for everything.

It's an old saw, but it still cuts: "A place for everything, and everything in its place" is a watchword for true home organization. Possessions, like people, need homes. Find them that home, defend their turf with labels, dividers, and organizers, and you've won most of the battle for an organized home.

> "It's an old saw, but it still cuts: 'A place for everything, and everything in its place.'"

Be creative when it comes to finding homes for household stuff—and rearrange your thinking. So what if stores sell towels in matched sets of three? Break up the trio and store them where they're needed: hand towels stacked in washrooms near living areas; bath towels and washcloths in the bathroom where they're most used. Don't hide pizza coupons and take-out menus away in a kitchen drawer where they'll get forgotten: store them in a folder near the phone where they'll be most useful.

2 Bring the family on board.

Getting organized is not simply a matter of domestic real estate; it's an integrated process involving all members of the household. Any organizing scheme or system will fail unless all family members understand it and can follow it. Bring the family on board as you organize your stuff and your surroundings. For example, when organizing where to put items in the kitchen, store plates, bowls, and unbreakable glasses in low cabinets. Younger family members can set the table only if they can reach the dishware; by storing tableware in an accessible place for them, you'll be helping all of the family to help you.

3 Create "centers" for household activities.

Looking for a model of a well-organized home? Head back to preschool! Preschool teachers are model organizers because they have to be. Without a plan for classroom structure, 18 or 20 energetic little people could create plaything havoc in mere moments.

To keep their schoolroom running smoothly, preschool teachers apply the concept of "centers": dedicated areas for a single activity, like blocks, dress-up, or sand play, with storage for all the playthings required by that activity. In the playhouse, kitchen toys, pots, and pans encourage role-playing; at the art table, paper, paints, and brushes are within easy reach. At pick-up time, children know to return costumes to the dress-up pole, and park the trucks in the "parking lot" storage area.

On the domestic front, you can set up centers that work the same way, to focus and support the everyday activities that are carried on in the home. To create them, you'll designate:

- **A focus.** Allocate one focused activity to each center.
- **A specified area.** Set aside a single place to perform the activity.
- **Storage for tools and supplies.** Ensure that all items needed are present and available in the center.

Creating centers

Consider establishing these activity centers for your home. Tailor them and their contents to your family's needs.

■ **Telephone** (phone directory, family address book, family calendar, message pad, pens, folder containing pizza coupons and take-out menus)
■ **Grooming** (skin-care products, shaving tools, cosmetics, and hair care implements near a bathroom sink and mirror)
■ **Outdoor clothing** (coats, hats, gloves, scarves, umbrellas, and galoshes in a closet near the door)
■ **Cleaning and caretaking** (mops, broom, and vacuum, cleaning tote with tools, cleaning products for refills, replacement light bulbs, cleaning cloths and sponges, specialty cleaners)
■ **Paper handling** (desk, telephone, computer, file box or file drawer, pens, paper, and checkbook)
■ **Correspondence basket** (stationery, selection of greeting cards, pens, envelopes and stamps)
■ **Recycling center** (bins for recycled materials, bags and twine for packaging, scissors)

■ **Reading** (comfortable chair, reading light, small table for beverage, reading glasses, pillow, highlighters, and page markers)
■ **Homework** (table, good lighting, pens and markers, paper, reference books)
■ **Entertainment** (television, remote controls, TV schedule, seating, snack trays, placemats)
■ **Fix-it desk** (workbench, lighting, toolboxes, organizers for hardware such as nails)
■ **Laundry** (washing machine, tumble dryer, folding space, stain pre-treatment, bleach, detergent, fabric softener, laundry sorter)
■ **Arts and crafts** (workspace, lighting, storage for paints, paper, glue, and embellishments)
■ **Mending** (sewing machine, iron and ironing board, sewing tools, fabrics and supplies)
■ **Planning and scheduling** (desk area, computer, planner or electronic organizer, office supplies, coupon organizer)
■ **Wrap and mail center** (mailing boxes, postal scale, gift wrap, ribbon and gift cards, scissors, tape, pens and marking pen)

bathroom center ▲ see pages 186–187   **play center** ▲ see pages 206–207   **paper center** ▲ see pages 220–221

Browsing the kitchenware aisle in any department store, it's easy to stray into a cluttered mindset—and from there, a cluttered kitchen. Trendy single-use gadgets or designer pan sets are a sure road to a clogged kitchen—and they won't make you a better cook.

When establishing centers in the kitchen, think "less is more" and limit each center to the bare-bones tools necessary to do the job. Pluck the three most-used saucepans and a good skillet from the big-box gift of matched pots and pans. Hone down the knife collection to the four or five knives you use most often. Focus on the favorite baking pans that see the inside of the oven on a regular basis.

Paring the contents of kitchen centers to essential tools makes the most of scarce kitchen real estate and simplifies food preparation—allowing the cook to focus on the food.

First principles:
organizing basics

As we get organized room-by-room around the house, keep these basic principles in mind. Whether it's crammed closets or cluttered counters, these central organization strategies will help keep order on the home front.

Hot, warm, or cold?

It's a simple but powerful premise: items that are used the most should be easiest to reach. Think of organized spaces as having storage locations that are hot, warm and cold, and store tools and supplies according to how often they're used.

■ **Hot zones**, like the fronts of drawers, shelves at eye level, and storage space on a counter, are home to the most used items. These are areas your hand can reach with little or no effort, such as the tool caddy next to the stove. This is where to store your favorite spoons, whisks, and ladles for easy access to these cooking best friends.

■ **Warm zones** are a bit harder to reach—like the space at the back of the drawer or the shelf near the top of the cabinet. You'll need to stretch or bend, or open doors wider to reach a warm zone. Send items you need infrequently, such as once a week or once a month, to the warm climes. Peelers, large pots, and baking dishes can all happily live here. You'll know where they are when you need them, but they won't impede your work the rest of the time.

■ **Cold zones** (otherwise known as Outer Siberia) are those storage places that must have been designed by a chiropractor to encourage business. They're dark. They're obscure. They're hard to reach without a step stool or assuming a posture on your hands and knees. The back recesses of the bottom shelf, or the cabinet above the refrigerator that can only be reached with a ladder, are cold-zone territories. Here's where you put those items that you use least, such as gelatin molds, seasonal baking pans, and serving platters for big parties. Think of it this way: the cold will keep them fresh!

Label, label, label

In the middle of a sort-and-toss-it session, an organizer's design seems obvious, but over time, that data can be lost. Facing a linen closet, our mental outline of "I'll stack the children's sheets here, the beach towels over here, and the winter blankets down here ..." lasts only until the first late-night rummage for clean sheets jumbles the tidy piles.

Solution? Labels, labels, and still more labels. Picture labels for children. Computer-printed labels. Labels by the sheet, or created one-by-one by electronic label-makers. Repeat after me: "There is no such thing as too many labels."

Labels make any organizing scheme crystal-clear. They show everyone, not just the organizer, where things belong. Babysitters or house guests will always know where to find the towels—and where to replace them—when the linen closet shelves are labeled.

When moving, labels on boxes help to get the contents to the right place in the new house. For seasonal storage, labels prevent the need to open-and-dig for the holiday lights. On the electrical panel, labels can show exactly which switch to throw to shut down the leaking hot water heater.

Harder to get out than to put away

Professional child-wranglers, such as day-care operators, know a simple secret: to keep things neat, make it harder to get something out than to put it away. It's just human nature. When we want something, we want it, and we'll work hard to get it, too. But when it comes to putting it back.... Take advantage of human nature and make things harder to get out than to put away.

▶ Children's toys and cards can be easily and quickly thrown into a sturdy basket at the end of the day. If you stick a photo label on the front of the basket, your child will begin to get into the habit of putting away his or her toys.

"Repeat after me: 'There is no such thing as too many labels.'"

Go vertical

For books, files, or papers, vertical storage beats horizontal storage every time. What is horizontal storage? It's a pile. A stack. One thin, rectangular object stored on top of another. A stack of books on a coffee table. Files in a tray on a desk. Magazines stacked next to a table, on the floor. To reach one book, one file, one magazine, you must move them all—and chances are, you won't take time to move them all back.

Vertical storage, like that offered by hanging files or bookcases or tabletop file boxes, makes it easy to find the file or letter you need. Simply flip through the hanging files, peeping at the papers within. In a vertical magazine file, it's easy to find the issue you want—and you won't disturb the rest of the magazines when you pull it from the storage box.

Our child's book flip-file illustrates the principle perfectly. Finding the right book is a matter of flipping through the covers; replacing it doesn't require moving the other books. Similarly, sewing enthusiasts know that hanging fabric lengths from clothes hangers makes it much simpler to find the fabric they're looking for—and with no need to disturb other lengths folded in a pile.

In geometry, there's no preference, but when organizing, take the vertical over the horizontal any day!

▶ Hanging file folders allow quick search-and-replace options for stored paperwork. Documents can be filed in alphabetical order, or simply by subject. Whichever way you decide to do it, label each section in the pop-up plastic sleeve so that you can quickly retrieve the file you need.

Saving money on
organizing products

Don't be fooled into thinking that buying specialty organizers is the only way to solve a clutter problem. Useful as these products can be, they'll become clutter themselves if you haven't done the heavy organizational lifting first. Shop sensibly and save money with these tips for choosing organizing products.

Organize, measure, buy

Take a common problem: magazine storage. Faced with a bookcase filled with favorites, it's tempting to say, "Oh, I must do something about those stacks of magazines," grab the car keys and head to the store. Once there, buying a set of 12 plastic magazine holders (in the same color as the family room drapes) appears to be the right solution.

Home you go—only to find that the holders are too big for the bookcase, and that the whole collection will require eight more containers to hold the entire stack. Wallet drained and energy depleted, you drop the whole project, leaving the new holders to swell the population of household clutter.

Smart organizers understand how the process works: they organize first, measure next, and buy—if they buy—last. First, they assess and sort the magazines, keeping only 20 percent: those periodicals to which they refer often.

After recycling the rejected 80 percent, our organizer plans and measures available storage areas. Only then does she shop for organizational products—and she does so with a list that enables her to buy exactly what she needs.

Put organizers to work for you by following these tips for making the most of the storage products available.

Corral and contain Cartons, boxes, baskets, and containers
are the organizer's foot soldiers in the war against chaos. Use them to sort and store magazine collections, children's toys, and arts-and-crafts materials. Open containers are ideal for often-used items, making them available but keeping them from spreading over living areas.

Climb the walls Hooks, pegs, and hangers provide bonus
storage in tight places. Pegs near an entryway allow children to hang coats and hats when they enter the house. The dog's leash and the car keys will never go missing if they have designated hooks near the back door. Narrow molding shelves intended for displaying picture frames are ideal to hold diaper and skin-care products near baby's changing table.

On the shelf Wall-mounted shelf units are hard-working
members of the get-organized team. Over-the-door shelving provides an instant pantry when stocked with canned goods. A shelf above the washing machine stores laundry products so they are accessible to adults but safe from children and pets.

For maximum storage power, combine plastic containers or wicker baskets with shelves. Color-coded containers help children keep their play spaces tidy. Low, flat wicker baskets make it easy to see and access toiletries in the bathroom.

Divide and conquer Drawers are great friends. There's only
one problem: open and close a drawer ten times, and you're apt to find a scrambled mess thereafter. Fix the problem with drawer dividers. Use short, straight lengths of cardboard or plastic to create divided areas or go for commercial drawer dividers: some offer different-sized trays that interlock to create custom dividers.

▶ **Reuse and repurpose** found items to get the benefit of commercial organizing products without the hefty price tag. Recycle product packaging, cardboard and containers, or visit yard sales for low-cost—and sustainable—organizing alternatives.

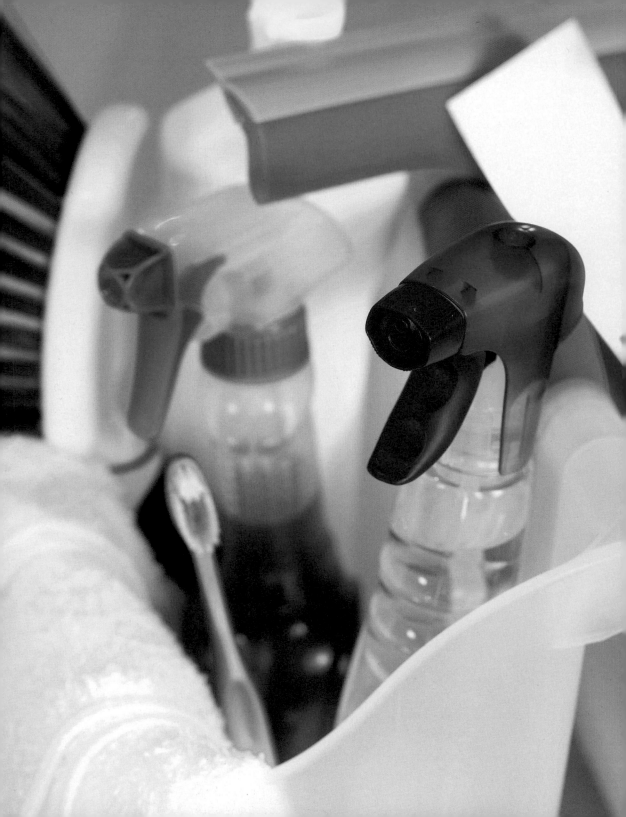

Cleaning house. It's a dirty job, but somebody has to do it. Chances are, dirt and disorder have taken over your home. Do you have the cleaning skills you need to keep a sparkling house?

Setting the right standard for "clean enough" brings a sensible reality check to the job of keeping a clean house. Learning to clean efficiently speeds house-cleaning chores and saves energy. Tapping family teamwork provides extra manpower (and woman- and child-power) to get the job done fast, while training younger family members in cleaning skills. Choosing the right cleaning products and tools—and using them effectively—matches the method to the mess, cuts costs, and helps preserve the environment. Scheduling cleaning chores helps deal with dirt and grime early, before it becomes entrenched and stubborn.

In this section, we'll learn the basic cleaning skills that keep a household healthy and happy. Got your apron and your cleaning tote? Ready, set ... clean!

Setting standards for
the "clean-enough" home

How clean is your house? It's a matter of choice: yours. While it may sound like heresy to the "cleanies" among us, the happiest families establish a standard for household cleanliness that suits their family composition, cleaning style, and personal preferences.

Set the right standard—for you

Some families—such as those with crawling babies or immuno-compromised elders—will need to reach for a very high standard of cleaning. Others, such as a clan of healthy young adults, can live quite happily in a home with a more-relaxed cleaning style. While nobody advocates ignoring cleaning to the point of health and safety problems, a realistic view of your family's cleaning standard prevents frustration—and helps get the work done faster.

Reach for family agreement on the issue of a cleaning standard. If most household members fall on the "relaxed" side of the equation, there'll be cleaning trouble if one member pushes for higher standards.

Negotiate a common-sense compromise. Food preparation areas require a high level of sanitation, but a teen's bedroom poses fewer health and safety concerns. Better to pick cleaning battles carefully, with an eye to general well being, than fight it out over every speck of dust.

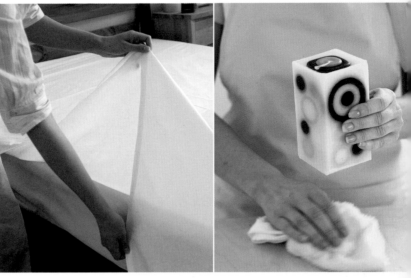

▲ **Clean smart** by setting a realistic cleaning standard for your home. Schedule chores to keep a clean house every day.

▲ **Be realistic** about where to insist on a higher cleaning standard. Children's rooms and kitchen areas demand a higher level of clean.

▲ **More relaxed** cleaning standards are appropriate in less-used areas. Go easier on the chores in guest bedrooms or utility areas.

Where does your family fall on the cleaning spectrum? Try this quiz: it will help you assess the sweet spot of "clean-enough" for your home. There are no right or wrong answers.

1 When dinner is over, what's the state of the kitchen?

A Pristine, of course. I load the dishwasher as I cook, and dinner dishes are done promptly. I can't relax if the kitchen doesn't sparkle when I turn out the lights. Who wants to come back to a dirty kitchen in the morning?

B I let the dinner dishes soak until next day. Who wants to ruin a good meal by spending time with their hands in hot water afterward?

C What's the difference? The counters are still covered with dirty dishes; I just washed the ones we needed before the meal.

2 How's your relationship with the vacuum cleaner?

A Who needs a man when I have my high-speed vacuum cleaner? Even the cat has learned to stand still for the daily vacuuming.

B Love-hate. I show it the carpet every week or so, or when friends are on the way over—but I do wish it would learn to lower its voice.

C What vacuum cleaner? I'm still hoping a cleaning reality show will stop by and dig us out. Public exposure would be a small price to pay!

3 Getting to the seat of the problem, how often do you scrub the toilet?

A As often as I use it, of course. Who wants to park themselves on anything less than sparkling?

B Hit or miss—a couple of times a week, more often if the fellows in the house forget to aim.

C Only when something snarls at me when I lift the lid ... say, every few weeks?

4 For sweetest dreams, how often do you change the sheets?

A Once a week—or twice a week in warm weather. I love the feel of crisp, fresh linens.

B When I remember, or the smell gets to me. Say, every couple of weeks or so?

C Only when I have a new boyfriend, if you know what I mean. Why waste good laundry powder and water if I'm going to be too sleepy to notice?

5 Are you a duster or a dabbler? How often do you remove dust from the home?

A Daily, of course; it's a ritual. Some of my finest ideas come to me while I stroke the furniture with my dust cloth.

B Once a week or so—or whenever the household joker writes "Dust Me" on the dining-room table with his finger.

C I'm a fan of the blow-it method. If I pick something up and it's covered with dust, I blow it off. Great household hint, huh?

If you answered mostly A, congratulations! You are a Clean Extreme, and happy to be so. Your house shines, and any dust mote so unwise to assert its presence is shown the door, pronto. Just be careful that militant cleaning doesn't come between you and other family members, who don't necessarily share your enjoyment of the process.

Mostly B answers show you're a Moderate Mopper, with a house that is clean enough to be healthy, dirty enough to be a home. Most of the time, you're happy with the balance between time spent cleaning and the domestic results, but occasionally, you slip a bit too far toward slapdash. Try a more scheduled approach to clean less and enjoy it more.

More than three C answers? You're a Dirt Dodger. Too often, you're discouraged about life on the home front. Remember this truth: if you don't wanna, you ain't gonna. To pull the household back from the dusty brink, focus on small changes: clearing kitchen counters once a day, setting aside an afternoon each weekend for cleaning chores.

Choosing and using
cleaning products

Cast your eyes down the cleaning aisle at the supermarket lately? An explosion of new cleaning products has created a dizzying array of choices for a clean house. Cut the confusion and save money by sticking to four basic cleaning products.

Together with a few specialty products, spray window cleaner, spray degreaser, tile and bathroom cleaner, and abrasive cleanser will handle everyday cleaning needs cheaply and well.

Window cleaner Don't be misled by the name "window cleaner;" this spray-on product cleans windows and a whole lot more, evaporating quickly and leaving no residue behind. Applied to glass or mirrors, it loosens surface dirt so you can remove it with a squeegee or cleaning cloth. Use on glass, mirrors, kitchen counters, sink fixtures, appliance fronts, refrigerator shelves, sealed cabinet fronts and any other liquid-safe surfaces with light, non-greasy soil.

Degreaser The tough guys of the cleaning world, these spray cleaners dissolve greasy soil so it can be lifted away and removed. Also known as "all-purpose cleaners," they will cut food soil on kitchen counters, greasy fingermarks on walls, doors and switch plates, oily dust on baseboards and moldings, and hard-to-remove dirt on outdoor furniture. Polish surfaces with a dry cloth to remove the slight film they leave behind.

Tile and bathroom cleaner The bathroom poses multiple cleaning challenges—sticky film from body oils, soap, and shampoo; mold and mildew from moisture and condensation; yellow, chalky, hard-water residues on fixtures

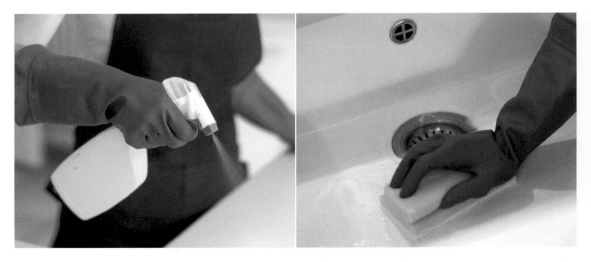

▲ **Save on spray cleaners** by diluting them with varying amounts of water. For many cleaning chores, full-strength cleanser is overkill; mix your own and save.

▲ **Elbow grease** provides even more cleaning power, but hold back. Allow cleaning products time to work before you scrub. Save your energy for other chores!

and fittings. Cut tough bathroom soil with a tile and bathroom cleaner: a potent, three-in-one product designed to fight soap film, mineral deposits, and mold and mildew.

A thick liquid, this cleaner requires standing time to sanitize surfaces, dissolve minerals, and cut greasy soil. Apply a thick coat using a squirt bottle. Allow it to stand for the time recommended on the product label, and then use a tile brush to scrub the product. Rinse thoroughly.

Abrasive cleanser Chemical-based cleaners—like window cleaner or degreasers—rely on chemical reactions to dissolve, lift, or loosen dirt. Sometimes, though, you need to add additional scrubbing power to deal with tough or dried-on dirt. Enter abrasive cleansers. These also contain small abrasive particles designed to enhance the scrubbing action. Like sandpaper, they use friction to remove hardened soil.

Abrasive cleansers are made in different strengths. Scouring powder is designed for most sinks; "soft scrub" cleansers feature smaller abrasive particles and are recommended for specialty finishes. Abrasive cleansers may be formulated with other cleaners, such as bleach, to fight stains; be sure to read labels and choose the appropriate variety for the job.

Because these products can be difficult to rinse clean, use them inside sinks, tubs, and toilets where rinsing is easier.

Specialty cleaners for special jobs

These special-use products are formulated for specific cleaning issues or specific surfaces. Be sure to read the labels and use as directed by the manufacturer.

■ **Gum, gunk, and goo remover.** A petroleum-distillate product designed to remove the greasy residues left by chewing gum, oily gunk, or adhesives.
■ **Lime and scale remover.** A highly corrosive solution to hard-water scale deposits.
■ **Rust removers.** Designed to remove the rust stains in sinks, tubs, and toilets that can occur in areas where the water supply has a high iron content.
■ **Stainless steel cleaner or polish.** Specialty products designed to clean, protect, and shine stainless-steel sinks, surfaces, pots, and pans.

Save money on cleaning products

Commercial cleaning products can make quick work of a clean house … but at a price! Costly cleaners don't have to break the bank. Try these tips to save money on cleaning supplies.

■ **Match the product to the job.** Why bring on the big guns for everyday dirt? Choose the right cleaner for the surface and soil involved; no sense wasting high-strength degreaser on a simple water spot—or trying to tackle stubborn grease stains using multiple spritzes of mild evaporative cleaner.
■ **Use just enough and no more.** No, more is not better! Using too much cleaning product wastes money and means extra time spent rinsing and wiping.
■ **Opt for half-measures.** Try using half as much product, and check the result. If you can't tell the difference, cut the amount in half again—until you find the sweet spot where cleaning and conservation meet.
■ **Can the caps.** With generous sizing and barely-visible markings, product caps are an inefficient way to measure cleaning products—and manufacturers know it. Use your own easy-read measuring cup—or mark caps with permanent marker—to guard against overuse.
■ **Buy in bulk.** With cleaning products, small sizes mean big per-unit prices, so buy supplies in bulk, and add a funnel to the cleaning cupboard. Fill your own bottles and save!
■ **Ditch the disposables.** Give these candidates for the landfill the cold shoulder. Replace disposable wipes with reusable cotton cleaning cloths, toilet bowl swabs with a good-quality toilet brush, and swipe-and-toss floor systems with a square-headed mop with replaceable terry covers.

Clean, green, and frugal:
homemade cleaning recipes

Store-bought cleaning products are effective, but contain harsh chemicals and can produce irritating fumes. Simple ingredients from the pantry can be used to make cleaners that are kinder to the environment—for a fraction of the cost.

Diluted white vinegar

Mildly acidic white vinegar dissolves dirt, soap scum, and hard water deposits from smooth surfaces, yet it is gentle enough to use in solution to clean hardwood flooring. White vinegar is a natural deodorizer, absorbing odors instead of covering them up. (And no, your bathroom won't smell like a salad. Any acid aroma disappears when dry.) With no coloring agents, white vinegar won't stain grout on tiled surfaces. Because it cuts detergent residue, white vinegar also makes a great fabric softener substitute for families with sensitive skin. In the kitchen, use vinegar-and-water spray (*see recipes, page 55*) to clean countertops, lightly soiled range surfaces and backsplash areas. In the bathroom, spray countertops, floors, and exterior surfaces of the toilet. For really tough bathroom surfaces such as shower walls, pump up the cleaning power by heating the solution in the microwave until barely hot. Spray shower walls generously with the warmed solution, allow to stand for 10–15 minutes, then scrub and rinse.

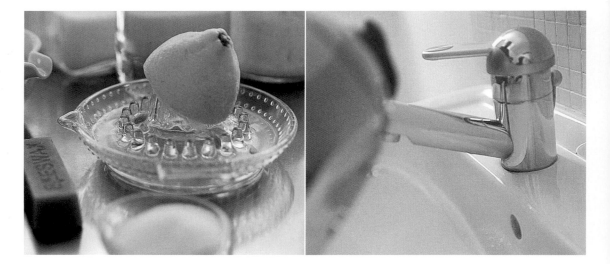

▲ **A mild acid,** lemon juice can be used instead of vinegar for general cleaning. Use the outer rind to polish porcelain surfaces and release fragrant lemon oil. If you have a garbage disposal unit, grind the rind in it while running cool water down the drain. The oils in the rind clean the disposal unit and sharpen the blades.

▲ **Keep bathroom drains** running freely and smelling sweet by pouring ½–¾ cup (20–40g) baking soda into the drain, and dribbling just enough hot water to wash the solution down. Let stand for 2 hours to overnight, and then flush thoroughly with hot water. (Do not use on blocked drains.)

Undiluted white vinegar

Used straight from the jug, undiluted white vinegar makes quick work of tougher cleaning problems involving hard water deposits or soap scum. Use it to clean the inside of the toilet bowl. Before you begin, dump a bucket of water into the toilet to force water out of the bowl and allow access to the sides. Pour undiluted white vinegar around the bowl and scrub with a toilet brush to remove stains and odor. Use a pumice stone to remove any remaining hard water rings.

Clean showerheads that have been clogged with mineral deposits with undiluted white vinegar. Place ¼–½ cup (60–120ml) vinegar in a plastic food storage bag, and secure the bag over the showerhead with a rubber band. Let stand for 2 hours to overnight, then rinse, and buff the fixture.

White vinegar softens clothes and cuts detergent residue. For family members with sensitive skin, add 1 cup (240ml) to the laundry rinse cycle instead of commercial fabric softener.

For general cleaning purposes, you can substitute lemon juice for white vinegar (*see caption on page 54*).

Baking soda

Baking soda's mild abrasive action and natural deodorizing properties make it a powerful replacement for harsh commercial scouring powders. Sprinkle baking soda onto a damp sponge to tackle grimy bathtub rings, scour vanity units, or remove food deposits from the kitchen sink.

For tougher grime, make a paste of baking soda and water, apply to the tub or sink, and allow to stand for 10–20 minutes until the deposits have softened and can be removed.

Rubbing alcohol

Rubbing (isopropyl) alcohol provides the base for an evaporating cleaner to rival commercial window and glass cleaning solutions. Use it on windows, mirrors, chrome fixtures, and for a shiny finish on hard-surface ceramic tiles (*see box, right*).

Ammonia

An alkaline solution, clear ammonia creates stronger window and all-purpose cleaning recipes than acidic vinegar (*see box, right*). Choose a non-sudsing type: suds may look as if they're working, but they're tough to rinse and remove.

Homemade green cleaners

Homemade cleaning products offer many advantages to cost-conscious households. Using on-hand ingredients can be far less expensive than buying commercial cleaners, won't generate discarded product packaging, and the household avoids exposure to harsh chemicals or toxic ingredients. Try these cleaning recipes as a starting point, increasing or decreasing their strength as your household's cleaning needs require.

■ **Homemade spray cleaner recipe**
Try this recipe to harness the cleaning power of white vinegar. Mix in a spray bottle:
1 cup (240ml) white vinegar
1 cup (240ml) water

■ **Homemade glass cleaner recipe**
Try this recipe to harness the cleaning power of rubbing alcohol. Mix in a spray bottle:
1 cup (240ml) rubbing (isopropyl) alcohol
1 cup (240ml) water
1 tablespoon white vinegar

Try the following formulations for spring cleaning or tough chores.

■ **Strong glass cleaner recipe**
Mix in a spray bottle:
1 cup (240ml) rubbing (isopropyl) alcohol
1 cup (240ml) water
1 tablespoon clear, non-sudsing ammonia

■ **Strong all-purpose cleaner recipe**
Mix in a spray bottle:
1 tablespoon clear, non-sudsing ammonia
1 tablespoon clear dishwashing liquid
2 cups (480ml) water

What's in your
cleaning tote?

Nothing stretches a cleaning session like having to run back and forth to the utility closet. Stay on the job—and make short work of it—by carrying commonly needed tools and supplies with you in a tote as you clean. Begin each cleaning session with a fresh stack of white cotton cleaning cloths.

A cleaning tote is a housecleaner's best friend. A plastic bucket or totable tray, it holds the tools and supplies needed to clean it right and clean it fast. What's inside? Check your cleaning tote for these top tools:

■ **Cleaning apron.** An apron protects clothing, keeps cleaning tools at hand and has pockets to hold spare garbage bags and collect trash or small out-of-place items. Choose a sturdy, comfortable, machine-washable apron.

"A cleaning tote is a housecleaner's best friend."

■ **Rubber gloves or washing-up gloves.** Protect hands from harsh cleaning products with rubber gloves. New colors make rubber gloves a bright addition to the cleaning tote—but steer clear of frou-frou decoration. Fur cuffs or rhinestone embellishments are fun to look at, but are not meant for serious cleaning.

■ **Cleaning cloths.** White cotton cleaning cloths are the cleaner's mainstay. Fold them for easy access, and then use them to wipe fixtures dry, make mirrors gleam, and remove fingermarks fast.

◀ **Carry your cleaning tote** with you as you move from room to room. You'll have everything you need at hand and can speed through the job in double-quick time.

■ **Scrubbing sponge.** This dual-duty sponge has an absorbent side and an abrasive side. Flip from soft to tough to take out stubborn, dried-on deposits in the sink.

■ **Squeegee.** Clean windows, mirrors, and glass the way the pros do. A rubber-bladed squeegee removes cleaning solution and soil with one quick swipe. Wipe the blade dry with a cleaning cloth between strokes.

■ **Scraper.** Dried-up gunk comes up fast when tackled with a smooth metal or plastic scraper. Keep the scraper handy in an apron pocket; it'll make quick work of blobs of jelly or dried-on oatmeal.

■ **Tile brush.** A handled brush with thick bristles cleans tiles, bathtub surrounds, and ceramic fixtures in a flash. Bristles reach into corners; the handle keeps your hands free and clear of the cleaning fray.

■ **Toothbrush.** Tiny spaces attract big-time dirt. Tackle them with a firm-bristle toothbrush. Use it to rout gunk from around sink fixtures, sink rims, or tight corners.

In addition to the above, if you are planning to buy cleaning products in bulk, you will also need the following:

■ **Squirt bottle.** Tile and bathroom cleaner works best when applied evenly and thickly. Use a funnel to decant the cleaner into a clean squirt-top bottle to get the right amount of product in the right spot—even underneath toilet rims.

■ **Spray bottle.** Whether you spritz it for light coverage or spray it for harder jobs, adjustable spray bottles make it easy to apply window cleaner or degreaser to surfaces. Use a color code or label bottles to tell them apart.

Cut costs in the broom closet:
cleaning tools

Supermarket sponge-mops and "as seen on TV" cleaning marvels may seem like bargains, but buying a succession of cheap tools and single-use gimcracks can be costly—and it won't get the house clean. Fill your broom closet with a set of durable, versatile cleaning tools, such as these tried-and-true workhorses of the cleaning world.

Floor cleaners

Mops Whether used for wet or dry cleaning, mops are the foot soldiers in the battle for clean floors. Every organized home needs at least two: a wet mop, to pick up wet spills and wash hard-surface floors; and a dry mop, to collect dry dust, dirt, and pet hair.

When choosing a mop for wet cleaning, bear in mind its purpose—not only should it dissolve dirt, but it must also lift it from the floor and remove it. For this reason, avoid string mops. They are heavy to lift, awkward to use, and nearly impossible to rinse clean.

Instead, look for large-headed wet mops with a swivel base and removable terry covers. These innovative tools do dual duty; a dry cover makes quick work of spilled liquids, while a cover wrung out in cleaning solution dissolves and lifts dirt easily. As the cover becomes soiled, simply replace it with a freshly wrung one.

To finish, a dry cover polishes away the last of the water—and since the terry covers can be machine-washed and dried, then reused, you'll avoid the expense and environmental problems of disposable mop liners.

Sponge mops, too, offer efficient cleaning for spills and floors. Larger cleaning heads make the job fly faster. Because these mops get a workout, make sure hinge mechanisms are made of metal; plastic won't stand up to the job.

◄ **Wet mops** with large, flat heads (*top*) swoop easily under furniture; reusable terry-cloth covers add versatility. Choose sponge mops with a hands-free wringing action (*bottom*) to stay dry.

▶ **The corn broom** (*back right*) has flexible bristles that reach easily into corners. A push broom (*front left*) clears large spaces quickly. A whisk broom makes short work of spills and crumbs.

Dry mops are available in many forms. Small disposable mops have the advantage of sliding easily into tight corners and are a favorite with young helpers, but they can be flimsy —and replacement pads are expensive.

Reusable microfiber mops offer a less costly alternative. Some microfiber mops use hook-and-loop tape to attach washable dry-mop pads to the mop face. Others replace disposable pads with reusable microfiber sheets. Use them on dry soil and to sweep up crumbs in the kitchen.

When buying a dry mop, examine the handle and hinge assembly. Mopping stresses these areas, so look for metal connectors and swivels.

Brooms These come in three basic types: push, synthetic, and corn. Push brooms are made from synthetic bristles arrayed in a wide flat base. They're used to sweep large areas like the center of indoor rooms, garages, and patios. Rougher bristles allow the push broom to tackle irregular surfaces.

Choose a push broom with tacked-in bristles, avoiding brooms that are merely glued together. Look for a metal coupling between the handle and the head; the stresses of sweeping will wear out plastic fittings quickly.

Angled synthetic brooms are lightweight and work well to clean near baseboards, behind furniture, and in corners. Use them indoors, as their lighter weight makes them impractical for heavier outdoor jobs. Store synthetic brooms head-up to avoid bending the bristles.

Corn brooms are made from natural bristles, and they're the all-purpose solution for sweeping chores. Pair them with a dustpan for quick kitchen clean-ups; the rough bristles do a superior job on flooring material with a coarse or pitted surface that holds dirt, such as brick or concrete.

When buying a corn broom, look for a smooth, strong handle, and multiple rows of stitching to hold the bristles in place. Store the corn broom head-up to prevent the bristles from bending. As the broom ages, trim the bristles an inch or so to restore it to youthful vigor.

Vacuum cleaner Equipped with proper filtration, a vacuum cleaner swoops up dust finally and forever and removes it from the home. Vacuum cleaners come in two basic styles: canister and upright. Generally, upright vacuums do a better job on carpeting, are less expensive, and easier to store, while the canister vac does a superior job on hard flooring, stairs, and hard-to-reach places, such as automobile seats. For dusting, use the vacuum's extension hose and specialty heads, such as an upholstery brush, dust brush, or crevice tool.

A handheld mini-vac comes in handy for stairs, tight corners, and small spills. Choose a mini-vac model with disposable bags for best air quality. Rechargeable mini-vacs are cordless—and convenient.

Dust-busters

Where there's life, there's dust! Household dust is an airborne mix of soil particles, lint, insect parts, animal dander, pollen, molds, and fungi. Dust comes in through the open window or door, or hitches a ride inside on shoes and clothing. It is stirred into the air by walking or careless dusting. Airborne dust irritates breathing passages, and triggers allergic reactions in sensitive people. As it falls, it settles on fixtures, surfaces, and floors, and clogs furnace filters and refrigerator coils, causing these appliances to work harder and consume more energy. Because dust is abrasive, walking on dusty floors can damage carpet, vinyl, or hardwood floors.

Regular dust removal is essential for a clean and well-kept home. Try the following tools and techniques to control dust.

Dust cloths What's the pedigree of a great dust cloth? It's white, and it's made of 100 percent cotton. Cotton is absorbent, trapping dust instead of scattering it, and it won't scratch fine furniture. White dust cloths show the dirt as you work and are washable, reusable, and may be bleached. For an Earth-friendly, frugal touch, recycle and repurpose old-fashioned unfolded diapers, squares of terry toweling, or stained damask napkins as durable dust cloths.

Lambswool duster A lambswool duster with a long handle extends your reach and is useful for dusting delicate, detailed items. Long wool fibers attract and hold fine dust until you release it outside by twirling the wand firmly between your palms.

How to clean a "dry" room

Cleaning a "dry" room—one with no sinks or water sources—comes down to a single word: dust. Because dust and dirt tend to fly when disturbed, a dry room is cleaned top to bottom. As the dust falls, the cleaner has a multiple chance to trap it and show it the door ... or the vacuum! Use your cleaning tote to work in place, a section at a time. Working around the room only once saves steps and makes cleaning chores fly. Try this step-by-step method to clean a dry room.

1 Toss the trash. Place the wastebasket outside the door to be emptied. When team cleaning, a team member empties all trash. If working alone, empty and replace the wastebasket at the end of the cleaning session. For team cleaning, divide chores between the duster, who circles the room dusting, and the vacuumer, who tosses trash and operates the vacuum cleaner.

2 Move around the room in sections, starting at the top. Using a long-handled lambswool duster, wipe down crown moldings, door tops, and the tops of hanging photos and artwork. Brighten photo glass and clean windows with a cleaning cloth lightly sprayed with glass cleaner; use degreaser to remove smudges and fingermarks.

Electrostatic dry cleaning cloths Made of special microfibers that attract and trap dust, these cloths are superb for cleaning electronic equipment or removing fine, blown-in soil. Choose washable, reusable cloths over disposables.

Tools to avoid Paper towels contain wood pulp products that can scratch delicate surfaces. Feather dusters move dust into the air instead of collecting it, they can't be washed, and a broken quill can scratch delicate surfaces.

Dusting rules

- **Collect, don't scatter.** The number one goal for dusting: to collect and remove dust, not scatter it. Forget images of flapping dust cloths. Instead, dust with the calm and controlled motions of a Tai Chi practitioner. Coax dust motes into your tools—don't disperse them into the air so that they resettle on the surfaces you are trying to clean.

- **Dust top to bottom.** When dusting, it's inevitable that some dust will fly, no matter how careful the cleaner. Give yourself a second chance to collect escaped dust particles by starting at the top and working down: ceiling fan or light fixtures, wall-hung artwork, window moldings, furniture, and baseboards.

- **Dust damp.** Use just-damp dust cloths as you work. The moisture will attract and hold dust. But beware of too much moisture. It can harm wood furniture and delicate surfaces. As an alternative, spritz your cloth with an aerosol dusting spray. Never spray surfaces directly; spray the cloth instead to avoid build-up and overuse of these products.

"Save money—and the environment—by choosing washable, reusable cleaning cloths over pricey disposable dusters."

3 Horizontal surfaces next. Gently dust knick-knacks or decorative items on mantles, shelves, or tabletops with a white cleaning cloth, then dust the surface beneath them. If needed, apply a light spray of cleaner to loosen soil on windowsills or countertops. Lean down to dust furniture legs and wipe dust from baseboards.

4 The final stage—center, vac, and out. After circling the room and working top-to-bottom, dust or clean any freestanding furniture in the center. Vacuum the floor from the room's furthest corner to the door ... then take the cleaner out of the room. Empty and replace the wastebasket. As a finishing touch, spray room freshener as you exit to leave the room smelling sweet.

Tools for wet cleaning

When it comes to cleaning, some household areas are all wet: rooms such as the bathroom or kitchen, which contain a water source and are home to food preparation, bathing, or grooming activities. Water splashes, soap film, air-borne grease and smoke from cooking, and overspray from personal-care products combine with household dust to up the cleaning ante in a wet room.

To clean a wet room, you'll use a greater number of cleaning products and cleaning tools than when cleaning a dry room. In the cleaning tote, rely on degreasers/all-purpose cleaners to cut through oily dirt and dissolve dried-on stains. Pair a degreasing spray with a good supply of fresh cleaning cloths; using a fresh cloth makes sure you remove the loosened soil, not just spread it about in a more even layer. To save money—and live green, too—stock cleaning totes with homemade window cleaner, white vinegar, and baking soda for sparkling kitchens and bathrooms.

Keep specialty tools like scrapers and abrasive scrubbing pads at the ready; they'll help you deal with sticky smears and blobs on counters and fixtures. Always spray the area generously with degreaser spray before scraping; the cleaner helps loosen dirt and protects the surface from scratching. A cleaning toothbrush reaches into cracks and crevices; use it in corners, the grout between tiles, and around the rim of sinks and fixtures. The toothbrush's long handle will keep your knuckles out of the fray; stiff bristles work best to scrape out hardened food or entrenched mold.

How to clean a "wet" room

"Wet" rooms—kitchens, bathrooms, and utility rooms—present more complex cleaning challenges than dry ones. Hard-water film, soap scum, and greasy deposits require amplified cleaning power; food preparation and personal care areas need to be sanitized. Instead of moving around the room in stages, stagger chores to give cleaning products time to work. This step-by-step method shows how to apply maximum power to cleaning a bathroom.

1 Place the wastebasket outside the room, to be emptied and replaced last. Add sanitizing pine cleaner or toilet bowl cleaner to the toilet bowl, and leave to stand. Apply a generous amount of bathroom spray or pine cleaner to the shower or bathtub walls. Leave cleaners to stand so they can get to work dissolving grease and grime while you turn your attention to the sink.

2 Dust any light fixture or mirror molding over the sink. Spray and squeegee the mirror, using glass cleaner. Spray and wipe towel racks or toothbrush holders, then spray the faucets and counter surface with bathroom cleaner. Let the cleaner stand while you scrub and rinse inside the sink, using powdered cleanser. Wipe the counter and polish faucets dry.

The presence of water often requires specialty cleaners. Depending on the content of the water supply, you may need to use limescale remover to treat hard-water deposits, or rust remover for reddish stains in areas with iron in the water supply. Handle these power cleaners with great respect, following the directions on the label.

Dressed to clean

A casual approach to cleaning can be risky—to your clothing! Tackling cleaning chores dressed in a nightgown or in office clothes isn't just haphazard—it's dangerous.

Take cleaning seriously and dress for the job. Avoid loose clothing that will catch on handles or interfere with tools. Comfortable clothing that provides a free range of motion keeps the cleaner on the job longer, and more happily. Washable clothing is a must; a white cotton T-shirt or top will be easiest to keep stain-free.

Wear sturdy, supportive shoes; these protect feet from injury. Avoid wearing footwear that is easy to slide out of, such as flip-flops, especially if using a step stool. Springy sneakers or lace-up walking shoes keep you on your feet, and protect toes from splashed cleaning solutions or a dropped tool. Add a cleaning apron with pockets for further protection, and to keep tools and cleaners close at hand. If your apron has side loops, hang spray bottles of cleaning solution from them ready for use. Line apron pockets with plastic bags to corral bits of trash. Stockpile a stack of cleaning cloths in one pocket, a cleaning sponge in another. You're dressed to clean.

"Stock cleaning totes with homemade window cleaner, white vinegar, and baking soda for sparkling kitchens and bathrooms."

3 Spray toilet surfaces with sanitizing bathroom cleaner: the toilet top, bowl cover top, bowl cover underneath, seat top, and finally seat underside. Leave the seat up while you scrub and rinse inside the bowl. A good toilet brush makes it easy to scrub under the rim, where mildew hides. Wipe toilet surfaces dry in reverse order with cleaning cloths.

4 Using a tile brush or scrubbing sponge, scrub to loosen deposits on shower or tub walls. Rinse walls clean. Use powdered cleanser or pine cleaner to scrub tub and shower bottoms, then rinse. Polish fixtures dry with a cleaning cloth. Using cleaning cloths or a small mop, clean and dry floors. Wipe dust from baseboards. Empty and replace the wastebasket—and take a second to admire your gleaming bathroom!

Top cleaning tips
from the pros

Paid cleaning services are masters of the art of speed cleaning. They're in and they're out, with only sparkling clean surfaces to show for it. Career cleaners work smart to get each job done as quickly and easily as possible. To clean your home in record time, try these tips from professional cleaners.

1 Schedule cleaning.
Nobody hires a cleaning service that promises to arrive "some Saturday or other when nothing else is happening." Take a tip from the pros, and set up a regular cleaning schedule. The pros don't quit until the job is done, and neither should you. Schedule the job and stick to it to get the work done in record time.

2 Get motivated.
You won't find paid cleaners pausing to follow television programs or check their e-mail. Use motivators to prevent distraction and head off boredom. Play upbeat music for an energy boost. Bookworms look forward to cleaning when a book-on-tape plays on a personal stereo. Clean as a team with friends or family members to stay on task.

3 Dress for success.
Professional cleaners dress for the job in comfortable, washable clothing designed for work. Supportive shoes and kneepads spare their bodies. Goggles and gloves protect against chemicals.
    End the era of bleach-stained sweatshirts and set aside a "cleaning uniform" instead—including shoes, gloves, and eye protection—and wear it!

◀ **Professional cleaners.** They have the tools, the talent, and the know-how to make short work of cleaning a house. Learn their secrets to speed cleaning chores in your organized home.

4 Invest in proper tools.

Professional cleaners don't use gadgets. You'll never find them toting specialized, one-use tools, or gee-whiz gimcracks hawked on some television infomercial. Buy good tools, once, and use them—you'll be finished in record time.

5 Tote your tools.

How does your cleaning session go? Is it fast and focused or more like this? Ooops! Forgot the powdered cleanser, so down the stairs you trot. The toilet brush? It's in the kids' bathroom down the hall. Run to the laundry room for more cleaning cloths, to the kitchen for a box of tissues. Where's the vacuum? Did the teenager take the squeegee to wash the car?

Professional cleaners tote their tools with them—all their tools, cleansers, brushes, and rags needed to finish the job are right there in the tote tray. Vacuum, mop, and mini-vac wait in the doorway. A plastic bag for trash is tucked into a pocket, next to the waving lambswool duster. That's why the pro has finished the entire bathroom before our amateur makes it back up the stairs with the powdered cleanser.

6 Simplify supplies.

There's a reason the pros can tote all the products they need in one tray: they've simplified their cleaning products. Professional cleaners go to work carrying the Big Four:

- Light-duty evaporating cleaner (glass cleaner or multi-surface cleaner)
- Heavy-duty degreasing cleaner
- Tile and bathroom cleaner
- Powdered abrasive cleanser

That's it! No soap scum remover, no special counter spray, no single-use products designed to clean only blinds or fans or walls. The professionals know that with these four simple products they'll be able to handle any ordinary cleaning chore.

7 Make every movement count.

Professional cleaners don't circle a room more than once. Taking their place before the bathroom sink, they'll spray and wipe the mirror, scrub the sink, wipe down counters, and polish fixtures before they move one inch to the right or left.

Don't get physical with your cleaning sessions—make every movement count. Stand fast and clean everything in your path before you move on.

8 Two hands are better than one.

Professional cleaners don't work as if one arm is in a sling, and neither should you. Get in the habit of using both hands to attack cleaning tasks.

Spray a mirror with one hand; wipe it down with the other. Scrub counters with two sponges or cleaning cloths. Dusting goes twice as fast when a lambswool duster in one hand cleans nooks and crannies while the cleaning cloth in the other skims flat surfaces.

9 Pick it up.

Professional cleaners come to clean—not to tidy—counters, furniture, appliances, and floors. They can't do the job if each horizontal surface in the home is covered with papers, toys, dirty dishes, and just plain clutter.

Pretend that you've hired a high-priced cleaning crew. You wouldn't make them relocate the clutter just to be able to do their job. Give yourself the same head start you would give professional cleaners: pick up before you clean.

10 Think teamwork.

Two people make a bed four times faster than a single cleaner working alone. Watch the pros at work. Working in teams of two or three, they make short work of an average home.

Where family circumstances permit, make cleaning a family affair. Family members are more reluctant to mess up a clean house when they have been part of the cleaning effort!

Children bring special cleaning challenges to any household—but their developing immune systems mean that kids can be more affected by chemical cleaners than adults. Meet the challenge of cleaning safely around children with these tips:

- **Avoid aerosols.** Fine mist emitted by aerosol products is easily absorbed in the lungs—and aerosol propellants can be highly irritating. Use pump sprayers instead.
- **Skip the scents.** Commercial cleaning products with added fragrance offer a double dose of potentially harmful chemicals. Often, fragrances are more toxic than the cleaner they're intended to mask! Opt for unscented to reduce chemical levels at home.
- **Home in on homemade.** Cleaning recipes from the pantry (*see page 54*) offer cleaning power without harsh chemicals—and are safe, inexpensive, and green alternatives to commercial cleaners.

Scheduling: the solution for
a clean and happy home

Clean houses have one thing in common: cleaning chores are tackled according to a schedule. Haphazard cleaning isn't only ineffective—it takes longer. The quickest and simplest route to a clean house is to schedule cleaning tasks on a daily, weekly, monthly, and seasonal basis.

I know, I know—you have a million reasons why you don't want to clean on a schedule. You're a free spirit. You're pregnant. Your spouse works odd shifts. You're an artistic type and sticking to a schedule would dampen your creativity.

Trust me; in over 10 years of teaching these skills, I have heard every rationale ever offered for resisting this truth. But truth it remains. There's only one reason to schedule housework: because doing so gets the job done fastest and most easily.

Little and often

Housework delayed is housework multiplied. Dust the breakfast nook weekly, and it's a quick-swipe, two-minute job. Wait a month, and enough air-borne grease has settled over the dust to require (a) oil soap, (b) elbow grease, and (c) an energetic half-hour to return the furniture to a state of clean. Better to schedule two easy minutes a week than to play catch-up with a sweaty half-hour once a month.

Whatever your mental roadblock to the idea, consider establishing a cleaning schedule. By scheduling chores so that they're performed regularly—before the problems mushroom exponentially—the house stays cleaner, and the house cleaners do less work to keep it that way. Use these sample checklists as a start-point to develop one that's right for your household:

Daily cleaning checklist

- Make beds
- Place dirty clothing in hampers
- Wash, dry, and put away one load of laundry
- Clear kitchen counters and wipe down stovetop
- Clean kitchen sink
- Take out kitchen garbage
- Sweep kitchen floor
- Pick up family room and play areas (put away toys, stack magazines, remove clutter)

Weekly cleaning checklist

- Change bed linens and bathroom towels
- Clean bathrooms
- Clean kitchen counters and wipe inside of microwave oven
- Wash or dust hard-surface floors
- Dust furniture
- Vacuum carpets and rugs
- Check entryway or porch; sweep if needed

The case against spring-cleaning

In Grandma's day, spring-cleaning was mandatory. It marked the end of the heating season, when the entire house was scrubbed clean of the smoky film given off by older heat sources. With today's heating technology, this rationale no longer applies. Modern lives, too, cannot sustain an old-fashioned cleaning marathon.

So how do we replace spring-cleaning? With a workable household cleaning schedule. Homes cleaned according to schedule stay reasonably clean all the time. A cleaning schedule integrates seasonal cleaning chores into daily or weekly cleaning sessions, and no task goes too long without being done. Result: a clean home all year around.

Even the best-run households experience rocky patches from time to time. Illness, special work assignments, absence of a family member, or volunteer commitments can throw a monkey wrench into the workings of a home.

There's a solution for busy times—a minimum maintenance shortlist to keep your home running smoothly. Think of it as a Magic Minimum: those essential tasks that must be done come Hell, high water, or soccer play-offs. Every family has different needs, but most Magic Minimums provide for:

- **Basic accounting chores** (bank deposits and bill-paying)
- **Meals and menus** (clean dishes, grocery shopping)
- **Laundry** (necessary clean clothing)
- **Home management** (once-a-day pick-up, weekly cleaning of bathrooms and kitchen)

To make your own Magic Minimum plan, list the rock-bottom essential maintenance chores that need to be tackled to keep the household clean, fed, and on time.

A sample list might look like this:

Every day:
- Load and run dishwasher
- Tidy kitchen
- Run one load of laundry, fold, and put away
- Family pick-up time

Every week:
- Review bank balances and pay bills
- Shop for groceries
- Clean bathrooms

Next step: delegate! Assign one or more minimum chores to each family member. Every family member has a stake in keeping the household functioning, so should be expected to help.

Finally, post your Magic Minimum list in a public place. Families using a Household Notebook (*see pages 84–87*) will include their list under the "home management" divider. Another choice is the refrigerator door, but use any central area. The written list aids accountability, because everyone knows what must be done to keep the household functioning during times of stress.

Minimum maintenance

laundry ▲ see pages 140–153

meals and menu planning ▲ see pages 92–97

Teaching
children to clean

"Clean your room!" It's the cry of parents everywhere. Toddlers to teens, it's a battle to get kids to help. The terrain is familiar: a dirty house, balky children, and frazzled, frustrated parents. What can parents do to create peace on the home front? Try these strategies to chill the chore wars.

The buck(et) stops here

An ambivalent mindset can keep us from successfully gaining kid cooperation around the house. Perhaps we grew up in a home heavy with sex-role stereotypes. Maybe we feel guilt because we work outside the home.

When ambivalence strikes remind yourself that, just as we prepare our children for adult life by sending them to school, so we need to prepare them to manage a home.

■ **Start small.** The easiest way to secure your children's assistance is to train them to it from the time they are small. A one-year-old will giggle if handed a clean diaper to dust the the furniture. Nothing can be such fun as washing a car with a five-year-old. Problem is, these little ones' efforts aren't yet much help. In truth, you'll probably have to follow behind that one-year-old with his diaper duster, removing the specks of dirt he's rearranged. Even when you match the chore to the child, the early years require some extra work from you. Listen up, parents of tiny children: just do it! An investment in your child's learning now will reap rewards in just a few years.

■ **Invoke change slowly.** Your children are at an age to be of help around the house—but their idea of "helping" is lifting their feet from the floor so you can vacuum beneath them. Resist the big blow-up and get children involved in chores slowly. For example, this month, decide that one child will assist with predinner preparation, the other will help with clean-up. Next month, begin a Saturday morning family "cleanathon." Gradual change gives you time to teach a child your household's standard for each task.

■ **Tap the power of choice.** Children who are given a choice of chores do them better and more happily. A child who dislikes the feeling of wet hands and gritty cleanser may be the World's Best Duster-and-Trash-Emptier. Another, with sensitive ears, may prefer bathroom duty to running the vacuum. A chore list of scheduled chores makes it easy to allow children to select jobs they'd prefer.

■ **Make housework a partnership.** The best motivator for a child is to work together with an adult. From a child's point of view, it's downright lonely to be sentenced to clean a bathroom each afternoon after school. Better to institute a family

"Invest in your child's learning now and you will be implanting skills for life."

Pick-up Time each day, a family Clean-up Time each week. Even if that same child is alone in that same bathroom, he knows that all the other family members are hard at work, too.

■ **Focus on the big picture.** Cleaning methods are a frequent bone of contention between parents and children. A parent's insistence on "the right way" can add another element of conflict to the housework issue. The answer? Avoid this by focusing on the "good-enough" job. A 10-year-old's skill with the vacuum cleaner will increase with practice ... if he's not derailed by arguments over too-high standards or demoralized when a parent redoes the work.

Who says kids can't do chores? Check this listing of age-appropriate chores to help children learn responsibility and habits of order:

Two- to three-year-olds can:
■ Pick up toys
■ Help make beds
■ Help feed pets
■ Dust lower shelves and furniture legs
■ Place spoons, napkins, and unbreakable dishes on the table
■ Carry dirty clothing to the laundry area
■ Sweep floors with a lightweight electrostatic dry mop

For four- to five-year-olds, add these chores to the list above:
■ Make beds (if using comforters)
■ Set the table
■ Dust table tops
■ Unload and put away groceries

Between six and eight years of age, children can master these additional tasks:
■ Keep their play areas or bedrooms tidy
■ Water house plants
■ Make beds (using bedspreads)
■ Sort laundry
■ Put clean clothing away
■ Assist with simple food preparation (tear lettuce, make sandwiches)
■ Fold socks, shirts, and pants
■ Help wash the car

Nine- to ten-year-olds are ready to:
■ Change sheets
■ Clean bathtub and sinks
■ Help cook meals

■ Prepare simple snacks
■ Wash dishes
■ Load the dishwasher
■ Polish silver
■ Vacuum
■ Sweep floors with broom and dustpan
■ Help with yard work (rake leaves, pull weeds)

From eleven and up, train teens to do "adult" chores. They'll squawk on the outside, but feel pride on the inside as they master real-life skills. With teaching, teens can:
■ Plan and cook family meals
■ Do their own laundry using the washing machine and dryer
■ Wash windows
■ Replace light bulbs
■ Polish furniture
■ Wash hard-surface floors
■ Clean garages and outbuildings
■ Wash, wax, and detail cars

family teamwork ▲ see also pages 66–67

Chores for children

top of the list! Add early-morning chores related to meals and laundry, and resolve to clear the kitchen counters before you leave the house. You'll thank yourself come day's end.

Evening Do-It checklist Do-Its in the evening wrap up the day and prepare for the morrow. In the kitchen, clean up from the evening meal and set the stage for the next morning. Think ahead! Prepare what you need for the morning's coffee or tea, make lunches, and set the table for breakfast. Avoid last-minute clothing crises by planning the next day's outfits. At the end of the day, list personal chores that will tuck you into a peaceful night's sleep: complexion care, prayer or meditation, or reading. Last on the list, remind yourself to take a quick look at the next day's schedule.

Daily Do-It checklists are your personal road map out of the aimless disorder of an unplanned day. Morning and evening, they'll remind you to do those basic, necessary minimums that keep life humming along.

"Daily Do-It checklists are your personal road map out of the aimless disorder of an unplanned day."

Weekly, monthly, and seasonal planning checklists

If Daily Do-Its keep each day running smoothly, weekly, monthly, and seasonal checklists get the big jobs done. What's on the checklist? Everything! From scheduled cleaning chores to menu planning to volunteer work. If you have to do it routinely, it belongs on your checklist.

Like the Daily Do-It, file your weekly, monthly, and seasonal checklists in plastic page protectors in your Household Notebook. Each week, month, and season, check the appropriate checklist to stay on-task and organized.

Use the sample checklists in the box (see right), as a guide to create your own checklists for routine chores to be done each week, month, and season.

Long-term checklists for weekly and seasonal chores are home to recurring to-do list items. Check your Master To-Do list to compile your household's checklists.

Weekly checklist
- Review calendar for the upcoming week
- Check Master To-Do list and add items to the running To-Do list (see pages 80–81)
- Plan weekly menus
- Clip coupons
- Pay bills
- Shop for groceries
- Run errands: visit the cleaners, the bank, the photo developers

Monthly checklist
- Review calendar for the upcoming month
- Check Master To-Do list and add items to the running To-Do list
- Reconcile bank accounts
- Check pantry and freezer inventories; rotate foods
- Change air conditioning or furnace filters

Seasonal checklist
- Review calendar for the upcoming season
- Check Master To-Do list and add items to the running To-Do list
- Make medical appointments
- Change out seasonal clothing and review family clothing needs
- Note vacation or travel plans and make travel arrangements, if needed
- Arrange for air conditioning, furnace maintenance
- Check smoke and carbon-monoxide detectors

Checklists for the long term

Smartphones, tablets and desktops are making quick inroads into the paper pileup. Ready to take your household management system to a virtual level? Try these resources to organize home life online:

■ **Family calendars** Web apps like Cozi.com or Google Calendar offer full-featured information management for electronically inclined families.

■ **Banking portals and apps** Check the full range of services offered by your bank to supercharge financial chores. Reminders, and apps that track recent charges and payments are among free services that may be offered by your bank.

■ **Home management apps** To-do lists, and cleaning and chore checklists are the focus of home management apps like RememberTheMilk.com and HoneyDo. Look for an app that shares tasks among household members. Dare to delegate!

Beyond the routine:
to-do lists

If checklists are a road map for the predictable activities of daily life, to-do lists organize the unexpected: one-time chores, extraneous jobs that must be done around the house, or ongoing projects. Working together with checklists, they'll make sure you tackle those jobs that don't show up on lists of routine chores.

For example, routine kitchen chores—clean refrigerator or scrub the sink—are daily or weekly checklist items (*see pages 76–77*). "Install wallpaper border in kitchen" is a to-do item, a single job broken down from a larger goal: "redecorate kitchen." You'll use to-do lists to identify these one-timers and schedule them into an organized life, and to break down and schedule bigger projects.

There are two kinds of to-do lists: a running to-do list for daily reference, and a Master To-Do list. The running list sets out a list of high-priority to-do items that must be done in the short term. The master list is the source: it's the place where you dump, sort, organize, and carry out the to-dos.

The Master To-Do list
To start a Master To-Do list, grab a sheet of lined paper and make three columns: assigned date, item, and completed date. Move to the middle column and list it all—and I do mean all—every must-do, should-do, want-to-do thought that crosses your mind.

A good Master To-Do list is a mix of goals and aspirations, errands and minutiae. It's a place to put those "oh yeah!" reminders circling your brain into concrete form. Don't worry if your list stretches for pages and pages. Better to put down buzzing thoughts on paper, than to carry them around with you. Better still, the Master To-Do list shows progress at a glance. You'll see what jobs you've completed, what tasks you're working on, and which items remain to be done.

You'll use the Master To-Do list to make frequent, short running to-do lists. As you add an item to the running to-do

Date assigned:	Item:	Date completed:
June 15	Return overdue library books	June 17
June 29	Repair floor in children's bathroom	
July 1	Make vet appointment for Duff	
July 10	Call about dance team costumes	July 14
July 14	Buy glitter trim for costumes	
August 1	Finish status report for event committee	

▲ **Power planner.** The Master To-Do list holds it all, big or small. By putting "gotta-do" jobs down on paper, it's easy to assign dates and translate them into action.

list, write the date in the "date assigned" column; when a job is completed, note the completion date. As time passes, you'll have a record of the good work you've accomplished.

Run with it: making the running to-do list

From the Master To-Do list comes the running to-do list: a short-term list of things to do that is consulted—and changed—often. Consult it daily along with your checklists to keep on top of goals and must-do jobs.

"A good Master To-Do list is a mix of goals and aspirations, errands and minutiae."

Making the running to-do list is simple. Check the Master To-Do list, and transfer two to ten "to-do" items to the running list. Some items will be time-sensitive: the "have-to-do" stuff that looms on the horizon. Sweeten the list by adding a few "want-to-do" jobs, those to-do items that forward a goal. As you add items to the running to-do list, note the date assigned on the Master List—and when you complete a job, cross it off the list! Add the list to your Household Notebook, calendar, or your personal planner. Together with checklists for routine chores, to-do lists guide efficient day-to-day planning for an organized home.

Daily To-Do Basics: Go, Call, Buy, and What's for Dinner?

Each day's to-do list has an internal rhythm that can help you get the work done fast. Most to-do lists set out where you need to go, whom you need to call, what you need to do, a list of things to buy, and what's for dinner.

Make your to-do list easy to follow. Group items on your list under these headings: Go, Call, Buy, and Do. Review dinner plans in a section labeled "What's for dinner?"

By grouping chores and reminding you about the evening's dinner plans, your to-do list gives an instant update on the important work of the day.

Time is a democratic asset; everyone is given the same 24 hours each day. Save your precious time with these tips:

■ **Don't go empty-handed.** Whether climbing the stairs, leaving the room, or going outside, take something with you to put away as you go. Trundle newspapers to the recycling bin when you go to the garage, carry a pair of shoes to the closet when you go upstairs, take out a bag of trash when you leave the house.

■ **Use small bits of time to do small jobs.** Fold socks during a television commercial. Give the sink a wipe-down as you leave the bathroom. Little efforts mount up.

■ **Do chores while you chat.** During telephone conversations, look for "busy-hands" jobs that can be done while talking. Chop a salad, sort a drawer, or return out-of-place items to their homes while you talk with family or friends.

■ **Double up on errands—or stay out of the store.** Never make a special trip to do one errand; instead, group them together. Visit the dry cleaner nearest the supermarket, or drive through the bank on the way home from work. Look for new-century time savings from online subscription services: have regular shipments of paper goods or personal care items made to your doorstep.

■ **Make good use of travel time.** Audio books are good companions for a driving commute; use trips to and from school to check in with children. Avoid talking on cell phones while driving, however; the timesaving isn't worth the safety risk to your family—and to others on the road.

Time-saving tips for every day

Habit, the household
wonder worker

Imagine the television pitch: "Special offer! The amazing Household Wonder Worker will take your house from chaos to castle in only 21 days. It'll speed your cleaning, calm your chaos, and cut your clutter. Backed by scientific research, our product is guaranteed to bring order and serenity to your disorganized home."

Habits: where to start?

You're sold on the power of habit, but where to begin? While every family's climb out of chaos will be different, focus on building these first habits for an orderly home:

■ **Check your lists.** Review each day's checklists and to-do lists each morning and evening. They'll keep you on-track and organized each day.

■ **Make the bed.** Invest 45 seconds to straighten sheets and tuck the covers to start the day on an organized note.

■ **Take time for self-care.** Morning or evening, no matter how busy, take 20 minutes for grooming and self-care. Care for yourself first; it'll give you confidence throughout the day.

■ **Welcome each morning.** The night before, check clothing for the next day. Set the table for breakfast, and set out items needed to prepare morning beverages.

■ **Keep meals in their place.** Clean kitchen counters and wash dirty dishes after each meal. Don't let clean-up chores from one meal invade cooking energy needed for the next one.

You say you have the phone in one hand and a credit card in the other? Sounds that good, does it? Sorry, television viewers. The Amazing Household Wonder Worker is the most powerful secret weapon in the war against disorganization and clutter, but you can't buy it, not in stores, or anywhere. You have to build your own, but it's free for the making. Put it to work for you, and it'll lead you, step-by-step, out of the darkness of disorganization and into the light. What is it? Habit.

Let the force of habit be with you

Habit is a small word for such a powerful force. It may start small, but habit works like a snowball, perched at the top of a snow-covered mountain. It takes a tiny little effort to push the snowball over the edge, but look out! By the time it reaches the bottom, that little snowball has gained the power of an avalanche.

So, too, with the habits we build into our daily life. Small steps forward, barely noticed, have a powerful effect on our homes and our lives. What's the secret? Momentum. It takes energy and thought to form a good habit, much like it takes energy and intention to push that little snowball over the edge. Once in place, however, a habit gains in strength and effect with each repetition, building strength and power behind it— and you don't even have to think about it.

Anatomy of a habit

Habits are powerful, but they're not mysterious. We all have a brace of them, for good or bad. Does each day begin with two cups of coffee and the newspaper? Habit! Do you sweeten weekly grocery shopping trips with a maple bar from the supermarket bakery? Habit! Do you always place your handbag or briefcase on the floor of the car, behind the driver's seat? There's that habit again!

If habits are familiar creatures, why are they so very difficult to start—or to change? Go back to the snowball. Yes, it's a bit of a nuisance to make it, isn't it? You have to get your hands wet, cold, and numb, and pack the snow tightly. You must perch the snowball on its ledge just so, and then give the silly thing a push. Once you do, though, look out!

"Once in place, a habit gains in strength and effect with each repetition, building strength and power behind it."

The analogy explains why good habits can be so difficult to start, and bad habits so difficult to end. Setting up good habits means creating conscious, intentional change. Ending bad ones means countering the tremendous, built-up force of a thousand repetitions.

21 days to success

How do you form a good habit? The concept is simple: decide what you want to do, and do it each day for 21 days. By the time you've repeated the habit daily for three weeks, you own it—or rather, it owns you. Put it in place and your habit will carry on without further thought.

Dr Maxwell Maltz, author of the book *Psycho-Cybernetics*, first noted the significance of this 21-day time period. A plastic surgeon, Dr Maltz knew that it took 21 days for amputees to stop feeling phantom sensations in the amputated limb. When he began working to help patients change their attitudes, not their appearance, he found that this time period applied to changes of thinking, too. It's a hard-wired interval needed to grow any change to fruition.

If the idea is simple (do it for 21 days!) the devil is in the details. Establishing a new habit is hard work. Each new habit must turn aside the formidable energy of an entrenched old habit in order to survive and thrive.

Old habits are not so easily dislodged. In practical terms, fresh new habits must be tended carefully and guarded from intruders. During their infancy and youth, good habits can be extinguished by a single episode of "Mañana, mañana—I don't wanna!" You have to cherish the new, good habit and fight the old bad one at the same time.

On the trail of good habits

Ready to bring the power of habit to your side in the war against domestic chaos? Try these three tips to help you form new habits:

■ **One habit at a time.** Tempting as it is to decide that today, you'll change your entire life from top to bottom, resist the urge. It's better to build a single helpful habit than try for a total overhaul of life—and fail.

Changing a habit takes undivided energy and commitment. To succeed, focus on a single habit. Only after you've established a new habit should you move on to another. Take heart, though. With 52 weeks in each year, you can build 17 new habits and still take two weeks vacation in a single year.

■ **Hitch your habit to a star.** A new habit stands a better chance of survival if it has a friend. Think of a habit you have now as a locomotive engine, and add the new one to the train. By building new habits in concert with established ones, you make the change easier to adopt.

Do you put your toddler down for a nap at 2 p.m. each afternoon? That's a perfect "prompt" to build your new habit—30 minutes of daily inspirational reading—into your schedule at 2:05 p.m.

■ **Seek out support.** When it comes to building new habits, a support network is worth a thousand words. Agree to trade "nags" with a good friend: you hold him or her accountable, he or she holds you accountable as you work to build new habits together.

Look for habit buddies to conquer tough habits side-by-side. Have you decided to walk for 45 minutes each day? Walking with a friend, a neighbor, or your spouse will double the motivation (and the fun!).

The Household Notebook:
planning an organized home

Organized people use a personal planner: a small book that contains information, calendars, and schedules to help them stay organized. Organized households need a planner, too: a Household Notebook. Containing calendars, schedules, checklists, and information of all kinds, a Household Notebook serves as "command central" for the entire family. It's the place to go, when you need to know.

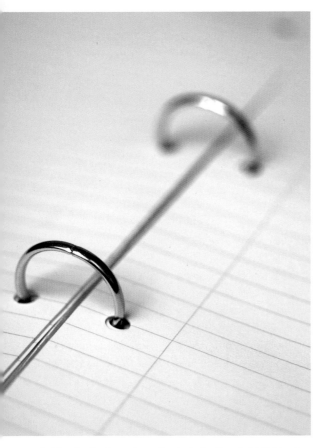

▲ **Simple, basic,** and even low-tech, the Household Notebook is a high-powered information manager. Do away with scrawled sticky notes, in favor of a central source for household information.

While each family's organizer will be unique, most are simple three-ring notebooks with several divider sections. Because they're infinitely expandable, household notebooks become as distinctive as the family that uses them. A family with school-aged children involved in dance, music, and sports will include organizer sections for rehearsal and practice schedules, summer

"A Household Notebook serves as 'command central' for the entire family."

activity ideas, and videos-to-rent lists. A two-career couple with preschool children may add baby-sitter and day-care dividers and an emergency telephone list to their household notebook. Empty nesters will rely on packing checklists for vacations, home repair records, and gift idea lists for far-flung children and grandchildren.

By compiling and storing family information in a central location, life at home benefits. No more searching for scraps of paper or mislaid permission slips. Information is always right where it belongs: in the Household Notebook.

Create Your Own Household Notebook

To create your family's Household Notebook, start with a three-ring binder, some clear plastic page protectors, paper, and tabbed dividers.

Add dividers Using tabbed dividers from the office supply store, set up dividers according to your family's needs. Each family grows their own family organizer; expect divider categories to change along with your family. Some suggested dividers are listed on the following pages, but your family is unique, so the dividers you choose will reflect that. Be sure to place a few clear page protectors behind each divider section.

Add paper Start with a calendar, and add pages or forms to record information. At OrganizedHome.com, you'll find hundreds of free printable calendars, planners and checklists to jumpstart your Household Notebook. Many of our forms are computer-fillable for ease of use. Computer users may use desktop publishing programs to create information forms; others can use simple lined paper to create pages for their notebook.

Finally, add clear plastic page protectors to each section. Found at office supply and variety stores, they make it easy to track checklists, display schedules, and view product manuals.

Ready to begin Once the dividers and page protectors are in place and you've added calendars and basic forms, you're ready to begin. Gather all scattered slips and scraps of paper: pizza menus and business cards, school hand-outs and church bulletins, class schedules and scout camp brochures. Enter information in the Notebook, writing phone numbers on the correct phone directory pages, punching and filing club calendars, slipping magazine articles into page protectors.

Be creative! Add dividers that express your household's priorities and needs. Planning home-improvement projects? Add a "House Beautiful" divider, and store snips and swatches in page protectors. Use Master To-Do and Daily To-Do lists in any divider to keep track of ongoing projects and goals, while blank lined pages hold information not covered by a specific form.

Keep your Household Notebook near the family calendar to guide family activities and decisions. A cupcake request from the Cub Scout den mother? Note it on the calendar, and add "cake mix" to the shopping list. Planning a Friday-night date with your spouse? Open the folder to the baby-sitter's information page and review emergency information with the baby-sitter before you leave.

Dividers for your Notebook

Every Notebook will reflect the unique family that builds it, but these suggested dividers will cover most information needs:

- **Emergency information.** Keep emergency information in the first section of the Household Notebook. Include a list of emergency phone numbers (including your home address, to assist rescue personnel; baby-sitter's checklists with contact information; phone listings for health care providers and information about emergency procedures.

- **Calendar and planning.** Calendar and planning notes are the heart of a Household Notebook, so set up a Calendar and Planning divider. What belongs here? A monthly calendar, a page protector with your checklists, and a section for to-do lists lives in Calendar and Planning. Use a three-hole punch to add work schedules, school calendars, and events lists for church and civic activities. Goal: to have a one-stop location for all planning information for each day, week, and month.

- **Contacts and information.** Fill out your Notebook with specialty dividers to track the family's information and contacts. Don't stop with mere names, addresses, and telephone numbers. Add personal information like babies' names, birthdays, and e-mail addresses to stay in touch with family and friends. File away copies of team rosters and club directories in the Telephone Directory divider. Add a Take-Out Menus divider for menus from your favorite restaurants. To prepare for the holiday season, add a "Christmas" divider for party planning, dinner menus, and gift lists.

Make it yours

With basic address book functions tucked away, custom-tailor the Notebook for your household's needs. Your Notebook may include dividers for these activities:

Family and school Family is where the heart is—and deserves its own divider. This section tracks the information needs of family members and family life:

- Personal information page for each family member
- Clothing sizes tracker
- Master occasions list (birthdays, anniversaries)
- Gift suggestion list
- Birthday party ideas
- Favorite take-out restaurants
- Videos to rent or stream
- List of books to read
- Library information

Families with school-aged children will want to add a school divider to hold:

- School schedules and holiday list
- Lunch menus
- Carpool schedule
- School information page
- School reading lists
- Summer programs information

Home management Bring it all back home! The Home Management divider holds information central to house and home. Cleaning, entertaining, decorating, and household storage information find a home here:

- Household cleaning schedule
- Seasonal chore checklists
- Children's chore checklists
- Home inventory
- Home decorating ideas
- Party guest lists and menus
- Car maintenance schedule
- Stain removal guide
- Recycling locations
- Home storage inventory

Meals and menus In the kitchen, the Household Notebook helps plan meals, create menus, and track inventory in the pantry and in the freezer. Use this section to hold:

- Weekly menu planners
- Grocery shopping lists
- Price book form (tracks grocery prices for frugal shopping)
- Freezer inventory forms
- Pantry inventory forms
- Recipes
- Index for cookbook recipes

Money and finance A section for tracking dollars and cents makes sense. Keep track of household finances here:

- Budget/spending record
- Bills to pay
- Checkbook register
- Credit card list
- Online service/online account information
- Home inventory
- Insurance information
- Safety deposit box inventory
- Utilities/services directory
- Magazine subscriptions
- Warranty information
- Vehicle records

Health and fitness Organize family health care with a Health and Fitness divider. Have a medical emergency? Grab the Household Notebook on the way to the Emergency Room. Visit to the pediatrician? Use this section to record illnesses, medication, and medical history. Types of information to file in the Health and Fitness section include:

- Diet trackers
- List of family allergens
- First aid kit checklist
- Medical information sheet for each family member
- Emergency directory
- Medical authorization form
- Prescription drug record
- Insurance information
- Pet health records

Travel, hobbies, and activities Time for fun! The Travel, Hobbies, and Activities divider covers the extra-curricular activities that make life worthwhile. Hobby, church, club, sports, volunteer, vacation, and travel ideas are included here. Your Household Notebook may have several dividers for this purpose. Are you part of a musical chorale? Give it a divider. Do the children play serious soccer? Divide it up!

What belongs in these sections? Any and every piece of paper pertaining to that activity. Prayer chain lists. Sports information sheets. Lists for travel and camping. These sections will vary from family to family, but here are some ideas:

- Picnic planner
- Travel packing checklist
- Before-we-leave checklist
- Camping checklist
- Vacation idea list
- House-sitter information sheet
- PTA newsletters and rosters
- Church prayer circle list
- Scouting or PTA materials
- Craft materials inventory
- Sewing pattern list
- Books to read
- Videos to watch

Holidays and seasons Make the holiday season bright with the planning power of a Household Notebook. Our sister site, OrganizedChristmas.Com, offers free printable forms for holiday planning, or make your own pages to keep tabs on holiday events. Throughout the year, keep track of important days, gift-giving, and holiday décor with pages to record:

- Family birthday calendar
- Birthday party planner
- Holiday gift list
- Seasonal greeting cards list
- Holiday menu planner
- Décor inventory
- Decorations to make list
- "Gifts to make" list
- Gift closet inventory for stored gifts
- Ornament memories journal

Life in view: the family calendar

What's the best way to keep track of hectic family schedules? A family calendar. Choose a large write-on calendar on which you'll track appointments, outings, kids' activities, family dinners, and carpool assignments. Use colored pens in a different color for each family member to color-code your entries.

If you can see the family's commitments at a glance, it will guide household planning. The week of soccer playoffs—with every night's dinner spent away from home at the soccer field—isn't the right time to tackle a new home-improvement project. A bonus: seeing family calendar dates in living color helps you say "No!" to new obligations, when they back up against existing plans.

Create a family information center
The best place to post your family calendar is in a family information center: a designated space in your home to review checklists, take phone messages, add items to a to-do list, and check calendars.

A family information center focuses on information handling and retrieval, so it should be located near a telephone, in a place that permits seating.

Hang the family calendar from the wall and place the Household Notebook near the telephone, if there is a landline. Arrange pens and pencils in a pretty mug or wall holder, and add a pad of paper for messages.

Alternatively, use a commercial "information center" whiteboard to take phone messages. Colored markers allow color-coding, while the whiteboard eraser makes it easy to change an entry.

cycles of an
organized home

What comes closer to the rhythm of life itself than the cycle of food? As the kitchen is the heart of the home, so food and food preparation stands at the center of our memories: holiday meals and special occasions; casual summer picnics and everyday family dinners. Make those memories happy ones with the ideas in this section, aimed to speed, streamline, and save money on the kitchen front.

Investigate menu and meal planning to save time and promote a healthy diet—while using smart supermarket strategies to keep the pocketbook plump. Learn proper food storage techniques to preserve your family's investment in foodstuffs.

Declutter cabinets, refrigerator, and freezer, then apply organizing principles to create kitchen "centers" that will speed food preparation and meal clean-up.

Harness the pantry principle for maximum savings—and to protect the family against natural disasters or hard times.

Planning
family menus

What are we having for dinner? It's the question of the hour. Too often, we find ourselves looking for answers in the supermarket at 5p.m. Harried and harassed by hungry children, we scan the aisles in desperation and rack our brains for a quick answer to the recurring dinnertime question.

Keeping the family fed can be daunting. Three meals a day. Seven dinners a week. From supermarket to pantry, refrigerator to table, sink to cupboard, the kitchen routine can get old, old, old. No wonder we hide our heads like ostriches from the plain and simple fact: into each day, one dinner must fall. What's the answer? A menu plan.

A menu plan saves money, because it cuts out last-ditch trips to the supermarket. A menu plan saves you time. No dash to the neighbors next-door for a missing ingredient, no frantic searches through the freezer for something—anything—to thaw for dinner.

Most important, a weekly (or monthly) menu plan conserves a home manager's most valuable resource: energy. Follow these strategies to put the power of menu and meal planning to work for you.

Dare to do it

Often, making a menu plan is something we intend to do . . . when we get around to it. Instead of seeing menu planning as an activity that adds to our quality of life, we dread sitting down to decide next Thursday's dinner. "I'll do that next week, when I'm more organized."

Wrong! Menu planning is the first line of defense in the fight against kitchen chaos. It's better to do menu planning in a single, 10-minute weekly session than to do it nightly—and in despair—standing in line at the market or peering into an open refrigerator.

Take the vow. "I [state your name], hereby promise not to visit the supermarket again until I've made a menu plan!"

Day	Main course	Dessert
Monday	Roast beef, baked potatoes, broccoli	Fresh fruit
Tuesday	Chicken breasts, steamed rice, stir-fried veggies	Apple pie and ice cream
Wednesday	French dip sandwiches (leftovers from roast), potato salad	Leftover apple pie
Thursday	Pasta with chicken and vegetables	Cookies and ice cream
Friday	Freezer lasagne, green salad	Frozen fruit bars
Saturday	Take-out chinese	Ice cream
Sunday	Baked salmon, wild rice, green beans	Layer cake

▲ **Paperless planning.** Internet menu planning services offer menu plans and shopping lists by email, integrating current coupon offers for maximum savings at the supermarket.

Start small and simple

Grandiose ideas of weekly new recipes and complex monthly schedules can scuttle the act of menu planning before it begins. Sure, it's fun to think about indexing your recipe collection, entering the data in a relational database and crunching menus until the next decade, but resist the urge.

"Take the vow: I promise not to visit the supermarket again without a menu plan."

Instead, think, "next week." Seven little dinners, one trip to the supermarket. Slow and steady builds menu-planning skills and shows you the benefits of the exercise. Elaborate and over-detailed menu plans become just another failed exercise: roadkill on the way to an organized kitchen.

The power of advertising

Where to begin to make menu plans? Start with what's on sale! Scan food flyers from the local newspapers or visit supermarket Web sites to get a feel for the week's sales and bargains. Build menus around loss leaders: items offered at below-market prices to attract traffic to the stores.

This week in my home town, for instance, two local chain supermarkets are offering whole fryers for a low, low price. To feed my family well and frugally, this is the week for Ginger Chicken and Fajitas, not a time to dream about Beef Stew and Grilled Pork Tenderloins. I'll serve those when roasts are the loss leader at the market.

Menu-planning tips

Here are some points to ponder as you bring menu planning under control—and take the "desperate" out of dinnertime.

Build a family shopping list Look in any gift store or browse mail-order catalogs and you'll find cute little shopping lists for all persuasions and occasions. Bear-shaped shopping lists. Long skinny shopping lists. Shopping lists with winsome graphics. Shopping lists with colored borders. Cute, colorful

OK, it's food ad day. Ready? Time to rough out a simple menu plan. The goal is two-fold: shop efficiently to obtain food required for seven dinner meals, while minimizing expenditure, cooking, shopping, and cleaning time. These are the bare bones of menu planning: make a draft plan, shop from a list, retain flexibility, firm up your plan, and hold yourself accountable.

■ **Scan the food ads** for specials and sales. Rough out a draft menu plan: seven main dinner meals that can be made from weekly specials, side dishes, and salads. Use a blank sheet of paper, or a menu planner form.
■ **Wander to the pantry** and the refrigerator to check for any of last week's purchases that are languishing beneath wilting lettuce or hardening tortillas. The best bargain is food you've already purchased—so plan to use it! Review your shopping list and note any condiments or spices that you will need for the week's meals.
■ **Ready, set, shop**—but shop with an open mind. That fryer on special offer won't look like such a bargain next to a marked-down mega-pack of boneless chicken breasts at less than a dollar a pound (0.5kg). Be ready to substitute.
■ **Return from shopping** and stock your shelves. As you put away groceries, flesh out the menu plan. Match it up with the family's calendar, saving the oven roast for a lazy Sunday, the quick-fix pizza for soccer night.
■ **Post the menu plan** on the refrigerator door. Refer to it during the coming week as you prepare meals.

Menu planning basics

freebies with pictures of kitty cats and teddy bears. Most homes have two or three pads of lists—or a dozen.

Only one problem: why aren't you using them?

Because they don't work, that's why! Teenaged sons play stuff-the-trash can with the empty cereal box, but have you ever known one to write "Cheerios" neatly on a shopping list? Pre-printed lists, moreover, fit about as well as one-size-fits-all stockings from the convenience store.

Solution? Build a family shopping list, noting all the foods and sundries your family consumes. Check your receipts. Computerized store receipts can help jog memories for items to include on the list. Include a few blank lines for new foods or unexpected ingredients.

When building your family shopping list, grab a handout supermarket map next time you visit the store. Organize your personal shopping list according to the departments where you shop in the store. Once you've made your family list, use a printer or copier to print 52 copies: a year's worth of shopping lists for the household.

Each week, post a fresh list on the refrigerator door or in the Family Information Center (see page 87). When today's breakfast empties the carton of orange juice, circle that item on the list. Boys who don't circle "Sugar Gaggers" on the list when they empty the box will soon learn the principle of cause-and-effect—not making a note means that they'll be eating hot cereal for the rest of the week.

On shopping day, grab the list and take it to the supermarket. You'll know at a glance that you need to buy more juice, cereal, and bread.

Making a personal shopping list can be an interesting— and revealing—exercise. During the years when we still had teen children at home, cereal, milk, and cookies headed the list, along with the entry "nuclear waste"—our family's slang for a cheap, luridly colored punch beverage sold in the dairy case. Sigh. The good old days. Now that our household is back-to-two (and we two are both a touch too round) "broccoli" and "salmon" head the list.

Court the calm of a routine Yes, there are some well-organized souls among us who don't make formal meal plans. But look closer and you'll discover that there's an underlying strategy behind this seemingly relaxed approach—the household meal service dances to a routine.

Sunday's a big dinner, and Tuesday gets the leftovers. Monday is burger night, and Wednesday sees spaghetti, year in and year out. Thursday's the day for a casserole, and Dad grills on Friday. Saturday night, it's take-out or pizza.

Create a routine around your menu planning. Sure, you can try new recipes—just don't let your enthusiasm for the glossy pages of the cookbook con you into doing so more than twice a month. Cooking tried-and-true speeds dinner preparation and streamlines menu planning.

To do it, look for cues in the family schedule. At-home days with more free time can handle a fancy meal—or can signal soup, sandwiches, and Cook's Night Off. Running the evening kid carpool is a great time to plan for pick-up burgers. Make the routine yours, and it will serve you well.

Stay flexible Menu plans aren't written in stone. So you're fighting fatigue on the "big" cooking day? Swap it with Pizza Night and go to bed early with a cup of herb tea. Family members will forgive you, as long as they get their postponed favorite a day or two later. Building flexibility into your plan can also serve the aims of thrift with Cook's Choice Night. Traditionally held the night before grocery shopping, you can slide a neglected dinner into Cook's Choice, or chop up the contents of the refrigerator for a clean-it-out stir-fry. Either way, you'll feel smug at your frugality and good planning.

Make it a habit Simple or not, a menu plan won't help you if you don't make one. Weekly menu planning is a good candidate for the weekly checklist. Get into the habit of planning before you shop, and you'll get hooked—one addiction that's worth cultivating!

Recycle not reinvent After you've made menu plans for a few weeks, the beauty of the activity shines through: you can recycle them! Your family won't mind, and you'll save even more time and energy. Instead of an ambitious plan for 30-day menus, tuck completed menu plans in a file folder or envelope. Next time fryers are on special offer at the market, pull out the plan you made this week. Done!

Your family loves home-cooked meals, but with a busy life, who has time to cook a full dinner every night? Enter freezer cooking: an organized method to cook once and eat many times by stockpiling pre-prepared main meals and side dishes in the freezer.

Also known as once-a-month cooking or investment cooking, the concept of freezer cooking is simple. When you do cook, cook multiple portions and freeze extra servings.

Problem is, this method is a bit haphazard. Who hasn't known the virtuous feeling of cooking up a big pot of baked beans and tucking a container or two deep in the bowels of Moby Dick, the great white freezer? Where, sad to say, it remains. Months later, a freezer clean-out yields an icy mountain of anonymous dribs and drabs of pre-cooked food. Without labels, planning, or portion control, the cook-ahead effort goes to waste.

Use the following tips to fine-tune your freezer cooking skills and avoid mystery meals.

■ **Plan multiple meals.** Ground beef and Italian sausage on sale this week? By all means, buy extra for freezer meals—but make it a plan. Two pounds (1kg) of beef and a pound (0.5kg) of sausage will make four meals for your family? Great! That's what you buy, not a smidgen more. Too often, a weak "I'll freeze the extra" leads to overbuying and waste.

■ **Package the freezer meals first.** Back to our hungry family, faced with a huge kettle of spaghetti sauce. Before you know it, a meat-loving teen has gutted the pot and put a serious dent in your meal forward-planning. To avoid this hazard, fill freezer containers before you serve the evening's meal. You'll have a tighter handle on portion control—and there will be no more scant cups of sauce marooned inside the freezer.

■ **Freeze casseroles before cooking.** A twice-cooked casserole is nobody's friend. After dinner, who wants to scoop the leavings into freezer bags? Efficient freezer cooks build their lasagna in three single-meal containers and freeze two while the current evening's dinner is in the oven.

■ **Package properly.** Ill-assorted margarine tubs and gaping plastic containers are for amateurs—and they won't protect your frozen assets from spoilage and freezer burn. Invest in three or four same-sized oven-safe casserole dishes. Is it beef stew tonight? Spritz the dishes with pan spray, and line with a sheet of foil long enough to wrap completely around the food. Spray the foil, too, then ladle in the stew. Gently tuck the foil up over the food. Freeze overnight, and then release the foil from the dish. Wrap, label, and freeze in freezer bags. To use, pop a foil-wrapped package into the casserole dish, thaw, and re-heat. Simple!

■ **Label, label, label!** An efficient freezer cook has assembled labeling supplies before he or she begins. Tuck a slip of paper with the name of the dish, cooking directions, today's date, and a use-by date to tell you how long to freeze the item between the foil-wrapped package and freezer bag. Better, use a permanent marker pen to label freezer bags. Computer-savvy cooks can print computer address labels for easy labeling of frozen foods.

■ **Track inventory.** "Out of sight, out of mind" defeats many would-be freezer cooks. Introduce inventory control with a whiteboard. Adding three dinners' worth of macaroni and cheese to your freezer hoard? Write 'em in. Visiting family has you drawing heavily on your inventory? Erase each meal as you use it. A small magnet-mounted whiteboard can be placed on the freezer door to track frozen assets. Or copy the freezer inventory and post it on the freezer door.

Save money on
grocery shopping

For most families, the food budget is the most elastic entry in the household budget. The rent is the rent, electricity costs may not change much from bill to bill, but smart shopping can reduce the cost of food—and cut the time and energy it takes to shop. Try these tips for frugal, efficient grocery shopping.

1 Never shop hungry.
Hunger pangs make it easier for snack food and impulse purchases to jump into the shopping cart.

2 Shop less, save more.
A quick stop for some milk usually turns into an hour's trip and a dozen grocery bags. Avoid small shopping trips.

3 Shop at home first.
When making menu plans, assess the contents of your refrigerator, freezer, and pantry before buying new foodstuffs.

4 Make a list, and live by it.
Grocery store marketers depend on the impulse buy. Protect your budget by shopping from a list.

5 Time trips for best savings.
Plan shopping trips for the day meat and produce managers mark down soon-to-expire items. You can save up to 50 percent on those purchases if you time it right.

◀ **Take charge** of your shopping and trips to the stores become an exciting challenge—but travel alone. With kids in tow, you'll be distracted and may be persuaded to buy more than you intended.

6
Be fickle and shop around.
Those who have a "favorite store" usually pay a price for their loyalty. Peruse supermarket ads and shop in two or three stores in order to make the greatest savings.

7
Love those brand names? Get over it!
Private store labels offer equivalent quality at a lower price than "nationally advertised" products.

8
Do the math on unit pricing.
Big boxes don't always mean big savings. Rely on the "unit price"—the item's cost per ounce/gram. It'll show you the carton with the best price, regardless of size.

9
Shop with the season.
Citrus in winter and strawberries in summer are much less expensive than the out-of-season reverse. Eat in season for freshness—and savings.

10
Buy in bulk …
but only if large sizes boast a lower unit price, and if your family can consume the product without waste.

11
Love those "loss leaders."
They're the sales items in the weekly food ads, offered below cost to lure shoppers to the store. Take the bait, but pass on higher-priced items.

12
Support local growers.
Farmers' markets and CSA farm shares offer fresh, local produce at competitive prices. "Eat local" to reduce transportation costs and energy use.

13
Equip the trunk.
For easy shopping, put an ice chest in your car's trunk for dairy products and frozen foods, and boxes to support plastic sacks.

Cutting costs with a price book

Even at the supermarket, knowledge is power—but how do you track prices and stay informed? With a price book.

A price book is a product-by-product record that tracks prices, sales, and buying opportunities for foods. Over time, you'll discover the "target price" for any item: the rock-bottom low price goal for purchases.

Second, the price book illustrates each product's sales cycle: the number of weeks between sales offering that target price. If canned tuna is offered for sale at a 4 for $1 target price every six weeks, smart shoppers will buy six weeks' worth of tuna—and they'll avoid this product during those high-price weeks where it sells for 59 cents.

To make your price book, use a small notebook or printable price book form from OrganizedHome.com. Assign one page to each staple product on your shopping list. On each page, list the date, store location, brand, item price, and unit price. As you shop, note each new "low price" for each product.

Product: TOMATO SAUCE

Date	Store brand	Size/price	Unit price
12/15	ALB Hunts	8oz (226g)/ $.32	$.04
1/5	COS Del Monte	28oz (85kg)/ $1.65	$.0128
2/28	ALB Hunts	8oz (226g)/ $.10	$.0225

Hint: Supermarket receipts make it easy to add entries to the price book. In the store, shelf labels often list unit prices for goods.

FRESH FOOD STORAGE GUIDELINES

Food	Time	Temperature	Packaging and tips
DAIRY			
Eggs Raw in shell Hard-cooked	3–5 weeks 1 week	Refrigerator (38°F/4°C)	Keep fresh eggs in the original carton; throw away any cracked or leaking eggs.
Milk	7 days	Refrigerator (38°F/4°C)	Always buy milk and dairy products at the end of your shopping trip to keep them cold and fresh.
Butter	1–3 months	Refrigerator (38°F/4°C)	Butter is very susceptible to picking up flavors from other foods. Store in original carton or covered container to prevent flavor loss.
Yogurt	7–14 days	Refrigerator (38°F/4°C)	Store yogurt in the original container.
Sour cream	7–21 days	Refrigerator (38°F/4°C)	Once opened, use sour cream within 7–10 days.
Cheese Hard (Cheddar, Swiss) Soft (Brie) Shredded cheese	6 months unopened 3-4 weeks opened 1 week	Refrigerator (38°F/4°C)	Wrap cheese tightly in original wrapping or plastic food storage wrap to protect against mold, flavor loss.
Cottage cheese, ricotta cheese	7–14 days	Refrigerator (38°F/4°C)	Keep cottage or ricotta cheese tightly covered in the original container. Store the container upside-down to seal out air and preserve freshness.
MEAT, POULTRY, AND FISH			
Beef Ground Roast Steaks Cooked beef (leftovers) Gravy and meat broth	1–2 days 3–5 days 3–5 days 3–4 days 1–2 days	Refrigerator (38°F/4°C)	Store meats in coldest part of the refrigerator. Store raw meat in original airtight packaging or plastic food storage bags.
Poultry Whole chicken or turkey Chicken parts Giblets	1–2 days 1–2 days 1–2 days	Refrigerator (38°F/4°C)	Juices can contaminate other foods. Store chicken and turkey in sealed packaging in lowest part of refrigerator.
Fish Lean fish (cod, sole) Fatty fish (salmon, halibut) Cooked fish	1–2 days 1–2 days 3–4 days	Refrigerator (38°F/4°C)	To prevent odor, store fresh fish in sealed packaging away from other foods.
Shellfish Shrimp, scallops, shucked clams or mussels Live clams or lobsters Cooked shellfish	1–2 days 2–3 days 3–4 days	Refrigerator (38°F/4°C)	Wash hands thoroughly with soap and water after handling raw shellfish.

Food	Time	Temperature	Packaging and tips
FRUITS AND VEGETABLES			
Fruits (cold storage):		Refrigerator (38°F/4°C)	Keep fruit juices tightly covered. Wrap melons and cantaloupes to prevent flavor transfer to other foods.
Apples	1–3 weeks		
Berries and cherries	1–2 days		
Citrus fruit (oranges, lemons, limes, etc)	3 weeks		
Grapes	5 days		
Fruit juices	6 days		
Melons (cantaloupe)	1 week		
Fruits (room temperature)		Room temperature	Ripen apricots, peaches, and pears at room temperature; store in refrigerator when ripe.
Avocados	3–5 days		
Bananas	3–5 days		
Peaches, pears, and apricots	3–5 days		
Vegetables (cold storage):		Refrigerator (38°F/4°C)	Store asparagus upright in plastic container containing 1–2in (2.5–5cm) water. Rinse leaf or shredded lettuce with water and store in sealed plastic storage containers. Add a paper towel to absorb excess moisture and promote crisping.
Asparagus	1–2 days		
Beans (green or wax)	1–2 days		
Carrots and beets	1–2 weeks		
Celery	1–2 weeks		
Corn (in husk)	1–2 days		
Lettuce (head)	3–5 days		
Lettuce (leaf or shredded)	1–2 days		
Mushrooms	1–2 days		
Spinach	5–7 days		
Vegetables (cool storage)		Cool storage (45–50°F/7–10°C)	Onions need a dry storage space, so don't store them with potatoes, which release moisture. Don't store potatoes or onions in plastic bags. Better air circulation promotes a longer shelf life.
Onions	Up to 4 weeks		
Potatoes	2–3 months		
Sweet potatoes or yams	2–3 weeks		
Vegetables (room temperature)			Ripen tomatoes at room temperature away from sunlight.
Tomatoes	1–3 days		
BREAD AND CEREALS			
Breads		Room temperature	Store sliced breads in original packaging or plastic food storage bag. Bread may be stored in the refrigerator for longer shelf life, but will become stale and dry more quickly.
Sliced sandwich bread	5–7 days		
French bread or baguettes	1 day		
Rye or artisan breads	2–3 days		
Cereals		Room temperature	"Decant" opened boxes of cereal from original packaging into airtight storage containers for longest shelf life. Keep rolled oats in an airtight container to guard against moisture and insects.
Cold cereal, opened	Up to 2 months		
Cold cereal, unopened	Up to 18 months		
Oatmeal (rolled oats)	Up to 3 months		

Looking for extra room in the grocery budget? Try these easy hacks to get the most value from your food dollar.

■ **Cool savings.** Plastic ice-cube trays are good friends in the frugal kitchen. Use them to freeze small portions of leftover broth, baby food, chopped fresh herbs, pesto, or tomato sauce. Pop frozen cubes into labeled freezer food storage bags. Since two cubes equal ¼ cup of liquid, they're pre-measured for use in soups or casseroles.

■ **Cultivate crumbs.** Bread ends and stale slices get new life—and spark new meals—if they're tossed into the oven to dry overnight after dinner. Use a flat roasting pan or cookie sheet, and arrange slices singly; place in a turned-off warm oven overnight. Next day, toss the crisp slices into a food storage bag and beat into dry breadcrumbs with a rolling pin. Store in an airtight container. Use in recipes or as a coating for chicken or fish.

The rules of
kitchen storage

The basic principle that underlies organized kitchens? Use it most, store it closest. Less used items are reached with a bit of bending or stretching, while specialty or seasonal tools are sent to the kitchen equivalent of the Black Hole of Calcutta. Assess kitchen contents and storage options according to these three rules.

Ready, rinse, **recycle!**

Embracing sustainable living means bringing recycling into the kitchen. Try these ideas to reduce your family's impact on the environment.

■ **Take it to the trash.** Make recycling as easy as tossing the trash by replacing the trash bin with a recycling organizer. Whether it's as simple as three small trash bins lined up in a row, or a specialty organizer that stacks bins for aluminum, plastic, and paper, enlarge the concept of "trash" to make room for recycling.

■ **Treasure compostable materials.** Adding a kitchen compost container makes it easy to recycle vegetable waste as you cook. Whether peeling potatoes, scraping the salad bowl, or tossing stale produce, a dedicated compost container turns scraps of vegetable matter into garden gold. Don't garden? Find a friend who does; they'll be thrilled to accept your donations on behalf of their plants.

■ **Put coffee grounds to work.** The coffee bean's natural deodorizing properties give it second life in a recycler's kitchen. After brewing, dry wet grounds in a mesh strainer. When dry, place them in open containers to deodorize cupboards or refrigerators; use dry grounds as a hand scrub to remove food odors after chopping onions or garlic.

1 **"A" is for every day.**
Every kitchen has a few best friends: dishware, tools, and equipment used each and every day. "A" kitchen items include plates and glasses, bowls and mugs, tableware and serving spoons, saucepans and skillets, kitchen knives and cutting boards, a can opener, teakettle or coffee pot.

They've earned a home in the prime storage spots in the kitchen. "A" storage areas are those easiest to reach: kitchen counters, the front areas of cabinet shelves, top drawers, and the fronts of lower drawers. Make the match, locating every-day kitchen tools in the prime real estate storage areas.

> "It's easy: choose the most accessible areas in your kitchen to store the items you use the most."

2 **"B" is for often.**
You love your crockery slow cooker—but use it only once a week or so. It's a member of the "B" contingent: kitchen items that are used often but not daily. In their ranks are items like graters, strainers, roasting pans, and mixing bowls.

Assign the "B" brigade to "B" level accommodations: lowest or highest shelves in the cabinets, or areas in the backs of drawers. To reach the land of "B," you'll stand on tiptoe or stoop a bit, but storage is reasonably accessible.

3 "C" is for seldom.

In the kitchen, "C" items are those arcane tools, seasonal items, or single-use gadgets that just barely earn house room by being used once or twice a year. These also include small kitchen appliances which, left to multiply, can overtake even the largest kitchen, dangling cords and all. Give all "C" items a thorough clutter scrutiny before assigning them storage space in the kitchen—if you have never used that pasta maker, donate it to a fettuccine-loving friend. Most should be decluttered, but if everything on your shortlist of "C" tools manages to come into use once a year, well and good. This group includes seasonal cookie-cutters, holiday dishware, single-use gadgets like potato ricers, oversized serving dishes, canning jars, or the waffle iron.

Consign "C" items to the dark reaches at the back of bottom shelves in the cabinets, or if they're decorative, perch them on top of soffits during the off-season. Small cabinets located over the refrigerator or oven, reachable only with a step stool, are a natural home for "C" items. Alternatively you can outsource them to other household storage areas. Store holiday dishes in the attic or basement, along with holiday decor items. Stack boxes of canning jars in the garage until time to make jelly, or tumble "C" cooking gadgets into a lidded plastic container in the attic, labeled "kitchen gadgets."

▼ **Everyday items,** like bowls used for soups or desserts, belong in "A" storage areas where you can reach them without undue effort, and where they can be easily replaced after washing up.

Kitchen
activity centers

In the kitchen, there's a primary rule: tools that work together should live together. Can you mix a cake, peel vegetables, or fry a burger without taking an extra step? Carry out this rule by creating activity centers in the kitchen: centralized places that group and organize tools needed for routine kitchen activities.

Each center will be organized according to an activity focus, be assigned a designated space, and encompass storage for tools needed for that particular activity.

In most kitchens, activity centers will overlap. A sink/cutting center—the zone for peeling, chopping, and washing food— may sit cheek-by-jowl with the cooking center focused on the nearby stove. Drawer and cabinet space may be shared between centers, and so may the tools and items they contain. Don't worry! The focus is on function, not boundaries. So long as you can get the job done without taking a step, overlap between activity centers is the norm.

Sink/cutting center

You're making potato salad for a picnic. In the next 15 minutes, you'll drain fresh-cooked potatoes, peel and grate hardboiled eggs, chop onion and celery, and mix a tasty dressing for your salad—and you'll do it all using the natural components of the kitchen's sink/cutting center.

This center's focus: washing, chopping, draining, and preparing food. Its designated area: the sink and a counter area next to the sink. Storage for this center can include the counter, sink storage areas, a drawer, and cabinet space.

Most-used cutting tools earn a home on valuable counter space. Paring knives, serrated knives, and butcher knives are close at hand—and attractive—stowed in a knife block. Hang a paper towel dispenser on the wall or beneath a cabinet to save space. To encourage hand washing and hygiene, decant liquid handwashing soap into a pretty pump dispenser, and assign it a home next to the sink.

Clean-up center

The potato salad is sitting pretty, garnished, and ready to chill. It's time to clean up—and to do so, we'll call on the activity focus, designated space, and storage in the clean-up center.

In this area is everything needed for cleaning up and trash collection. The designated location is under the sink, and includes the center's storage; in households with young children, be sure to secure the cabinet with childproof locks or choose an inaccessible, high-up storage location close by.

Moisture is a persistent issue in a cabinet beneath the sink, so a cabinet liner is a must. Scraps of vinyl flooring, cut to fit the base of the cabinet, make it easy to wipe up spills and keep the area sanitized.

Large under-sink turntables make it easy to store items in the inaccessible back of the under-sink cabinet. Increase under-sink storage by mounting specialty organizers to the cabinet doors. A towel rack keeps hand towels at the ready; small shelves stow dishwashing liquid, sponge, and rubber gloves for easy access at washing-up time.

When it's time to toss the trash in the under-sink garbage can, plastic liners are clean and convenient. Make it easy to change liners by storing a good handful at the bottom of each can, underneath the current liner. When you remove the full bag, a fresh bag is always available.

Cooking center

Focused on the stove top and oven (and maybe a microwave oven), the cooking center is the place to fry chicken, simmer chili, or bake a batch of cupcakes. It's home to the pots and

pans, whisks and spatulas used to heat, cook, and bake food. Because the cooking center's tools are many and large, look hard for storage options near the stove that can be included in this activity center. Above the stove hood, store baking pans and cookie sheets. Some stoves feature under-store drawers that are natural homes for the broiler pan and large bakeware. Put pots in their place with hanging racks that store cookware in plain sight—and within easy reach.

Spoons and spatulas are durable friends; store them in the easiest-to-reach drawer, or stand them upright in a stoneware crock near the stove. Affix a hook in the wall or underneath the cabinet for hanging potholders at the ready—but not too close to heat sources!

Store cooling racks, muffin tins, cookie sheets, and broiler pans vertically on their sides in the cabinet. You'll be able to reach just the pan you need, without having to lift, sort—and scratch—the rest of the group.

▲ **The sink/cutting center** is where much food preparation begins. Here you'll house all the tools you'll need for slicing, chopping, cutting, grating, sieving, and squeezing.

Herbs and spices need to be conveniently located for easy seasoning, but make sure they are in a cool place: they'll lose their savor stored under hot conditions.

Mixing center

In the words of an old song, "Can she bake cherry pie, Billy Boy, Billy Boy?" She can—if her organized kitchen includes a well-planned mixing center.

The focus: mixing, preparing, and assembling food. The mixing center is the place where cookie dough and piecrusts, marinades and muffins make their appearance. Star player in the drama will be the electric mixer, with supporting roles filled by measuring cups, baking supplies, canisters, and sifters.

The mixing center is the most movable of all the kitchen activity centers. Since it's not tied to a fixture, such as the sink or stove, it can be located in any designated area with counter space available. Storage includes cabinet, drawer, and wall areas around the designated counter space.

Dishwashing/tableware center

The meal is over and it's time to clean up—and turn to the dishwashing/tableware center to get the job done. Chances are, this activity center will lie right next to the cutting center, since both share the kitchen sink as a designated space and use the same washing tools. The automatic dishwasher is the second compass point for this activity center.

The center's focus is the washing and storage of dishes and tableware—in a manner that will help family members to get the job done fast. Find storage for these items in drawers and cabinets convenient to the dishwasher. Shelf paper helps prevent scratching when putting dishes away; plastic skid-resistant shelf-liner cushions delicate china and glasses, preventing breakage. Assign dishes a home according to their function and use. Just because you purchase dishes as a set doesn't mean you should store them that way. A "breakfast shelf" holds cereal bowls, salad plates, and mugs—and lets children set the breakfast table each morning.

Seldom-used serving dishes live in the inaccessible way-back of the cabinet shelf, while plates and soup bowls enjoy the air and light of the shelf front.

Keep plastic food storage containers nested and handy. They'll help build the next day's lunches from the evening's leftovers. Corral lids separately in a plastic basket or drawer to prevent fallout—the descent of multiple containers onto your feet when the cabinet door is opened.

▼ **Keep children's bowls, mugs,** and other breakfast requirements together on a low shelf where they can be reached easily and quickly laid out in the morning.

Organizing the kitchen according to activity centers helps to speed cooking chores by storing tools in the area where they're most likely to be used. There's a natural logic to activity centres that makes it easy for others to find what they need—and to put them away. While some tools will span more than one center, the categories below give a rough guide to who's who in the kitchen.

Sink/cutting center
- Knives
- Cutting boards
- Grater
- Strainers
- Colander
- Juice squeezer
- Mixing spoons
- Rubber scraper
- Garlic press
- Vegetable peeler
- Vegetable brush
- Melon scoop/melon baller
- Paper towels
- Liquid handwashing soap

Clean-up center
- Garbage can
- Garbage can liners
- Dishwashing liquid
- Dishwasher detergent
- Rubber gloves
- Dish pan
- Dish drainer
- Cleaning cloths
- Cleaning supplies or cleaning tote
- Abrasive cleanser (scouring powder)
- Sponge
- Silver polish
- Houseplant watering can
- Houseplant fertilizer

Cooking center
- Pots, pans, and lids
- Baking pans
- Microwave cookware
- Loaf pans
- Muffin tins
- Pie pans
- Roasting racks
- Spice rack with spices
- Wooden spoons
- Spatulas and lifters
- Wire whisks
- Ladles
- Instant-read thermometer
- Candy thermometer
- Meat thermometer
- Cooling racks
- Cookie sheets
- Broiler pan
- Covered roaster

Mixing center
- Electric stand mixer or hand mixer
- Food processor
- Automatic bread machine
- Mixing bowls
- Batter bowls
- Measuring cups and spoons
- Mixing spoon
- Rubber spatula
- Rolling pin

- Cookie cutters
- Biscuit cutters
- Canisters for bulk baking supplies (flour, sugar, brown sugar, yeast, cornstarch)
- Baking staples: baking soda, baking powder, salt, vanilla, pan spray
- Herbs and spices
- Shortening
- Sweeteners (honey, molasses)
- Cupcake papers
- Cake decorating tools

Dishwashing/ tableware center
- Plates
- Bowls
- Glassware
- Mugs and teacups
- Serving dishes
- Knives, forks, and spoons
- Serving utensils
- Plastic food storage containers
- Napkins (cloth or paper)
- Dishpan and dish drainer
- Rubber gloves
- Liquid dishwashing soap
- Automatic dishwasher detergent
- Hand towels
- Dish towels

Kitchen centers **tools and equipment**

Special kitchen
cleaning challenges

The kitchen. It's the heart of the home—and home to the household's toughest cleaning challenges. Slinging hash from day to day feeds the family—and the grime gremlins, too. Rout the dirt and bring sparkle to the kitchen with these cleaning tips for ovens, stove tops, and sink and counter areas.

Oven

Heat plus grease plus food spills equal a tough cleaning chore: the oven. Baked-on food and spattered grease require additional firepower in the form of specialty cleaners. Commercial oven cleaners do the job well—but are formulated with corrosive products such as sodium hydroxide (lye), and should be handled with extreme care.

■ **Safety first.** Whatever the cleaning method, protect eyes, skin, and clothing while cleaning the oven. Wear long sleeves and rubber gloves to protect arms and hands; safety goggles or glasses prevent injury to the eyes. A painter's mask guards against corrosive fumes, particularly when using spray oven cleaner products. Where possible, use a liquid formulation.

■ **Follow directions.** If using commercial oven cleaners, read the directions first, then follow them. Oven cleaners may be formulated to work on warm ovens or cold ones, so get the method straight before you begin. Newer versions offer fume-free cleaning for a healthier home.

■ **Rinse clean.** After cleaning, use a spray bottle filled with water to rinse the oven walls, then wipe them dry with a

> ## "Kitchen dirt heads straight for the sheltered hideouts offered by stove knobs, rings, and burner pans."

cleaning cloth. This process removes the last traces of oven cleaner, and prevents your next meal from tasting like cleaning chemicals! Similarly, be careful to remove all traces of oven cleaner from around the oven door gasket and seal.

■ **Try green alternatives.** If you don't like the idea of corrosive commercial oven cleaners, there is a greener option: baking soda. Sprinkle an even ¼ in (5-mm) layer of baking soda in the bottom of a cold oven, then lightly dampen the soda with water; it should be moist, but not wet. Spread the paste over the walls and ceiling.

Let the soda paste stand for 12–24 hours, re-wetting if it dries out. The paste dissolves grease and softens burned-on food, and makes it easier to remove next day. You will need to apply some elbow grease to the job, but you'll avoid working with corrosive cleaners.

To clean oven racks and drip pan the green way, soften them up with an ammonia bath. Place the racks and pan in a large, leak-proof black garbage bag, and add ¼ cup (60ml) non-sudsy ammonia. Seal the garbage bag, and place it outdoors or in a garage overnight. The ammonia will soften baked-on food and make for easy cleaning the next morning. Rinse thoroughly and remove any remaining food, then dry the racks and drip pan before replacing them in the oven.

Stove

The top of the stove is a homing ground for kitchen dirt. Pans boil over and skillets pop grease; stirring spoons deposit little lakes of dried sauce after the meal—and all of it heads straight

Cleaning the kitchen

Nothing says "good morning!" like a clean and sparkling kitchen. Achieving cleanliness in the face of an endless parade of hungry family members is another matter. Tackle kitchen grime and gunk quickly with this step-by-step guide to a clean kitchen.

1 Empty the garbage can, and replace any can liners. Pre-spray all counters and the stove top before you begin to clean using a degreaser or a multi-surface spray cleaner. Move around the room and spritz flat surfaces lightly.

2 Wipe down walls and backsplashes, cabinet faces, and the fronts of kitchen appliances with a cleaner-dampened cleaning cloth. Use an extra spritz of multi-surface cleaner to remove fingermarks, smears, and stains.

3 Scrub the interior of the sink with a powdered cleanser or a spray degreaser. Use a toothbrush to rout out dirt around sink rims and drains. Rinse, then use degreaser to clean fixtures and the sink apron. Wipe dry with a clean cloth.

4 Back to the counters, this time to wipe them clean and dry. Use a scraper to remove dried-on foods, and a small tile brush to loosen soil where the backsplash meets the countertops.

5 Return to the stove top, and use the toothbrush to remove softened food from around the burners, knobs, and dials. Tackle stubborn blobs with a scraper. Wipe dry with a fresh cleaning cloth.

6 Sweep or vacuum the floor, then damp-mop. Pay extra attention to the areas beneath the sink (water spots) and stove (grease). Shake and replace any mats or rugs. Put away tools, cleaners, and apron.

for the sheltered hideouts offered by stove knobs, rings, and burner pans, where it dries and hardens.

■ **Prevention, not cure.** As in the game of life, the best defense against stove-top dirt is offense. Wipe up stove spills immediately, before heat has a chance to harden them. Consider covering burners on gas ranges and older stoves to protect them from kitchen-borne grease.

■ **Take your time.** When you do have to clean, use tools and time to help the job along. Spritz cold stove tops with a thick coat of degreaser spray, then give the product 10 minutes or so to soften dirt. Use a toothbrush to get into nooks and crannies and rout out the soil.

■ **Overnight treatment.** Spattered stove rings and drip pans may be cleaned in a similar way to oven racks. Remove them from the stovetop and place them in a large black plastic garbage bag. Add ¼ cup (60ml) of non-sudsy ammonia, seal the bag, and store it outside overnight. Next day, use a scrubbing sponge to remove the last traces of soil.

■ **Special needs.** Newer sealed stove tops or ceramic stovetops require special cleaning methods to preserve their beauty. Check with your stove's manufacturer for the recommended cleaning products for these stoves.

Microwave oven

Because microwaves cook food from the inside out, there's less heat build-up to harden foods inside the oven. Take a gradual approach to microwave cleaning.

> ## "As in the game of life, the best defense against stove-top dirt is offense. Wipe up stove spills immediately."

■ **Steam-clean.** For light soil, boil a cup of water in a heatproof microwave container in the oven for 5 minutes. The steam will soften the dirt; use fresh cleaning cloths to wipe the oven dry.

■ **Degrease and deodorize.** For more cleaning power, use the steam-clean method above with a 50–50 solution of lemon

▲ **Shiny and safe.** A paste made up of a solution of 50–50 baking soda and water makes stainless steel fixtures sparkle and avoids the use of harsh abrasive cleansers.

juice and water, or vinegar and water. The acid will help cut stubborn grease, and the deodorizing properties of the lemon juice or the vinegar will help take away the lingering scent of last week's microwave popcorn.

■ **Heavy-duty cleaning.** If there is hardened soil inside the oven which requires abrasive cleaning, use a baking soda paste (*see page 108*) to loosen and remove it. Take care to apply light pressure when wiping up the paste to avoid scratching the oven interior.

Sink and under-sink area

Sanitation is the name of the game when it comes to cleaning sinks and the areas beneath them. Moisture, food waste, and the hygiene challenges of meat and poultry preparation mean that the wet area of the kitchen can become a happy breeding ground for bacteria. Under the sink, drainpipes and garbage

▲ **Cutting boards** require special care. To remove odors, rub with half a lemon; to clean and sanitize them, soak in a mild bleach solution (1 teaspoon chlorine bleach to 1 quart/1 liter hot water).

▲ **Counter care.** Remove spilled food from kitchen counters using disinfectant all-purpose spray cleaners. Allow the spray to sit for several minutes to loosen dried-on soil.

disposal units harbor germs and odors. The presence of moisture combined with holes necessary for plumbing fixtures creates an attractive home for insects, mold, and mildew.

■ **Spray and wipe.** Use a disinfecting all-purpose cleaner in a spray bottle to clean sink surfaces, fixtures, and rim. Rout dirt from the base of the faucet, or around the rim, with a cleaning toothbrush, then wipe dry with a cleaning cloth.

■ **Get tough.** If stubborn deposits or stains require an abrasive cleaner, use powdered cleanser on ceramic sinks—but only inside the sink. It's too hard to rinse powdered cleanser from sink rims or countertops.

■ **Keep the shine.** For stainless steel sinks, use a paste of baking soda and water applied with a cotton cleaning cloth, or use a commercial product specially formulated for cleaning these sinks. Avoid powdered cleanser—its abrasive qualities can scratch the surface of the steel.

■ **Out damned spot.** Use full-strength white vinegar to tackle water spots in the sink. Spray or pour it on generously, let stand, then rub the spots with a scrubbing pad.

■ **Clean and fresh.** Under the sink, clean the cabinet walls, doors, and the cabinet floor with a disinfecting all-purpose cleaner. Wipe them dry with cleaning cloths, then leave the cabinet doors open for at least two hours, to permit the area to dry completely.

Food preparation surfaces

Public health officials recommend sanitizing food preparation surfaces by washing with hot, soapy water. Rinse with clear water, then sanitize the cleaned surfaces with a solution of 1 tablespoon of chlorine bleach to 1 quart (1 liter) of water. Use this method on counters, in sinks, and for cutting boards —wherever food may be placed during preparation.

Decluttering
the refrigerator

He's big, he's stainless steel, and he spouts water and icebergs: **Moby Dick, the Great White Refrigerator.** Staring into his chock-full innards, you know what you must do. Plastic food storage containers pile in unsteady ziggurats in every corner. Leftovers huddle in back corners. Shriveled fruit and wilted lettuce snuggle into the vegetable crisper. Time to declutter the refrigerator!

A refrigerator is not just an appliance: it's a central artifact of life. As you declutter it, you'll find evidence of your values (hospitality), aspirations (weight loss), resolutions (financial prudence), and self-indulgence (chocolate raspberry mousse cheesecake). A session of spearing the Great White does more than clear clutter: it can be a valuable peep into the state of the house in general—and of your mind.

To declutter the refrigerator, follow the STOP clutter in the fridge steps outlined on page 113. Before you begin, turn your refrigerator off—and unplug it, too, for good measure. The only shocks you want to receive are those from the expired use-by dates of some of the discarded food.

The moment of truth

You are standing in your kitchen, face-to-face with a clean and empty refrigerator, a garbage can brimming with discarded food, a dishwasher full of plastic food containers, and the few hardy survivors of your harpooning session. What can we learn from all this?

Lean back against the kitchen counter and take a hard look at what the Whale has been hiding in its dark little innards. The implications will hit you in the face. Has your family changed—but your shopping habits haven't? The day I tossed out four jars of dried-out jelly and a jar of peanut butter

manufactured in the last decade, it was clear that my children had turned a culinary corner, and the days of peanut butter and jelly sandwiches were no more.

You'll wring a few unpleasant admissions from yourself, too. Look carefully at what foods have been wasted, especially from the vegetable crisper. Are you doing what I've been doing? I'm Miss Nutritional Virtue herself at the grocery store, but the baby carrots and heart-healthy spreads languish uneaten in Moby's dark corners.

▶ **Chill out** with a well-organized refrigerator. Spare and spacious, a clutter-free refrigerator helps speed food preparation, while free air circulation helps save on energy costs.

Use pen and notepad to jot down your discoveries and track your new resolves. Is healthy eating on your wish list? Toss the sugary condiments and high-calorie dressings for natural alternatives.

Do you want to tighten the budget? Focus on the waste you've discovered. Do you buy grapefruit only to toss the shriveled husks, months later? Are you overbuying milk, or

"A well-organized refrigerator helps speed food preparation, while free air circulation saves on energy costs."

cheese, or meat? If you've tossed it out today, make a note to yourself to buy less—if any—on your next shopping trip. Have family members come to expect weekly cases of soda as a staple, not a treat? Cut back, and substitute fruit juices and iced tea for those high-priced soft drinks. (I will maintain a respectful silence on the subject of chocolate raspberry mousse cheesecake. A rich life must have some indulgences.)

Staying organized

Now that you've sorted, tossed, cleaned, and replaced, you'll want your fridge to stay organized. These tips will help:

■ **Create meal centers.** Make it easy to build a sandwich by tucking mayonnaise, mustard, cheese slices, and cold cuts into a flat-bottomed plastic basket and storing them together. Ditto a "morning toast" grouping of butter, jelly, and honey; pull it out to top your toast.

■ **Keep leftovers in the clear.** Don't bury leftovers in sealed containers; place them in clear food storage bags. If you can see them, they'll remind you of their existence and be more likely to be eaten.

■ **Stay on top of the Whale.** A weekly refrigerator clean-out, done just before making menu plans, will keep Moby under control for good. Toss expired foods, wipe up smears and spills, and rearrange fridge contents before you shop.

STOP clutter in the fridge

Gather your tools: a lined garbage can, a sink-full of hot, soapy water, degreaser and window sprays, and cleaning cloths. Clear the kitchen counters so you can spread out, and empty the dishwasher.

1 Sort and toss

Start at the top. Remove everything from the top shelf. Set aside what still has some life in it, but send all leftovers to the garbage. Working your way to the bottom, you'll build up enough steam to tackle the vegetable crisper. Amazing, isn't it, how innocent little tomatoes and shy stalks of celery undergo such a malign transformation in that place? Unless you bought the vegetable desperado in question within the last week, throw it out. Then turn to the door shelves.

2 Clean

Rinse emptied plastic food containers and consign them to the dishwasher. Shelves go directly to the sink's soapy water. While it soaks off the grime, use degreaser spray to clean the refrigerator's ceiling, walls, and door. Rinse, dry, and replace the shelves. Use spray window cleaner to remove greasy fingerprints from chrome and see-through plastic. Wipe down the door gasket and front, then clean the top of the Whale.

3 Put away

Time to replace the few food items that survived your scrutiny at the Sort and Toss stage. Done correctly, the Spearing of the Great White should all but empty the refrigerator. Don't be afraid of that stark look! A fridge is most energy-efficient when it has adequate airflow.

Declutter
the freezer

The freezer is a cold and lonely place, a natural refuge for forgotten food. Bulging containers with gaping lids join icy, unlabeled parcels in the Arctic wastes of this House of Mystery Food. The goal of a freezer declutter: to cull the contents to remove unusable food, and return the survivors to an organized space that makes the most of your household's frozen assets.

Freezer: to defrost or not to defrost?

Most modern freezers don't require defrosting, but what about the older refrigerator that's hanging out in many garages? These garage or basement appliances still require defrosting. If your unit does not offer manual defrosting, try these do-and-don't tips to defrost freezer areas safely.

Defrosting do's:

■ **Schedule the job** Defrost manual defrost freezers when ice build-up reaches ¼ to ½ inch (5mm to 1.25cm), or when ice builds up on compressor coils.

■ **Cut the power.** Before defrosting, turn off the power to the freezer unit, and unplug the freezer from the wall.

■ **Empty the contents.** Remove all the food from the freezer. Store it in ice chests while defrosting and cleaning the freezer.

■ **Melt the ice.** Either leave the freezer door open until the ice melts naturally (be sure to cover the floor with newspaper to guard against melt water and falling ice) or add heat to speed the process. Use pans of warm water from the sink to melt ice, or wield a blow dryer to force warm air onto the ice (*see also Defrosting don'ts*). As the ice melts, soak up drips with a sponge, utility towels, or cleaning cloths.

■ **Clean up.** When the freezer is ice-free, scrub out the entire interior with a light paste of baking soda and water. Wipe clean and dry with a fresh cleaning cloth. The soda will absorb any lingering food odors and remove any food spills. If necessary, wash the shelves or the freezer baskets in warm,

soapy water. Dry them thoroughly before returning them to the freezer.

■ **Return to power.** Close the freezer door, plug it in, and turn the power back on. Let the freezer run for at least 15 minutes to allow it to cool before returning the frozen food stored in the ice chests.

Defrosting don'ts:

■ **Gently does it.** Don't use picks, knives, or sharp instruments to remove ice from freezer walls. A slip can cause injuries, to you and to delicate freezer coils.

■ **Safety first.** If using a hair dryer to melt ice, be cautious about electric shock. Do not stand in puddled water or allow watery drips to touch the hair dryer.

■ **Skip the suds.** Don't wash freezer walls with soapy water. Soap is difficult to rinse clean; a soapy residue can affect the taste of stored food.

Organizing the freezer

Unlike refrigerators, which need a free flow of air to stay cool, freezers operate most efficiently when they are full. However, a full freezer is a dangerous landscape that allows food to go hidden until it is no longer edible. Keep an organized freezer with these tips:

■ **Label, label, label!** Labeling frozen foods is key to keeping an organized freezer. Label each package—homemade or commercial—with the food's name, number of servings, and the date it was added to the freezer. Use

▲ **Zipper seal freezer bags.** These are perfect because the food is clearly visible. Also you can write directly on the bag using a permanent marker pen, so you don't need to worry about labels smudging or falling off.

a permanent marker pen to write directly on zipper freezer storage bags or freezer paper; stick a computer address label on freezer containers. Hint for computer users: print label sheets of commonly frozen foods ("hamburger patties," "spaghetti sauce," "chicken pieces") to make quick work of feeding the freezer.

■ **Date everything.** To manage frozen foods efficiently, you need to know whether they are fresh. Remember to always write a date on every package added to the freezer. Make sure that you rotate foodstuffs so that new foods go behind older packages.

■ **Organize a large freezer by category.** Keep all casseroles in one area; frozen beef roasts and steaks in another part of the freezer. Frozen chicken and turkey should live in the bottom basket of the freezer where they are easy to grab.

■ **Use freezer baskets.** Flat-bottomed baskets support floppy freezer bags and organize freezer contents. Place all frozen vegetables in one basket, upended loaves of sandwich

STOP clutter in the freezer

Gather your tools: a double-lined trash can for rejected foods, ice chests to hold declutter survivors, a sink of hot soapy water, baking soda, and cleaning cloths.

1
Sort
Turn off the freezer, and unplug it from the wall. Start at the top, and remove each parcel of food. One by one, decide if the container stays or goes. The freezer declutter rule is simple: if it's sealed, labeled, and fresh, it stays. If it's Mystery Meat of unknown age, freezer-burned, or an open container, out it goes.

2
Toss
Declutter all foods with torn or open packaging, freezer-burned meat, or any chunk of food you can't identify and date. Run reusable containers holding the rejects under a hot stream of water to loosen the food-icicle from the carton. Pop the food into the double-lined trash can, and soak the container in the sink's sudsy water. Tuck any keepers into the holding area of ice chests.

3
Clean and put away
When the freezer's empty, wipe it out with a paste of baking soda and water. Wipe dry with fresh cleaning cloths. If necessary, remove and wash shelves or organizer baskets in hot soapy water. Rinse thoroughly and dry before returning them to the freezer. Clean door storage units. Soak and rinse door racks, then dry before returning; wipe door compartments with baking soda paste, then dry. When the freezer is clean and dry, plug it in and turn it on for 15 minutes before replacing food.

bread in another. Specialty freezer organizers are designed to fit together, and won't crack in cold temperatures; they're a good option for chest freezers.

■ **Think square.** When freezing homemade soups or stews, use square or rectangular plastic freezer containers to store them in rather than round ones. Squared-off containers fit together neatly and take up considerably less space than cylindrical shapes.

■ **Rotate for freshness.** When adding new foods to the freezer, store them behind existing products, and use the oldest foods first.

freezer inventory

Item

Bread dough			✓	✗ ✗
Bread rolls		✓	✓ ✓	✗
Chicken casserole	✓	✓	✓	✗ ✗
Beef, raw ground			✓	✗
Beef, sausage		✓	✗ ✗	
Ice cream, (chocolate)	✓ ✓	✗ ✗	✗	
Soup, chicken			✓ ✓	✗
Soup, lentil			✓	✗

Use a slash mark to record each freezer meal or frozen item stored in the freezer. Cross out each item as used.

✓ **Item in**   ✗ **Item out**

▲ **Track freezer contents** with a simple write-on, wipe-off whiteboard or make a freezer inventory list. A free printable form is available from OrganizedHome.Com.

Freezer inventory

When it comes to the freezer, out of sight is too frequently out of mind. Expensive frozen food goes to waste because no one remembers it's there to be eaten.

Solution: a freezer inventory (*see form below and check out OrganizedHome.Com*). Post the inventory on the outside of the freezer door, and check it regularly when you make menu plans. Remember: the best bargain at the supermarket is the food you've already bought and paid for.

Selecting and buying a refrigerator/freezer

A refrigerator/freezer is more than a place to store food; it's a major financial investment and a big consumer of energy in any household. If you're in the market for a new refrigerator, keep these pointers in mind while shopping.

Capacity For the best value, match the refrigerator's capacity to your family size. Buying too large or too small costs money, both up front and in additional energy costs. A too-large refrigerator wastes energy cooling empty space; an over-filled, too-small refrigerator has to work too hard to keep food cool without proper air circulation.

Appliance manufacturers measure refrigerator capacity in cubic feet (liters). To gauge the correct capacity for your household, follow this rule of thumb: a household of two people requires 8–10 cubic feet (250–300 liters) of refrigerator space. For each extra person, add an additional 1–2 cubic feet (30–60 liters).

Size Your kitchen's built-in cabinetry and floor plan will determine the maximum size of a new refrigerator. Measure the available space, and shop with a tape measure. You'll avoid falling in love with a gleaming behemoth that's just a fraction too tall for the space available!

A refrigerator's depth is important, too; you'll need to make sure that there's enough room to open doors fully in your kitchen space. Note whether doors open to the right or left; some refrigerator models feature adjustable doors. When judging depth, be sure to allow for an adequate clearance from the kitchen wall. A refrigerator needs 4–6in (10–15cm) of air space for air circulation over the compressor coils.

FREEZER FOOD STORAGE GUIDELINES

Food item	Time at 0°F (−18°C)	Packaging tips
BAKED GOODS		
Bread, baked	12 months	
Bread dough, (yeast, unbaked)	2 weeks	
Quick breads (nut bread, banana bread)	3 months	Wrap loaves tightly in plastic wrap, then insert in zipper freezer storage bags to avoid moisture loss.
Rolls, unbaked	2 weeks	
Rolls, baked	12–15 months	
Muffins	3 months	
Pancakes or waffles	6 months	
DAIRY PRODUCTS		
Butter, salted	3 months	The "salty" taste of salted butter may intensify with freezing; store unopened butter packages in moisture-proof freezer wrap or freezer storage bags.
Butter, unsalted	6–9 months	
Margarine	12 months	
Cheese (Cheddar, Swiss, Jack)	4 months	Thaw in refrigerator.
Cheese, cottage	3 months	Thaw in refrigerator.
Cheese (Roquefort, blue)	3 months	Freezing will affect texture, crumbling.
Cream (heavy, half-and-half, light)	2 months	Cream will not whip after freezing.
Eggs (raw and out of shell)	6–12 months	Do not freeze eggs in shell; freezing will affect texture. Freeze in covered container.
Ice cream, ice milk	2 months	
Milk	1 month	Allow room for expansion in freezer container; freezing will affect flavor and texture of milk.

Food item	Time at 0°F (−18°C)	Packaging tips
MEAT, POULTRY, AND FISH		
Beef, raw ground	3–4 months	
Beef, roast	6–12 months	
Beef, steak	6–12 months	
Beef, sausage	1–2 months	
Beef, cooked dishes	2–3 months	
Pork, raw ground	3–4 months	
Pork, chops	4–6 months	
Pork, roast	4–6 months	
Pork, sausage (fresh)	1–2 months	
Pork, sausage (smoked)	1–2 months	
Ham, fully cooked (whole or half)	1–2 months	Do not freeze ham slices or canned ham; freezing will affect texture and flavor.
Casseroles with ham	1 month	
Bacon	1 month	
Chicken, whole	12 months	If freezing for more than 2 months, over-wrap original packaging with freezer wrap or freezer food storage bags.
Chicken, parts (raw)	9 months	
Chicken, parts (cooked)	4 months	
Turkey, whole	12 months	
Casseroles, poultry	2–3 months	
Fish, fresh (whole, filets, or steaks)	6 months	Freeze fresh fish in sealed containers or wrap to prevent moisture loss.
Fish, cooked	3 months	
MISCELLANEOUS		
Pasta, cooked	3–4 months	
Rice, cooked	3–4 months	
Soups and stews (vegetable and/or meat)	2–3 months	

Cut food costs with
pantry power

It's the secret weapon of a frugal kitchen: a well-planned pantry. By creating a reserve of bought-on-sale foodstuffs and household supplies, a pantry saves time, money, and stress in the kitchen. Think you don't have room? If there's so much as a spare roll of toilet paper tucked beneath a sink, your home holds a pantry. A pantry's not a place, it's an attitude!

What's the goal of establishing and maintaining a pantry? It's two-fold: household convenience and protection against unexpected events. A well-planned pantry means that the household will never run out of commonly used products such as toilet paper. More important, a pantry is a reserve against hard times. Whether it's job loss, illness, or natural disaster, a pantry ensures that the family will continue to be fed, clean, and comfortable in the face of adversity.

Beginner, intermediate, or advanced?

A beginner's pantry focuses on convenience and contains back-up products for each storable item used in the home. The standard is simple: for each open bag, box, or carton, the pantry contains a second, back-up product. A good first goal: a three-day supply of food and hygiene supplies adequate to support your family plus one additional person.

More robust pantries serve additional aims. In case of emergency, a mid-range pantry can feed a family for a period of two weeks to a month. This pantry includes substitutes for fresh foods, such as powdered milk, dried fruits and vegetables, and protein products.

The most comprehensive home pantries are designed to meet long-term food storage needs. For instance, members of the Church of Jesus Christ of Latter-Day Saints (LDS) are taught to maintain a one-year supply of food and clothing for their families. To do so, these premier pantry managers stock versatile foodstuffs with long shelf life, such as whole wheat berries, together with a variety of preserved and dried foods.

Stocking the pantry

Whether it's Chef Boy-ar-dee brand ravioli or Wolfgang Puck's upscale condensed soups, build your pantry to suit your family, your finances, and the storage space you have available.

Single-income households with young children will build pantries replete with cold cereal, formula, disposable diapers, and child-friendly snack foods. Empty nesters with an active social life and his-and-hers diets will lean toward pickled asparagus, low-sodium veggies, and tiny jars of cocktail nibbles for pick-up appetizers and hostess gifts. Dedicated home bakers will include specialty flours, gluten, and dried buttermilk powder in their pantries, while non-cooks will rely heavily on microwave entrees and freezer pizza. And just about every family can stockpile basics for kitchen and bath, such as toilet paper, toothpaste, detergent, and paper napkins.

Check the grocery list

Where's the best place to discover your family's pantry preferences? Your grocery list. If you buy it, use it, and it can be stored, it's a pantry candidate. Building a pantry from the grocery list is also a powerful antidote to Pantry Mania: the indiscriminate purchase of case lots of canned turkey chili or house brand soups that no one in the household will eat.

An expansive view of the pantry principle also allows for freezer storage and a limited amount of refrigerator real estate. Carrots, potatoes, oranges, and apples enter the pantry zone when bought on sale and tucked into corners of the vegetable bin, while freezer convenience entrees qualify, too.

To work the pantry principle, you've got to get organized! Maximum pantry power requires that you know what you have, how long it will keep, and how to store it safely.

■ **Starting a pantry** does not require complex organization. Create it by buying twice as many of each item as needed for weekly use, then store the extras. When you've used up the mayo in today's tuna salad, retrieve the back-up jar from the pantry, and add "mayo" to the week's shopping list.

■ **The beginner's pantry** can often be stored side-by-side with opened or in-use items. For example, stack the open box of detergent on top of the pantry box or line up cans of chicken noodle soup front to back on the canned goods shelf.

■ **Rotate the contents** of the pantry by placing just-purchased items at the back of the stack or row; use the front items first.

■ **A dedicated pantry area** can be a big help. Set aside a cabinet or shelf to hold pantry items. Organize them by category, stacking cans and boxes. Flat-bottomed plastic baskets support and contain bags of dried beans, rice, or pasta.

■ **Complete pantry meals** are one exception to the "store by category" rule. On a section of pantry shelf, assemble all the makings for three to five pantry meals: a family-sized can of clam chowder, an extra can of chopped clams, and the box of oyster crackers shelved together make it easy to spot the empty spaces after use, and restock.

■ **Larger pantries** require more storage space and may be sited in multiple locations around the house, depending on different foods' storage needs. Root vegetables and apples need to be cool and dry; canned goods can tolerate greater temperature fluctuations. A written inventory can remind forgetful cooks of the location of pantry items.

Pantry organization tips

pantry storage guidelines ▲ see pages 120–121.

PANTRY STORAGE GUIDELINES

Food item	Storage time	Packaging tips
Baking powder	18 months	Unopened
	6 months	Opened
Baking soda	2 years	Unopened
	6 months	Opened
Beans and peas, dried	18 months	
Biscuit mix	12–18 months	
Breakfast cereals, ready-to-eat (corn flakes)	6–12 months	Unopened
	2–3 months	Opened
Breakfast cereals, hot (oatmeal, farina)	1 year	
Brownie mix	1 year	
Cake mix	1 year	
Canned fruit	1 year	
Canned vegetables	1 year	
Catsup, chili sauce, barbeque sauce	1 year	
Chocolate chips, semi-sweet	12 months	
Chocolate, unsweetened	18 months	
Cocoa	Indefinitely	
Coconut, grated	1 year	Unopened in original packaging
Coffee, ground	2 years	
Coffee, instant	1 year	Unopened in original packaging
Cornmeal, regular or self-rising	1 year	
Cornstarch	18 months	
Crackers	6 months	
Flour, cake	6 months	
Flour, white	10–15 months	Opened in airtight container
Flour, whole wheat	6–8 months	Opened in refrigerator
Gelatin	12–18 months	
Grits, instant	8 months	
Grits; regular	10 months	

Food item	Storage time	Packaging tips
Herbs and spices, dried	6 months–1 year	Discard spices when their scent fades; store in airtight containers
Honey	1 year	
Infant formula	12–18 months	
Jelly, jam and preserves	1 year	Unopened in original packaging
Juice, canned citrus	6 months	
Juice, canned non-citrus	1 year	
Marshmallows	3 months	
Mayonnaise	4 months	Unopened in original packaging
Meat and poultry, canned	12–18 months	
Milk, condensed	1 year	
Milk, non-fat dry	6 months	
Milk, sweetened condensed	1 year	
Molasses, unopened	1 year	Unopened
	6 months	Opened
Nuts, unshelled	8 months	
Oils (canola oil, corn oil, vegetable oil)	18 months, 6–8 months	Unopened, Opened. Store in cool place
Oil, olive	9 months	
Olives	1 year	
Pancake mix	6 months	
Pasta, dried	2 years	Store opened pasta in sealed containers or airtight jars
Peanut butter	6–9 months	
Pickles	1 year	Commercially prepared, unopened in original packaging
Popcorn, unpopped kernels	1–2 years	
Potatoes, instant	18 months	

Food item	Storage time	Packaging tips
Pudding mixes	12–18 months	
Rice, brown	1 year	
Rice, mixes	6 months	
Rice, white	2 years	
Salad dressing	10 months	Unopened in original packaging
Salt	Indefinitely	
Sauces, condiments, and relishes	1 year	Unopened
Shortening	8 months 6 months	Unopened Opened
Soft drinks	3 months	Unopened in original packaging
Stuffing mix or croutons	6 months	

Food item	Storage time	Packaging tips
Sugar, brown	4 months	
Sugar, granulated	2 years	
Sugar, powdered	18 months	
Syrup	1 year	
Tea, bags	18 months	
Tea, instant	3 years	
Tea, loose	2 years	
Tomato sauce or paste	12–18 months	
Vinegar (balsamic, cider, rice, red wine, white, white wine)	Indefinitely	Store vinegar in original packaging or in glass containers; do not store in metal

How to store pantry items

Select pantry storage areas in cool locations; canned food and pantry items should be kept at 70°F (21°C) or below; don't store them in direct light. Newer packaged foods now include a use-by date as a guideline for product freshness. Where dates are unavailable, observe the food storage guidelines given here for best quality.

Product code dates: what do they mean?

- **Sell-by date.** A sell-by date sets the last date of sale for perishable products, such as milk. A period for safe home use follows. Newer products often list both the sell-by date, after which the food should not be sold, and an expiration date, after which the food should not be eaten.
- **Use-by date.** A use-by date is a guideline for best quality for foods with a longer shelf life. The use-by date is not a safety date. The food remains edible for some time after that date, but food quality will begin to decline.
- **Expiration date.** Commonly used for highly perishable foods like meats and dairy goods, the expiration date is the last date on which the product should be consumed.
- **Pack date.** Pack dates for canned goods and processed products indicate when they were packed. Use specific food storage recommendations to determine how long the food remains edible after packing.

Building a pantry on a budget

Investing in the pantry principle pays off in savings of time and money, but it does involve an up-front cost. Try these tips to spread the load:
- **"Tithe" for the pantry.** Set aside a regular percentage of each week's grocery budget for pantry building.
- **Buy on sale.** Take advantage of supermarket loss leaders—tuna, tomato sauce, canned soup, and canned beans—to stock up.
- **Buy in bulk.** Bulk-buying for the pantry really pays off. A 25-lb (11-kg) sack of bread flour at the warehouse store will be better value than the supermarket's pricier 5-lb (2-kg) bag. You'll save and stock up at the same time.

Clothing! For most of us, clothes are much, much more than just something to cover our nakedness. Shopping for clothes, wearing clothes, and caring for clothes travels through deep emotional shoals. Our closets bulge with sartorial remnants of earlier selves—thinner, younger, with different interests and vocations.

In many homes, the cycle of clothing becomes bogged down. Mt. Washmore—a teetering tower of unlaundered garments—erupts in the laundry area with volcanic speed. Overstuffed closets and bulging drawers betray the presence of clothing clutter—and in the midst of it all, we stand and wail, "But I haven't a thing to wear!"

By observing the cycle of clothing—plan, shop, launder, and store—we'll plan and shop carefully to maximize the family's clothing dollars. We'll free closets and drawers from the clutter of clothing that is out of style, out of season, or simply out of place. New laundry systems will keep clothing fresh, mended, and ready to wear, while well-planned storage will keep out-of-season clothing ready for use.

Save money with
wardrobe planning

Clothing, clothing everywhere … but not a thing to wear? Save on clothing costs and cut closet chaos with a wardrobe plan. Before you shop, a wardrobe plan helps assess clothing requirements, and identify clothing needs. At the store, a wardrobe plan saves money by relying on style principles—not impulse buying—to guide clothing choices.

Children's clothing needs

Grandmother Betty had a very simple rule of thumb when it came to clothing her three children in the 1930s: "One to wear, one to wash, and one to have clean!"

Times, if not toddlers, have changed. Busy lives and lower clothing costs mean many families buy—and buy and buy and buy. Clothing stacks up and backs up and is often outgrown before it's outworn—or worn at all. Too much clothing clogs closets and drawers, and makes it harder for a child to keep his possessions tidy.

How many clothes do your children really need?

Let the laundry schedule be your guide. If you wash children's clothing once a week, seven to ten T-shirts and trousers will see them through with accidents to spare. If you wash more often, you can reduce that number to five to six outfits.

Double up on socks and underwear, especially for toddlers and preschool-aged children. Accidents happen, and usually on the way to Grandmother's house.

Wardrobe plan basics

To create a simple family wardrobe plan, start with a piece of lined paper (or a free printable wardrobe planning form from OrganizedHome.com) for each family member.

Focus on activities School and work, sports and play, church and committee; the heart of any wardrobe plan is the activities the clothing must cover. For each family member, list the activities that require clothing: school, work, church, sports, dance, or volunteer. Add an additional topic for basics: socks, underwear, nightclothes, coats, and weather gear.

Inventory clothes on hand Next step: inventory the clothing you have, listing each item under the appropriate category. For growing children, check sizes; a growth spurt can see a child outgrow most of a closet in just a few weeks.

As you build your list, you'll see who needs what quite quickly. In your closet, casual jeans abound, but you've had trouble getting dressed for committee meetings. A young son has a plethora of T-shirts, but can't manage to button his dress slacks for church services or dining out. A daughter has lots of pretty dresses, but needs tights, tops, and trousers for school days and play dates.

Make a shopping list From the inventory sheets, make a running shopping list of family clothing needs. Your list will alert you to current clothing needs, and help control spending. Don't leave for the department store without it.

Wardrobe planning pointers

A good wardrobe plan requires every new item to pull its own weight in the clothes closet. No more unworn garments!

Consider color Following a wardrobe color scheme can make the difference between a working wardrobe and nothing to wear (with a closet full of clothes). Sure, that shell pink blouse looks marvelous in the store with its companion grey skirt, but it'll turn wallflower when paired with the beige-brown colors predominant in your closet. Avoid color mistakes and closet orphans by developing a color scheme as part of your wardrobe plan. For each family member, select a basic neutral color—black, brown, navy, tan—and coordinate shoes, coats, belts, and handbags with that color. Accent colors harmonize with the basic neutral: rely on them when selecting tops.

Reach for flexibility Look for flexible clothing that will do double-duty in the closet: a summer shell can take a turn in winter as a chemise under a suit jacket, a child's simple shift dress doubles up as a jumper in cooler weather with the addition of tights and a turtleneck. The more uses the garment has, the better value it will give you for your money.

Rely on classic designs Sure, it's fun to splurge on the latest thing, but no one can build an efficient wardrobe by relying on hot trends. For big-ticket items, choose classic. The timeless look of a well-cut woman's suit will see you through meeting after meeting in style.

▼ **Shop smart.** Build a wardrobe around classic styles and solid colors; inexpensive accents update the look from year to year.

More dash for your cash:
buying quality clothing

Today, it's hard to spot quality clothing based on the price tag alone. Costly designer garments can be shoddily made; modestly priced clothing can be of top quality. To get the most for your money, look for good fabric, appropriate styling, and proper construction and finishing—and good buys can be found at every price point. Try these tricks to sort the right stuff from the schlock.

1 **Examine fiber content and care labels.**
Quality fabric has more natural fiber, and can endure normal laundering or cleaning processes.

2 **Assess the over-all appearance.**
Gathers or puckers at collar, cuffs, or waistband signal a poorly made item. Topstitching should be flat and even, zippers should be hidden and smooth.

3 **Check buttons, buttonholes, and fasteners.**
Bulging buttonholes are a bad sign; closures should be neat, tight, and adequately attached to the clothing. Check that buttons are firmly sewn.

4 **Check hems.**
Unless a visible hem is part of the garment's design, hems should be invisible. A hem that rolls or twists is a warning that the fabric was cut off-grain —and the garment will follow.

5 **Eyeball the seams.**
Look for straight, smooth seam lines and even stitching. Seams that are stretched, skipped, scanty, or bubbled will look even worse when worn.

◀ **Dress smart!** Buying quality clothing is a good investment, in financial terms and when it comes to your self-confidence. You're right ... if your clothes are right.

6 Finger the finishes.
Flip up the hem and check seam and hem finishes. A well-finished seam won't ravel; a generous hem will allow alterations and will help a garment hang properly.

Save money on clothing

Clothing, like food, is an "elastic" expense in the family budget: it can be stretched or squandered. Save money and keep the family well-clothed with these tips:

1 Shop seasonally.
Best buys on clothing occur at the end of each season, when clearance sales move out winter clothing to usher in spring styles. Retailing seasons are falling further and further out-of-whack with the real world, so pay attention! Shop for clothing bargains when retailers move from one season to the next.

2 Don't buy just to buy.
Shopping for clothing can be part outing, part therapy, and part social event. Stick to your list, and if you don't find what you're looking for, don't buy something else just to buy something. That's a prescription for "14 white twin sets in the closet," all bought in desperation "because I can always use another twin set."

3 Know when to mend.
Clothing in need of a stitch or two can be found at great prices, but be smart about taking on garments that need repairs. Know your sewing skill level and let it guide you. There is no point in buying pants that need a new zipper if you've never touched the zipper foot ... let alone the sewing machine!

4 Shop at thrift or consignment stores.
Quality "pre-owned" clothing may be purchased inexpensively at thrift or consignment stores. A bonus is that the consignor will check incoming clothing, and will reject stained or very worn garments.

Garage sales, consignment stores, and online auction sites can be good sources for inexpensive clothing—and buying recycled clothes makes sense ... and cents! Shop smart for second-hand clothes:

- **Stick with reputable sellers.** At yard sales, do judge a book by the cover; a seller offering carefully hung clothing beats the neighbor's jumble of dusty garments. Online, check a seller's feedback, and look for photographs and honest descriptions before you bid.
- **Dress the part.** Yard sales may not offer fitting rooms, so slip into leggings and a slim-fit T-shirt before you leave. You'll be able to check the fit on the scene.
- **Follow your nose.** Give second-hand items a good sniff. If you can smell the previous owner's perfume (or worse), take a pass.
- **Look for quality labels.** Brand-name labels can shortcut the search for good quality in pre-owned clothing.
- **Check fastenings carefully.** Even if a garment passes muster, a broken zipper or missing button can move it from "deal" to "dud." Inspect closures and zippers for signs of wear before buying.
- **Measure, measure, measure.** Tote a tape measure, and use it to measure garment dimensions. Size labels can be deceptive—or missing altogether. A quick run of the tape tells the true story about sizing.
- **Shop your friends' closets.** An overlooked source for inexpensive clothing? Your friends! Organize clothing swap parties with friends; their closet wallflower is your new friend—and the price is right. Free!

Clothing the family for less

Declutter the
closet

Stacked, packed, and bulging, the clothes closet looms. When it takes too long to dress for a special occasion—or to find jeans and a T-shirt on Saturday morning—it's time to STOP clutter in the clothes closet.

The STOP clutter rules

In closets, as in life, less is more. Specifically, the venerable 80–20 rule applies: we wear 20 percent of our clothing 80 percent of the time, while the remaining 80 percent—impulse purchases, orphaned blouses, and the one-size-too-small brigade—represent the freeloaders of the wardrobe clan. Guiding principle: pare it down! Does each garment in your closet pull its own weight? Apply these STOP clutter rules to determine whether to keep, toss, sell, donate, or repair clothing.

Keep an item of clothing if:

■ It fits ... today. Not "10 pounds from now" and not "last year after I had the flu and lost all that weight." Today!
■ It's clean, unstained, and in good repair.
■ You've worn it within the last year.
■ You love it unconditionally.

Toss any garment that is:

■ Worn, stained, or in need of major repairs such as broken zippers, fabric tears, or shredded seams. Items eligible for the repair basket include those with hanging hems, torn pockets, and opened seams.

Identify a candidate for the consignment store if:

■ You haven't worn it in the last year.
■ It's out of style.
■ It's not your color.
■ It doesn't fit, it's uncomfortable, or just unflattering.

before decluttering ▲

STOP clutter in the clothes closet

Gather your tools: timer, STOP declutter boxes (marked Put Away, Sell/Donate, and Storage), a garbage bag for trash, and an extra box for Repair items. Set the timer for 20 minutes. Yes, I know that clothing consultants recommend trying on every single item with every other single item, culling the unacceptable, mending the ragged and tattered, and hanging the survivors in descending order according to color. Yeah, right. Twenty-minute nibbles get the job done in controllable bites.

1 Sort
One garment at a time, make a decision using the STOP clutter rules. Start small: one shelf, 1ft (30cm) of hanging rod. Examine each garment and decide whether to keep, toss, sell, repair, or store it. If necessary, try on the garment to make the decision.

2 Toss
If it's a keeper, hang it back on the rack or return it to the shelf. If not, put it in the appropriate box or toss it in the trash can.

3 Organize
Out-of-place items—sports equipment, fishing poles, hairbrushes, safety pins, the stapler you used for an emergency hem repair—go to the Put Away box. Arrange the remaining garments according to color on the newly spacious hanging rod or cleared shelf.

4 Put away
When the timer rings, stop. The timer's bell is your friend, seeing to it that you don't bite off more clutter energy than you can chew. Empty the trash, take the Repair items to the sewing area, and circle the house with the Put Away box.

after decluttering ▲

Organizing
the clothes closet

You've weeded your closet of the freeloaders, the ill-fitting, the orphans, and the ugly. Time to think about the remaining clothing, and the word is cluster. Organizing your clothing into compatible groups that work together maximizes wardrobe options and versatility, and helps you get the most mileage from each garment.

Thrifty tips for an **organized closet**

Cringing at clutter in the clothes closet? Commercial closet systems may seem like the answer, but too often their cost isn't sustainable on a real-world budget. Try these low-cost options for efficient clothing storage:

■ **Double up.** Suspend a second hanging rod from a too-tall closet rod to increase hanging capacity for shirts, skirts, or slacks, and make good use of space in the closet.

■ **Cube creations.** Modular wire grid cube units are inexpensive—and have multiple applications in the clothes closet. Build them horizontally to stack sweaters or shoes; assembled vertically, cubes create cubbyholes for handbags or boots, or subdivide too-large shelves. Use curtain rod brackets to suspend a single grid panel on the wall to display jewelry, belts, and scarves.

■ **Hanging helpers.** Low-cost organizers designed to fill unused hanging space offer cheap, easy storage for sweaters, T-shirts, handbags, and shoes.

■ **Don't forget the door.** Over-the-door hooks, hanger racks and shoe bags solve storage problems by tapping unused space behind the closet door.

Guiding principle: store by cluster

A clothing "cluster" is a core group of five to eight clothing pieces that work together. A typical cluster might contain a plaid wool blazer with tones of camel, red, and navy, a coordinating navy skirt, navy dress slacks, dark blue jeans, a red T-shirt, and an ivory blouse. Dress it up and you have a suit look with blazer, skirt, and blouse. Dress it down with the T-shirt and jeans, and toss the blazer over your shoulders for a casual outfit. Layer the blouse over the T-shirt and add the slacks for a committee meeting—you've mastered the art of the cluster!

Look at your culled closet with an eye to forming several clusters from your existing clothes. The main organizing principle is color, not season or style. Group similar-colored garments together, and think, "What could I add to this group to form a cluster?" A stay-at-home mom might cluster her pale denim jeans and white T-shirts with a pieced jean jacket, a coordinating vest, and a long red tunic dress/sweater.

Thinking "cluster" simplifies the process of buying clothes. No longer will you buy in terms of "outfit"—that's how you get in the position of having a closet stuffed with clothes and nothing to wear. Adding another piece to a cluster means you can wear the garment several different ways, using the clothing already in the closet.

Guiding principle: simplify storage

Let's face it. Many traditional methods of clothing storage just don't work. Drawers stick and squeak and are usually overloaded. Long hanging garments brush against shoes and wrinkle on the floor. Wire hangers grab one another with pointy metal edges, snagging delicate garments in their eagerness to spring apart. Shoes tumble over the floor, tripping the unwary. Try these tips to simplify your clothes storage:

■ **Make it easier to put away.** Liberate your thinking about clothing storage. There's a principle here, too: in storage, it should be easier to put something away than it is to get it out. With this principle in mind, put underpants and brassieres in an open-topped plastic basket on a shelf, rather than confining them in a too-small lingerie drawer. Hang long nightgowns and robes from hooks and they'll be easy to find each bleary-eyed morning. Invest in the marvelous modern multi-level closet systems, and your delicate blouses will never again catch on the hooks holding your skirts.

"In storage, it should be easier to put something away than it is to get it out!"

■ **Think cluster.** If possible, hang clothing in clusters, rather than segregating it by shirts and slacks and dresses. When the interesting multi-stripe shirt is hidden between two old jean shirts, it's hard to remember how well it works with those stone chinos. Store clothes by cluster, and you simplify the process of getting dressed.

■ **Stay open.** Stack jeans, shorts, and T-shirts on open shelves, and you'll never again lose a favorite pair in the dark corners of an over-stuffed drawer. Socks deserve their own open basket; store pantyhose by color, with each color confined to a separate large zipper food-storage bag.

■ **Hang it right.** Finally, invest in proper hangers for the life of your clothing (*see page 134*), and recycle those wire hangers at your local dry-cleaners.

▶ **Bring order to your closet** Use suitable hangers to hang clothes, and fold T-shirts and sweaters. If you can see your clothes at a glance, you don't need to search the whole closet.

Tips for organized closets

If you can see it, you can find it ... and wear it, too. Try these tips to get organized in the clothes closet:

■ **Boost storage with specialty organizers.** In the closet, space is at a premium—yet many closets teem with unused areas. Specialty organizers can tap that empty space. Double the room for shirts and blouses by hanging a second rod for twice the storage. Stackable shelves subdivide over-tall shelving and add a second layer of storage. Hanging sweater bags convert extra space into shelves for sweaters, handbags, or folded jeans.

■ **Round up shoes with shoe racks.** Shoe storage can cause even the most organized among us to stumble, so get shoes up and off the floor. Use shoe racks or shoe bags to store shoes in small spaces.

Tips for organizing dressers and drawers

Crammed bureau drawers can lead to snagged hosiery, rumpled garments, and pinched fingers—so put the following tips to work to declutter and organize clothing stored in chest of drawers and dressers:

■ **Declutter, declutter, declutter.** As storage devices, drawers function best when they have breathing room; when they are jammed and crowded, they damage clothing and make it hard to find garments. Keep drawer contents lean by decluttering them. Use the STOP clutter method (*see pages 20–23 and 128-129*) to trash singleton socks and torn knickers. Don't let clothing clutter bring drawer storage to a standstill!

■ **Labels point the way.** Keep the drawer contents tidy —and where they belong—with labels. Label drawers on dresser fronts or the upper edge of the drawer lip. Use labels with pictures on to help small children put away clothing in the proper drawer.

■ **Divide and conquer.** Drawer dividers keep knickers neat, stockings folded, and T-shirts in their stack. Use narrow strips of cardboard to subdivide drawers, or stow lingerie and socks in shallow, flat-bottomed plastic baskets. Commercial drawer organizers can make a neat drawer out of a jumbled mess.

■ **On a roll!** For neat storage, roll garments instead of folding them. Mate socks, and then roll them together; they'll be easy to find, and you won't stretch elastic edges. Rolled T-shirts are simple to sort and stow; no more flipping through folded piles to find a favorite. Rolled garments take up less room in the drawer; rolling lessens creases and rumpling.

■ **Turf it.** To pare down excess clothing in the chest of drawers, find alternate storage locations in less crowded areas. Toss rolled socks and leggings into a flat-bottomed basket, and slide beneath the dresser or a nearby bed. Bulky jeans can claim more than their fair share of drawer space; consider hanging them in the closet instead. Don't hang sweaters, though; they should be stored flat to retain their shape.

◀ **Divvy it up.** Drawer dividers make it easy to find clothing you need quickly, and frustrate the tendency of small items to shift when dresser drawers are opened and closed.

Clothes storage tips for **clutter personalities**

Try these tips for clutter personalities. They'll help sort out the closet clutter that holds you back:

■ **Perfectionist.** The perfectionist has the world's most organized clothes closet ... in her head. Because her dream of color-coordinated storage systems is so lofty, she won't throw herself into the yawning void between what she has and what she imagines. In the meantime, she's diving beneath winter's fleece jackets to try to find the bathing suits.

The perfectionist needs to cut herself some slack! A "good enough" job is truly good enough. Keep in mind the 20–80 rule: 20 percent of the effort to do any job will reap 80 percent of the benefits.

■ **Deferrer.** The deferrer dreams of an organized clothes closet, too—but the job seems so overwhelming that she spins her wheels at the thought. Break the thrall of procrastination by making one tiny start. Declutter half a hanger rod or half a drawer. Tomorrow, do it again ... and again ... and again. The remedy of action is usually enough to get the deferrer going; taking many little steps will build a bridge to the goal: a clean and organized closet.

■ **Rebel.** Mom was a tyrant, all right—she insisted that clothing be hung up or put away neatly. Out on her own, the rebel continues the war, tossing clothing with abandon. After a while, rummaging through piles on the floor to get dressed in the morning loses any appeal—but the rebel's behavior pattern is entrenched.

To make peace with the internal rebel, remind yourself of the power of choice. "I choose to store my clothing in a way that protects it, and makes it easy for me to dress well," will send the rebel back into the past, where she belongs.

Storing
seasonal clothing

Unless your family lives in a balmy equatorial region, seasonal clothing must be rotated and stored between hot-weather and cold-weather seasons. Be alert for storage options that will keep out-of-season clothing safely and provide easy access for the next season's closet changeover.

Before you store

Launder or dry-clean clothing before storing it for the season —even if it looks clean. Hidden stains may not be evident now, but you'll see them in six months, after the stain has set. Body oils attract clothes moths and cause a deep-set odor if not removed from clothing before storage.

Remove dry-cleaned garments from plastic bags, as the bags trap moisture and encourage mildew. Cotton garment bags or old cotton sheets protect stored clothing from dust, while allowing air circulation.

Choose a storage location that is cool, dry, and well ventilated. Beware of the attic when storing winter clothing. Hot summer attic temperatures can cause fiber damage, while the heat will set any hidden stains. Avoid storing clothing in an area receiving direct sunlight; it can fade clothing.

Choosing hangers Select the right hangers when storing clothes for the season. Avoid storing clothing on thin wire hangers (*see page 136*). Store jackets and coats on padded hangers or wooden suit hangers. Hang trousers by the cuff or hem, hanging straight, to avoid creases. Hang skirts from waistbands using skirt hangers. Wooden or plastic hangers may be used for blouses or shirts. Dresses and skirts often include hanger loops designed to support the garment's weight; place them around the head of the hanger or on hanger hooks.

◀ **Bed 'em down.** Space beneath the bed works well for seasonal clothing storage. Use under-bed storage organizers, and if necessary raise the bed with bed risers to make room for them.

Boxing clothes When boxing clothes for storage avoid boxes made from cardboard. Cardboard is acidic, and the glue it contains is attractive to pests and insects. Lidded plastic storage containers will hold clothing safely, without attracting pests or damaging fibers. Use labels or a permanent marker to label containers to help you identify the contents later.

Clothes moths In areas where moths are prevalent, mothballs can help protect clothes made from natural fibers, but treat them with extreme respect. Mothballs kill moth larvae with chemical fumes, so they should be used only in sealed containers. Do not place mothballs directly on stored clothing.

The fumes are hazardous to humans, so do not wear clothing immediately if it has been stored with mothballs. Clean clothing or air it in a well-ventilated location for at least a day before wearing. Always keep mothballs away from children and pets.

Cedar blocks, shavings, or cedar oil offers less toxic protection against moths when storing clothing. Like mothballs, clothing must be stored in a closed container when using cedar, so that the fumes will deter moths.

Where to store out-of-season clothes?

Try these tips to stash seasonal clothing out of the way when not in use.

■ **Rack 'em up.** Rolling garment racks are inexpensive, sturdy, and make seasonal closet changeovers easy. Roll the rack to the closet, and load it up with winter jackets, suits, and trousers. Add a sweater hanger to provide shelf space on the rack. When you are finished, roll the rack to an alternate storage location; cover it with a cotton bed sheet to protect the clothing from dust.

■ **Suitcase solution.** Suitcases are ideal containers for transporting clothing—and for storing it, too. During the off-season, tuck seasonal clothing inside suitcases. A label or sticky note affixed outside of the suitcase identifies clothing inside.

■ **Hang 'em high.** If you're blessed with a closet that has a high ceiling, tap that empty space for seasonal storage. Add a hanging rod near the closet ceiling; store out-of-season clothes up in the nosebleed seats for safe, accessible storage.

Saving strategy: kids' clothing archive

A growing child means outgrown clothes—and too often, an outgrown clothing budget. To keep costs under control, many families retain baby clothes and hand-me-down clothing for use by the next youngster. Frugal parents "buy up", purchasing sale clothing in larger sizes for children's use as they grow; garage sale shoppers can collect an entire wardrobe of quality children's clothing as they cruise the yard sales.

Problem is, where do you store the bargains? Most children's bedrooms have inadequate storage for clothing in active use, much less an added cache of "grow-into" clothes. Solution: set up a simple clothing archive to sort, store, and organize kids' clothes.

Ready to wear

To create a kids' clothing archive, collect or purchase eight to ten lidded plastic storage containers. Containers should be clean, dry, and stack easily.

Sort clothing by gender—boy or girl —and then by size. Assign each pile to a box, and label accordingly: Boy–Size 6; Girl–Size 8. Stack boxes in an accessible storage area in basement, garage or attic, arranging them by gender and size.

Did you find a great bargain on toddler coveralls? Stash them away in the "Boy–3T" box until the baby is ready to cruise the house. When daughter's dresses are all too short, check the "Girl–Size 6" archive box before you shop for new clothes; add her outgrown dresses in good condition to the "Girl–Size 4" archive for use next year by her younger sister.

Cut costs in the closet:
clothing care

Whether you love your clothes—or simply hate to shop—it makes sense to maintain clothing properly. Clothing represents a substantial investment of money, time, and energy, and no one likes to see the premature demise of a favorite garment. Good care prolongs the life of your clothing and keeps it looking good longer.

Here are basic pointers to protect your clothing investment:

■ **Air out clothing before wearing it.** Wait! Don't tuck that expensive suit or pretty dress back into the closet right away. When you've worn a garment, hang it up to air outside the closet overnight before putting it away. An airing will smooth out wrinkles. By removing moisture and odors, it also reduces the need for costly dry-cleaning.

■ **Kiss wire hangers good-bye.** Dry-cleaning freebies are hard on good clothes. Hanger ends poke into blouse sleeves, stressing the fabric, while rough wire edges snag a fabric's delicate weave. Skinny wires cut into shoulder pads and don't support heavier garments. For advice on which type of hanger to use for which type of garment, see page 136 and the caption below. Earth-friendly tip: many dry-cleaners will recycle wire hangers; check with your cleaners to see if they will accept surplus wire hangers for re-use.

■ **Dress dry.** Deodorants, body lotions, and perfumes are a treat for your body but hard on your clothes. Chemicals used

> "An airing will smooth out wrinkles and reduce the need for costly dry-cleaning."

◄ **Happy hang-ups.** Use sturdy, shaped wooden hangers to support the weight of jackets and coats; slender wood or plastic hangers keep blouses wrinkle-free and ready to wear.

in cosmetics can harm clothing fibers, so get dry before you get dressed. After you apply them, allow deodorants, sprays, and cologne to dry thoroughly before donning clothing—and never apply perfumes or lotions directly to your clothes.

■ **Treat stains quickly.** Stains are harder—or impossible—to remove once they have set. Launder stained garments, or deliver stained clothing to the dry-cleaners as soon as possible after the stain occurs. You'll stand the best chance of erasing the mishap if you move quickly.

"It's an old home truth: 'A stitch in time saves nine.'"

■ **Dust ... your clothing?** Dust and lint are more than just unsightly on your clothes; these abrasive particles can damage fibers. Use a lint roller and a clothes brush to remove dust and lint from clothing regularly.

■ **Mend your ways.** It's an old home truth: "A stitch in time saves nine." Mend small tears or rips quickly, before they become big ones. A quick stitch to a sagging hem will prevent an embarrassing downfall later down the road.

■ **Keep order in the closet.** Crowded closets are more than just inconvenient—they damage clothing, as well. Crushed too tightly together, clothes wrinkle unnecessarily, and moisture and odors are trapped in the fabric. Give your clothing breathing room in the clothes closet to preserve it.

■ **Go for the Gobi ... closet.** In humid climates, closet storage can get downright funky. Moisture in the air settles on clothing and encourages mold and mildew; the closet's enclosed space magnifies the destructive effect. Result: musty smells and damaged clothing. Investigate dehumidifier products to dry closet interiors and preserve your wardrobe. These plastic containers hold moisture-attracting crystals and can be placed in a corner where they'll absorb excess humidity.

■ **Repel pests.** Moths and carpet beetles love the confines of the clothes closet where they attack natural fibers like wool and cotton. Keep them out safely with environmentally friendly cedar blocks. Hung from hangers or clothing rods, cedar's essential oils repel pests. When the scent fades, restore it by lightly sanding the blocks to expose new surface.

Your money's worth: dry-cleaning

Professional dry-cleaning is a valuable tool for preserving the life of your clothing, but it helps to be in the know. Get the most for your dry-cleaning dollar with these tips:

■ **Dry-clean sparingly.** The dry-cleaning process is harsh and costly. Subject clothing to it only when absolutely necessary.

■ **Double or nothing.** Because dry-cleaning can fade or alter fabric color, always dry-clean both pieces of a two-piece garment such as a suit, not just one.

■ **Come clean with your cleaner.** When you take clothing to the dry-cleaner, point out stains and spots. and identify what caused them, if possible. If he or she has to guess, it's less likely that the cleaner will be able to remove the stain.

■ **Put a stop to staples.** Ask the cleaner to use a safety pin to attach cleaning tickets to your garment, not a staple. The stapler shreds garment tags unnecessarily.

■ **Tap the cleaners' clothing-care talent.** Many dry-cleaners also offer clothing repair and alterations, shoe repair, and special treatments for bridal gowns, quilts, suede, or leather. Ask them about any specialty services you may need; they are a great source of wardrobe talent.

■ **Pitch the plastic bags.** Once home, remove clothing from the dry-cleaner's plastic bags. Fumes from solvents used in the dry-cleaning process need air circulation to dissipate, while plastic bags hold in moisture that can harm clothing during storage.

■ **Recycler's tip.** Tie a knot in the bottom of the plastic bag, and use it to line a trash can.

Cost calculation:
the mending matrix

Grandmother Betty was quick to pick up her needle as a young mother in the 1930s, but whether or not to repair clothing is a more complex question in today's world. Cheaper global labor has brought down the relative cost of clothing, while overall clothing quality has declined—and sewing skills are no longer part of an ordinary school curriculum. When is it worth your time to mend or alter clothing?

Mastering mending basics

Growing up in the home of a hobby seamstress, my son was fascinated by sewing machines from an early age. By the time he turned eight, son Ryan had learned to machine-sew most of the seams of his favorite shorts: bright-colored cotton "jams."

I was happy to encourage his interest, because everyone—male, female, fashionista, or fad-adverse—needs a set of basic mending skills. When he entered boot camp for the United States Marine Corps, Ryan came to agree with me as he watched fellow recruits struggle with the simplest mending chores.

Here is a list of mending basics that everyone—even big, strong Marines—should know how to do. These simple sewing jobs require very few tools, and will keep clothing on the job and functional:

- Sew a button
- Mend a straight seam
- Patch a hole
- Take a hem
- Darn a tear or a rip
- Replace hooks, eyes, and snaps

These days, it's hard to know whether it's time or cost-effective to mend clothing. High repair charges versus lower clothing costs weigh against mending, lower-quality clothing is harder to mend, and we may not own the sewing tools—or possess the sewing skills—necessary to complete the job. Consider these questions to determine whether to mend or alter clothing:

- **Is the garment in good condition?** Repairing a slight tear in a new pair of child's cotton overalls makes sense—but the identical repair will be hard to justify if the garment is worn and the fabric is thin. Mend garments only if they're in good condition, because worn fabric won't hold a repair for very long.
- **How extensive is the needed repair?** Taking up a frayed hem or reinforcing a split seam is a quick and easy job; removing and replacing a broken zipper is difficult and time-consuming. Save major mending jobs for expensive clothing that will justify the effort.
- **Do I know how to make this repair?** Even a simple mending chore will weigh heavy if the task is above your skill level. Nothing can be more frustrating than struggling at sewing, so take a reality check when it comes to sewing skills. Some of us have them; some don't—so be honest with yourself about your sewing competence when you contemplate making repairs.
- **What tools will I need to repair this item?** A simple hem requires only needle and thread, but repairing a broken invisible zipper may be impossible without a special adapter

foot for the sewing machine. Be sure to factor in the cost of any tools you will need for the job when you evaluate whether to mend an item of clothing.

■ **What would a professional charge for this repair?** To get a true grasp of the economics of mending clothing, find out what a professional would charge to do the repair. Balance that amount against what the garment is worth for a good rule of thumb on the question of to mend, or not to mend?

"Even a simple mending chore will weigh heavy if the task is above your skill level."

Make a mending center

The mending basket can be a black hole that swallows garments for years, giving them back only when time and styles have passed forever. Make mending chores fly by creating a mending center for your organized home. The center's focus: a one-stop place to store garments in need of mending, and the tools to complete the repairs.

Locate a mending center in or near the laundry room or laundry center (*see pages 140–141*). A quick stitch to a sagging hem before washing makes sure the problem isn't exacerbated. Set aside a hanger area, or designate a basket or hamper to hold items in need of repair. Store mending tools in a basket or tote with a handle.

A basic kit should comprise:

■ Scissors
■ Needles and thread
■ Measuring tape
■ Thimble
■ Seam ripper

When a mending job needs more than a minute or two, the tote makes it easy to relocate to a comfortable chair with your sewing. Choose one with good light, and your eyes will thank you; make it near a television or radio, and you'll enjoy your sewing more.

Mine the mending for clothing cash

Let's face it: few of us look forward to mending clothes. As a to-do list item, "empty mending basket" ranks as a lower-than-low priority. Think again! Clothing that is already purchased but in need of repair represents a hidden asset in terms of time and money. To change your thinking (and free your clothes), try this method to keep mending in bounds.

■ **Get real.** If you're using the mending basket to avoid decisions (or even just stall ironing chores), you're misusing it. Use the tips on this page to be realistic about when and whether to mend.

■ **Shop at home first.** Before hitting the mall, check the mending. Often, those "new black travel slacks" on your list can be found in the basket—and it takes less time to shorten them than it does to drive to the shopping center.

■ **Check when the seasons change.** Some garments bought at season's end never see closet space because they've been tucked into the mending basket for a quick alteration to make them wearable. Hunt them out when the seasons change and new wardrobe needs are fresh in your mind.

▲ **Basic sewing tools.** Needle, thimble, and thread are inexpensive allies in the fight to get the most use from your clothing. A basic sewing kit keeps clothing in good repair.

Laundry
activity center

Where there's life, there are clothes—and where there are clothes, there's laundry! Does Mt. Washmore erupt and rise from the floor in your home on a regular basis? Laundry nerds may revel in the act of folding freshly dried sheets, but the rest of us need a laundry reality check. Stay on top of the laundry mountain with these tips.

Schedule laundry chores regularly

The equation is simple: you wear clothes? You wash clothes— and towels, sheets, and bedding, too. Put off the laundry side of the equation, and the job becomes much harder. In the laundry hamper, stains and wrinkles have a chance to settle in and make themselves permanent. A load of wet laundry, left to itself in the washing machine, invites mildew. The dryer load, forgotten and unfolded, settles back into rumpled comfort once the heat dies down. As the laundry mountain grows, family members scrabble up its sides, looking for socks, jeans or underpants that are clean enough for a reprise wearing.

Solution: schedule laundry chores regularly. How often to do laundry will depend on your family's needs. Households with young children may have to launder multiple loads each day, while singletons can go for a week at a time between laundry sessions—as long as laundry operations are conducted regularly.

Create a laundry activity center

A laundry activity center combines the equipment, tools, and supplies needed to get in and get the job done—quickly. Establish a space to assemble, sort, wash, dry, fold, and return clean clothing and bedding.

- **Location, location.** Look to the location of the washing machine (if you have one) to set up the laundry center. Clear space around the machine; folding laundry is an active process, so you'll need as much clear counter space as you can create. A sink nearby will make it easier to treat stains and presoak soiled clothing.

- **Let there be light!** Good lighting will help you find and identify stains, so supplement existing lighting if it's dark or dreary. Can you read the fine print on a garment label? If not, provide additional lamps or lighting fixtures.

- **Find the upper reaches.** Store detergents and laundry products in an overhead cabinet, or mount a shelf unit on the wall above the washing machine. Households with small children will need to locate cleaning products up and away from little hands, but within reach of preteens and up, to make it easy for growing youngsters to take over their own laundry chores.

- **Get hung-up.** Install a closet rod in the laundry center to hang permanent-press garments. If cabinetry permits, an expandable shower-curtain rod will hold clean shirts and extra hangers in smaller spaces.

- **Fold and retract.** If space permits, add a retractable clothesline or folding drying rack to the laundry center. Even if the house has an automatic dryer, a clothesline or rack makes it a quick matter to dry sweaters and underthings that should not be placed in the dryer.

- **Color-matching.** Code laundry baskets with a different color for each family member—and place baskets in every bedroom and bathroom. On laundry days, family members who can toddle can toddle their own baskets to the laundry center, and return the clean and folded clothing to their own closets at day's end.

▶ **Cut costs** and corral clothing with a set of laundry-room baskets. They'll separate lights from darks and hold garments until there are enough for a full wash-load to save water and energy.

Laundry
basics

Our grandmothers knew the drudgery of washing clothing by hand; they'd envy the wealth of laundry appliances and products available today—and the ease and speed we take for granted. Ready to tackle the family wash? Here's the fast track to clean clothes: sort and prepare, treat or mend, wash, dry, fold, and put away.

Sort and prepare

Skip the sort step before starting the wash, and you know what'll happen: red jumper plus white undies equals pink panties (or worse, pink jockey shorts).

To sort laundry, start with color. Separate clothing into white, light-colored, bright, and dark divisions to avoid dye transfer—the pink panties problem. Wash white and light clothing separately to keep dye transfer at bay.

Separating synthetics (polyester, nylon, acrylic) from natural fibers (cotton, linen) can also cure dye transfer problems; synthetic fibers can be dye magnets, absorbing the cast-offs from dye-rich natural fibers.

Troubled by lint in the wash? Keep lint-generators (sweatshirts, towels, flannel fabrics) away from lint-attractors (nylon blouses, microfibers) in the laundry process.

For cleaner clothes, sort clothing by soil level. Jeans worn while planting out seedlings in the garden aren't good wash-mates for lightly soiled blouses. Fabric weight, too, should be considered; the heavy stitching, brads, and buttons on jeans are too rough-and-tumble to share a wash cycle with lighter-weight or delicate clothing.

Treat or mend

As you load the washer, check each item of clothing. Close zippers, remove belts and ties, and check pockets for forgotten items that don't belong in the wash.

Eyeball each garment, searching for stains and treat them before you wash (*see pages 148–149*). Check if items need a quick mend (*see pages 138–139*). Keep the mending center in or near the laundry area so that it's easy to make repairs.

sort and prepare ▲   **treat or mend** ▲

Wash

You're ready to wash—but how well do you know your washing machine? Your washer's product manual has a wealth of information about how to get clothes clean effectively. Washing recommendations vary from machine to machine. For instance, filling a front-loading spin-cycle washer more fully gets clothes cleaner, but overloading a top-loader that uses an agitator will impede the cleaning process and could damage clothing.

Clothing loaded, add detergent. Detergent use is among those "know-your-machine" issues where it pays to be informed. Washing machines vary in capacity, and are designed to use

"Skip the sort step and you know what'll happen: red jumper plus white undies equals ... pink jockey shorts."

differing amounts of detergent. Consult the washer's product manual first, then read the detergent box to determine how much detergent to add—and do measure carefully, using a measuring cup. You may need to use more detergent for large loads, very dirty clothing, or if you live in an area with hard water. Use a bit less detergent for soft water, small loads, or lightly soiled clothing.

Add any fabric additives or softener. Follow manufacturer's recommendations to use bleach, non-chlorine bleach, or fabric brighteners; these toxic products must be used with care and according to label directions. Fabric softener should be added during the final rinse cycle.

Select the appropriate water temperature for the clothes in the washer (*see pages 146–147*). Start the washer!

Dry

When the washer cycle has finished, time to dry. Place clothing in an automatic dryer, and select the appropriate heat level and cycle duration. Give any twisted garments a good shake as you load them; you'll give them a head start to dry smooth and wrinkle-free. Hang delicate clothing from hangers, a dryer rack, or from a clothesline to air-dry. (*For more information on drying, see pages 146–147 and 149.*)

Fold and put away

Make sure that you fold or hang clothing quickly after removing it from the dryer; the last bit of heat in the garment will help to smooth out wrinkles (and prevent the need to iron). Watch out for metal buttons or zippers. They can be very hot after a tumble in the dryer.

Using color-coded baskets, place each family member's clothing in a separate basket as you fold. You'll make it easy for everyone to put away their own clothing if they only have to grab a basket and go.

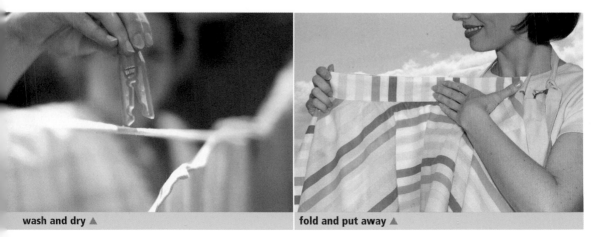

wash and dry ▲   **fold and put away** ▲

Clothing manufacture places big demands on the environment, so green living calls for recycling or repurposing unneeded clothes. Try these ideas to breathe new life into old clothes:

■ **Get good clothes into the right hands.** In good condition, unwanted clothing is ripe for recycling. Donate business clothes to organizations that assist job seekers; and give outgrown kids' clothes to the local children's charity.

■ **Get creative with worn-out clothing.** Turn the cut-off legs of tattered jeans into plastic bag organizers, and seam up the top to create a messenger bag. Old fleece garments make cute stuffed toys, while creative quilters can make "memory quilts" from children's outworn character T-shirts.

■ **Add to your cleaning arsenal.** Ragged terry robes make stellar cleaning cloths if cut apart into large squares—and holey cotton socks find new life as over-the-hand dusters.

Clothing care for
different fabrics

New advances in fiber technology have created garments that are more functional than ever before, but caring for them can be confusing. Clothing care labels offer a dazzling array of choices. Hand wash. Delicate cycle. Line-dry. No iron. Read the labels—then follow these guidelines to care for the range of fabrics in your closet.

Acetate

Acetate is a man-made fiber, often found blended with other fibers to create beautiful, easy-to-drape clothing. Acetate and acetate blends clean up well, but can be very sensitive to dye transfer. Check the care label, and then wash garments containing acetate fibers in cold water.

Acetate is a weak fiber, and can be damaged by twisting, wringing, or heat. Hand-wash acetate blends, or use the gentle cycle of the washer for machine-washable garments.

Iron garments containing acetate using a low-heat setting. Press on the wrong side and use a press cloth to avoid shine and preserve the beauty of the fabric.

Cotton

Cotton is a worldwide favorite for comfortable, versatile clothing. A natural fiber, cotton can be found in garments as casual as a T-shirt or as elaborate as a ball gown.

Cotton fibers will shrink unless the fabric has been pre-shrunk or processed, so start with the care label. "Cold water only" may signal that your ankle-length cotton trousers will convert themselves to capri pants if not washed correctly.

Cotton items that are pre-shrunk may be washed in hot, warm, or cold water, depending on the color of the garment and care label recommendations.

If care labels agree, add chlorine bleach to white cotton wash loads to remove stains; colored cottons may be brightened by non-chlorine bleach formulated for colored clothing. Cold-water washing will protect the deep color of cotton jeans, and preserve the pep of brightly colored Hawaiian shirts.

Over-drying cotton will encourage shrinkage; dry cotton garments at a lower heat and remove them from the dryer while still fairly cool.

"'Cold water only' may signal that your ankle-length trousers will convert into capri pants if not washed correctly!"

Linen

Linen is a natural fiber, made from the flax plant. Check care labels on linen garments to determine whether the garment must be dry-cleaned. If machine-washable, wash according to label instructions, using water appropriate to the garment's color. Linen absorbs more water during the washing process than other fibers, so guard against overcrowding in the washer and dryer. Iron linen from the inside out, using steam at a hot iron setting.

Polyester

The last century's "wonder fiber," polyester creates colorful, durable, easy-care garments. Most polyester fabrics may be machine-washed using warm water, but check care labels first.

Tumble-dry polyester garments on low heat. Remove them from the dryer while still slightly damp to prevent wrinkles and avoid a static build-up. If ironing is required, use a low heat: polyester will melt beneath a hot iron.

Silk

Supple, strong, and lustrous, this natural fiber is among the world's oldest clothing materials. While silk fiber itself is washable, many weave patterns used for silk fabric will tighten or pucker if washed, and deep dye tones may not be color-fast.

Let garment labels guide you when cleaning silk garments. "Dry Clean Only" signals a fabric or construction that will not survive washing. Launder washable silk garments using products formulated for hand-washing or delicate fabrics. Mild baby shampoo (without conditioning additives that may add wax or oils) is a good choice for hand-washable silk fabrics. It will clean the natural protein and revitalize the fiber.

Never tumble silk in the dryer. Instead, roll the item in a towel to press out moisture, and then hang to dry. Press silk garments with a warm iron.

Spandex

A touch of stretch makes clothing fit and feel better. Enter spandex, an elastic fiber now incorporated in small amounts in many types of fabric to add stretch and comfort. While spandex is hand- or machine-washable, avoid hot water and chlorine bleach. Both will damage the spandex fibers. Unless care labels provide otherwise, hang spandex garments to dry, and avoid machine drying.

The heat of the dryer can cause some spandex-blends to pucker or bubble. If ironing is necessary, press the item quickly with a warm iron.

Wool

Sheep love it, and we do, too: the soft, warm fiber made from wool. Naturally insulating and easy to dye, wool fabric runs the gamut from rugged tweeds to floating wool challis.

In the natural state, wool is washable, but because many wool garments incorporate construction methods that cannot be washed, dry-clean wool clothing where the label requires. If washable, use a gentle detergent and hand- or machine-wash as directed by the clothing care label.

A tip from a venerable Shetland Islands' knitter: wash and rinse wool fibers in lukewarm water. Using cold water to rinse can cause shrinkage when it comes to wool.

FABRIC WASH AND DRY GUIDELINES

Fabric type	WASH				DRY			
	Hand	Cool	Warm	Boil	Dry naturally	Tumble cool	Tumble warm	Tumble hot
Acetate	●				●			
Cotton				●			●	
Linen		●			●	●		
Polyester		●			●	●	●	
Rayon			●		●			
Silk	●	●			●	●		
Nylon				●	●	●		
Spandex	●				●			
Wool	●				●			

Out, out, **damned spot!**

Life is like an ice cream cone: it's cool, it's sweet—but there are always going to be a few drips. When they land on your clothes, will you know how to handle them? Prompt and proper stain treatment will keep clothing looking new longer; delay or the wrong response can make the stain a permanent addition.

Pretreat promptly. As you sort laundry, be on the lookout for stained items; pretreating is the best and easiest way to remove stains. A trip through the washer and dryer can turn a dribble of salad dressing into a permanent addition to a blouse if it's not treated first.

Pretreat properly. When it lands on your pants and must be removed, sauce for the goose isn't always sauce for the gander. Different stains require different pretreatment methods. Here are some of the most common stain problems and how to pretreat them:

■ **Oily stains.** Salad dressing, lipstick, and auto grease create oily stains on clothing—and so does your neck on the inside of a shirt collar. To treat collar rings and oily stains, apply liquid detergent directly to the soiled area. Allow the item to stand for 15 minutes before laundering. The detergent will loosen and dissolve the soil so that it can be lifted away in the wash.

■ **Protein stains.** When Baby spits up on your shoulder, you've got a protein stain. Blood, milk, and dairy products, and most body soil contain organic matter that will harden and set over time or when exposed to hot water. Soak protein stains in cold water for at least 30 minutes before laundering. A tip from the nursing profession: stubborn, dried-on blood stains may be removed by applying a 3 percent hydrogen peroxide solution (sold in drugstores for wound care) to the stain, but pretest fabric for color-fastness, first.

■ **Tannin stains.** Tannin puts the pucker in your tea—and permanent color on your clothing if you spill it. Wine, coffee, tea, soft drinks, fruits, and fruit juices commonly cause tannin

▲ **Easy does it.** Treating stains is one time when a light touch is best. Rubbing or scrubbing at stained fabric can harm fibers or lighten dye. Blot stains for best results.

stains. Pretreat them by soaking in cold water, then wash in the hottest temperature appropriate for the garment.

■ **Dye stains.** Loll on the grass some summer afternoon, and you're apt to get up with a grass-green dye stain, compliments of the lovely turf. Foods with strong colors, such as blueberries or mustard, create dye stains. So does direct transfer from fabric or leather, such as the blue cast rubbed off on white undergarments worn beneath new jeans. Pretreat dye stains with direct application of detergent to the stained area, then wash in the hottest water appropriate for the fabric.

Keeping a family in clean clothes isn't just a never-ending chore; it's a major consumer of energy and natural resources in the household. Focus on these strategies to stay clean and green in the laundry area.

Using the washing machine

As an energy user, the washing machine is a household front-runner. Rein in the beast's use of water and power with these energy-saving tips:

■ **Chill out.** Heating water for household use is a costly proposition, so turn down the thermostat on the hot water heater. For most households, a setting of 120°F (49°C) is adequate—and lower hot-water temperatures make scald injuries much less likely to occur. By turning down the thermostat, you'll save energy whenever you launder with heated water.

■ **Stay cool.** Wash in cold water whenever possible. New detergent formulations for cold-water washing dissolve well and get clothes clean at lower temperatures. Even when heavy soil or fabric type requires washing in hot or warm water, a cold-water rinse saves energy. Bonus: cold-water washing preserves fabric colors.

■ **Fill 'er up.** Wash full loads of laundry—you'll use proportionately less water and energy than doing several partial loads.

■ **Cycle down.** Make good use of the washing machine's alternate cycles for best energy savings. Permanent press or delicate cycles are shorter, and agitate and spin less than "heavy wash" ones. Use them for lighter-weight or lightly soiled garments.

■ **Measure twice, wash once.** In the laundry room, more isn't better when it comes to the amount of detergent or other laundry additives you use, so measure carefully. Too much detergent won't clean clothing any better and will be hard to rinse away. Chlorine bleach eats away fibers if overused. Too much fabric softener can stain clothing; rewash to remove spotting.

■ **Clean and green.** A green hint: use a cup of white vinegar instead of commercial fabric softeners. Vinegar cuts detergent residue, softens clothing, and removes odor—and at a price point far less than commercial products.

Drying clothes

When drying laundry, convenience costs! Duck high power bills with these tips for efficient dryer use:

■ **Let the sun shine.** Sunlight and fresh air dry clothing for free—and the warm scent of sun-dried clothes is a sensory bonus. When possible, hang laundry outdoors to dry.

■ **Hang loose.** Don't over-fill an automatic dryer. Crowded with clothing, the dryer will have to work much too hard, and leave clothing with wrinkles that can require ironing. Let clothes tumble freely for most efficient dryer use.

■ **Enough is enough!** When using an automatic dryer, don't over-dry clothing. "Auto" settings sense moisture levels and temperature inside the dryer, so use them when possible. Over-drying clothing can cause shrinkage and fabric damage, so save your clothes and the environment by removing dried clothing promptly.

■ **Free the filter.** Clean the dryer's lint filter with every load. A lint build-up impedes air circulation and forces the dryer to work longer and hotter. Every month, rinse the filter; you'll be amazed at the volume of lint that you'll remove.

■ **Vent it.** Check the dryer's vent hoses and outlet hood for lint build-up or obstruction. If the hood cover won't open freely, replace it. Proper ventilation is necessary for efficient drying and will save energy.

Clean and green in the laundry room

TREATING STAINS

For this stain	use this product	and this method
Adhesive tape, chewing gum	Prewash stain remover	Rub the stained area with ice to harden the gummy residue; gently remove as much as possible with a dull knife. Saturate the stain with prewash stain remover. Rinse thoroughly before laundering.
Baby formula	Enzyme-based laundry presoak	Soak the stained item in a solution of enzyme-based presoak and water for 30 minutes to several hours.
Blood and bodily fluids	Enzyme-based laundry presoak; chlorine, non-chlorine or oxygen bleach product; hydrogen peroxide (3 percent solution, sold in drugstores for wound care)	Soak fresh stains in cold water for 30 minutes or until the blood is gone. For dried stains, presoak the garment in a solution of enzyme-based presoak and water, then launder. If the stain remains, launder the garment using non-chlorine bleach, chlorine bleach, or oxygen bleach, as appropriate for the fabric type. To remove set stains on a colorfast garment, apply hydrogen peroxide to the stained area using an eyedropper. Reapply until the stain is dissolved, then rinse and launder the garment. [Note: as hydrogen peroxide is a bleach, test the garment for color-fastness first.]
Coffee, tea, soft drinks	Prewash stain remover or liquid detergent; non-chlorine bleach	Use prewash stain remover or liquid detergent; soak garments with fresh stains in cold water before laundering. For set-in stains, apply a prewash stain remover or liquid detergent; allow to stand for 15 minutes before laundering. Wash the garment using non-chlorine bleach where appropriate for the fabric type.
Candle wax, crayon marks	Paper towels and iron; chlorine or non-chlorine bleach	Apply ice to the stain to harden it, then remove as much wax as possible with a dull knife. Place the stained fabric between two layers of paper towels, and iron with a warm iron to remove wax. Repeat with fresh paper towels until the wax is removed. Launder, using chlorine or non-chlorine bleach where appropriate for the fabric type.
Chocolate	Enzyme-based laundry presoak	Presoak in an enzyme-based laundry presoak before laundering as usual.
Dye transfer	Color-remover laundry additive	Use commercial color-remover laundry additives as directed to remove dye transfer stains from light-colored or dye-magnet fabrics, such as light-colored garments and synthetics.
Eggs	Enzyme-based laundry presoak	Presoak egg stains in an enzyme-based laundry presoak for 30 minutes to several hours. Launder as usual.
Fruit or fruit juices	Prewash stain remover or liquid detergent; chlorine or non-chlorine bleach	Soak fresh stains in cold water before laundering. For set-in stains, apply a prewash stain remover or liquid detergent directly to the stained area; allow to stand 15 minutes before laundering. Wash garment using chlorine or non-chlorine bleach where appropriate for fabric type.
Grass	Enzyme-based laundry presoak	Presoak grass-stained items in an enzyme-based laundry presoak for 30 minutes to several hours. Launder as usual.

For this stain	use this product	and this method
Grease or oil	Prewash stain remover or liquid detergent	Apply a prewash stain remover or liquid detergent directly to stained area. Allow to sit for 15 minutes, and then launder in the hottest water appropriate for the fabric type.
Mildew	Chlorine or non-chlorine bleach.	Launder mildewed garments in the hottest water appropriate for the fabric type, using the bleach product safe for that fabric. Mildew stains may be permanent.
Milk and dairy products	Enzyme-based laundry presoak	Presoak stained garments in an enzyme-based laundry presoak for 30 minutes to several hours. Launder as usual.
Mustard	Prewash stain remover	Pretreat mustard stains with a prewash stain remover; launder as usual.
Perfume	Prewash stain remover or liquid detergent	Apply a prewash stain remover or liquid detergent directly to the stained area. Allow the item sit for 15 minutes, and then wash as usual.
Rust or iron stains	Commercial iron remover	Treat rust or iron stains with a commercial iron remover, according to package directions. Do not use chlorine bleach to try to remove iron stains, since bleach will set them permanently.
Sauces (catsup, tomato sauce, barbeque sauce)	Prewash stain remover or liquid detergent; chlorine or non-chlorine bleach	Apply a prewash stain remover or liquid detergent directly to the stained area; allow to stand 15 minutes before laundering. Wash the garment using chlorine or non-chlorine bleach where appropriate for the fabric type.
Tobacco	Enzyme-based laundry presoak	Presoak in an enzyme-based laundry presoak before laundering as usual.

Treating stains on the run

In a perfect life, spots and stains would occur right there in the laundry area, where the means to treat them was close at hand. In reality, stains love life on the fly: while traveling, eating out, or away from home. Try these ideas to deal with stains on the run:

■ **Duck them!** Simple as it sounds, avoiding stains prevents the need to treat them. Sit down to eat, when possible, instead of juggling drippy burgers behind the wheel (and wearing the catsup for the rest of the day). Tuck napkins into children's T-shirts to soak up the inevitable restaurant spills.

■ **Carry a first-aid kit for stains.** Whether it's car travel or just the daily commute, tuck an emergency stain kit into the car. Fold a few paper towels into the bottom of a plastic food storage bag; they'll help you soak up spills and blot fresh stains with cool water. Add a disposable plastic knife for scraping away solid materials. Some prepacked stain-removal towelettes will also come in handy.

■ **Be ready for vacation mishaps.** Pack a travel-sized bottle of liquid detergent or pre-packed stain-removal towelettes so that you can treat a stain on the spot. In an emergency, try using talcum powder from your washbag to treat an oily stain. Cover the stain with a layer of powder, then leave it for at least half an hour for the powder to absorb the oil. Brush the powder away with a clean, dry washcloth—if there's still some staining, repeat the procedure until the mark has gone.

Press on!
top tips for easy ironing

The tools: iron, ironing board, sprayer, and starch. The job: remove wrinkles from clothing. The goal: get the job done, fast and smoothly. The problem: wilting resolve behind the ironing board. Speed household ironing chores by knowing what to press and how to press it. Try these tips to take the heat out of ironing.

1 **I iron, ergo I am.**
Proper ergonomic alignment speeds the ironing process and avoids backache. Adjust the ironing board to hip level; when holding the iron, your elbow should be bent at a 90-degree angle and your shoulder should move freely.

2 **Clean the scene.**
Before turning on the heat, check the iron's soleplate for built-up residue. Remove any deposits before ironing: scorch or soil is a drag on the soleplate, and can be transferred to clean clothing.

3 **Know your clothes.**
Read clothing care labels and match iron temperatures to the garment's fiber content. If in doubt about a garment's fiber content, set the iron on the low side of the temperature dial.

4 **Duck a dirty job.**
Never press soiled or dirty clothing. The iron's heat will set stains and body soil, and intensify odors in the fabric. Heat plus dirt equals a fine mess, so keep clothing sweet by washing or dry-cleaning before you press.

◀ **Buying an iron.** When replacing an iron, new choices enhance safety and usability. Look for auto-shutoff features, labeled heat settings, roomy water reservoirs, and built-in sprayers.

5 Into the mist.
Keep a spray bottle filled with water close at hand. A quick spritz of water releases any accidental creases and makes pressing chores fly. For a scent-ual touch, fill the ironing spray bottle with linen water: water infused with non-staining fragrances. Find linen water at bath-and-bedding shops.

6 Go with the grain.
Just as you sand a wooden table, iron with the grain, not against it. Ironing across thread diagonals causes fabric to buckle and stretch.

7 A pressing matter.
The press cloth is your friend! Use this rectangle of tightly woven cotton cloth as an intermediary between the iron and the garment to guard against shine when pressing on the right side of wool or delicate fabrics.

8 Keep it moving, keep it light.
Keep the iron moving and the pressure light. Pressing too hard flattens fiber nap and stresses reinforced areas like pockets, while a slow iron is more apt to scorch or burn fabric.

9 Hang 'em high!
When you've finished pressing, hang the garment immediately. Freshly ironed clothing is vulnerable to wrinkling in the first several hours. Allow clothing to cool and dry completely before placing them in a closet or bureau drawer.

Keep cool: no-iron strategies

A hot iron is nobody's cup of tea—and it's a household power hog. Save time and energy by heading off ironing in the first place.

■ **Buy smart.** When shopping for clothes, look for labels that promise "no-iron" or "permanent press" fabric finishes; they're your ticket to ironing freedom.

■ **Enlist the aid of the washer.** Special washing machine cycles for permanent-press clothing use cool rinse temperatures to encourage clothing to shed wrinkles— so use them!

■ **Shake it, baby, shake it.** Shake out each garment before adding it to the washer. Untwist spirals of trouser leg, and unwind clumps of bathrobe ties, tights, and pantyhose.

■ **Stay cool.** Over-drying clothing in the automatic dryer shrinks seams and sets wrinkles, so stop the dryer when clothing is just dry and not yet hot. Barely damp clothing will release wrinkles as it hangs, avoiding the need for touch-ups.

■ **Dance attendance on the dryer.** Remove clothing from the dryer promptly, and hang immediately. As you remove clothing, smooth collars and cuffs, and stretch seams for a smooth look.

TEMPERATURE GUIDELINES									
Fabric type	Acetate	Acrylic	Cotton	Linen	Nylon	Polyester	Rayon	Silk	Wool
Iron setting	Cool	Cool	Medium to high heat with steam	Medium to high heat with steam	Low	Low to medium heat	Low to medium heat (iron inside out)	Low heat (iron inside out)	Medium heat with steam

Today's homes are a treat for the senses. Rich rugs glow atop gleaming wood floors. Chrome fixtures reflect the sheen of ceramic sinks and granite countertops. Plush chenille pillows contrast with sleek, cushy leather sofas, while wood furniture invites the eye with the depth and richness of wood grain.

Beneath the surface lie a home's systems: the powerful friends that keep us cool in summer, warm in winter, and supplied with water and power year-round.

In this section, we focus on the surfaces and systems that make a home. We'll discover easy ways to preserve our housing investment: keeping walls, windows, floors, and ceilings clean and furniture well cared for. We'll learn to maintain household systems for best energy efficiency and savings.

Finally, we'll focus on safety, adopting simple checklists to keep the home a safe place to live. A household emergency plan will ensure that family members are prepared and informed in the face of fire, flood, or disaster.

Surfaces and systems
select, save, maintain, clean

Cleaning **walls**

Soft with paint or bright with wallpaper, walls frame the life of the household—but too often, they also wear it! Daily living tends to deposit smudges, smears, and fingermarks (especially if there are small children in the household), marring the beauty of walls and woodwork. Painted or papered, keep walls clean and gleaming with these tips for wall cleaning and maintenance.

How to clean painted walls

On your mark, get set, prep! Cleaning painted walls is a big job, so be prepared. Push furniture to the center of the room, and lay down old sheets or canvas drop cloths to catch soapy drips. Avoid plastic tarps; they don't absorb water and become slippery when wet. To protect your hands and to remind you where pictures belong, cover picture nails with a chunk of household sponge.

Assemble your wall-washing tools: lambswool duster, white cleaning cloths, a natural sponge (avoid colored sponges, since they can deposit dyes on light-colored walls), and two buckets: one filled with cleaning solution (*see below*) and one filled with clear water for rinsing. Rubber gloves or washing-up gloves protect your hands; be sure to turn up glove cuffs to help contain drips. A step stool makes it easier to get to the high reaches for easy cleaning; tools with handles keep wall cleaning sessions safe.

Ready to clean In one bucket, mix a wall-cleaning solution. For normal soil levels, try a mild detergent solution to clean walls that consists of:

- 1 gallon (4 liters) warm water, to which you add
- a good squeeze of liquid dishwashing detergent

For more heavily soiled walls, you'll need a stronger alkali solution—but spot-test any cleaning mixture first to ensure

◄ **Take it easy.** A soft approach is best when cleaning walls and moldings. Harsh cleaners, abrasives, or an oversupply of elbow grease can mar painted surfaces or damage delicate wallpaper.

it won't remove or lighten paint. Add all of the following to your bucket and give it a good stir before you start:

- 1 gallon (4 liters) warm water
- 1 cup (250ml) clear non-sudsing ammonia
- 1 cup (250ml) white vinegar
- 1 cup (250ml) washing soda (borax)

The second bucket should hold clean water, to be used for rinsing. Change the water if it starts to look very dirty as you work around the room.

Ditch the dust Dust is always easier to remove than mud, so remove any loose dust before bringing moisture into the mix. Circle the room with the lambswool duster, wiping walls and woodwork from the top down. When the duster is covered with dust, take it outside and spin the handle between your palms to release the dust.

Alternately, use a vacuum cleaner's extension wand and bristle brush head (used for upholstery) to remove dust and cobwebs from walls and woodwork.

Bottoms up Drips are inevitable when washing walls. Should they run down dry, dirty surfaces, they'll dry—and create long muddy stains. Avoid drip issues by washing walls from the bottom up. Yes, you'll drip onto already-cleaned areas, but the solution will be a quick swipe with a sponge, not a tough cleaning job.

Dip the natural sponge into the bucket of cleaning solution, and rub the wall gently to avoid removing paint. Work in small areas, washing, and then using the sponge to rinse the area with clear water. Last, blot excess moisture with white cleaning cloths.

Take it to the end When washing walls, always wash the entire wall, bottom to top and side-to-side. If you need a breather, take it between walls, not in the middle. Stopping the job before you finish the entire wall can cause "wash marks": a wave effect caused by stop-and-go wall washing. Avoid this effect by washing an entire wall in a single session, and use the same type and strength of cleaning solution for each wall.

Wallpaper cleaning tips and tricks

Wallpaper's bright colors and varied textures enliven any room—but that same color and texture can cause problems when it's time to clean. Protect your investment with these wallpaper cleaning tips:

- **Check manufacturer's guidelines.** Because wallpapers differ in content and coating, follow the manufacturer's advice for appropriate cleaning methods.
- **Dust carefully.** Use a lambswool duster, or tie a dry cleaning cloth over a broom to dust the walls before cleaning.
- **Older, non-coated wallpaper.** Use a "dry sponge," found at the hardware store. This product lifts and removes surface dirt without moisture. Rub it lightly against the surface in long strokes to remove dirt.
- **Scrubbable or washable wallpaper.** Use a natural sponge lightly dampened with a solution of warm water and a small amount of liquid dishwashing detergent. Before cleaning, test the solution in an inconspicuous corner to be sure it won't remove paper or coating. Don't scrub too hard or allow the paper to get too wet to avoid damage. Use cleaning cloths to absorb extra moisture after rinsing.
- **Fingermarks or smudges.** Remove by rubbing them gently with an art gum eraser. Use a light touch to avoid damaging the area. Commercial wallpaper cleaners may also be used to lift the small stuff.
- **Cleaners to avoid.** Never use abrasive cleaners—scouring powder or "soft-scrub" cleanser—to clean wallpaper. The abrasive granules which they contain can scratch the wallpaper's coating.

Caring for
specialty surfaces

Marble floors, tile counters, brick fireplaces, or stone entryways bring a unique feel to any home, but require special care and cleaning methods. Preserve the appeal of specialty surfaces with these maintenance tips.

Marble

This stone is soft, porous, and relatively weak. Marble will scratch easily, absorb standing stains, and must be treated with care. For routine cleaning, dust, then buff with a barely damp cleaning cloth to restore the shine.

When more intense cleaning is required, pour a little clear non-sudsing ammonia onto a cleaning cloth, wipe the marble surface and buff dry. When finished, use a commercial marble polish to restore the shine.

Never use abrasive cleaners on marble surfaces. Avoid acid-based cleaning solutions, such as any product containing white vinegar; acids can dull or etch bright finishes.

Ceramic tile

Tile comes in two types: glazed and unglazed. Smooth glazed tile is tough, but brittle and easily scratched, while the surface of unglazed tile can absorb cleaning products. Finally, grout, used to set tile in place, is porous and traps moisture, mold, and mildew.

For regular cleaning of glazed ceramic tile—the shiny tile most commonly used in kitchens and bathrooms—use a non-abrasive spray cleaner. Spray window cleaner leaves a nice finish, but avoid heavily colored commercial sprays, as the bright-colored cleaning solution can discolor porous grout.

Heavily soiled glazed ceramic tile requires bigger guns: an abrasive cleanser or scouring powder. For a seriously stained kitchen counter or grimy shower wall, apply a thin paste of cleanser containing a bleaching agent and water, and allow to stand for 15 minutes to several hours before wiping away cleanser haze. Rinse the area well with water, then wipe dry.

Clean unglazed ceramic tile with a natural sponge lightly dampened with a solution of water and non-soap detergent or commercial tile cleaner.

Avoid using acid-based cleaners, such as white vinegar, on tiled areas. Acid attacks the grout, causing it to crumble. Stay away from steel wool! It will scratch the surface of ceramic tiles.

Brick

Made from clay, brick is porous with open pores that can trap dust and dirt. Use a vacuum extension wand with a long-bristled upholstery brush to remove dust and dirt from interior brick on a regular basis. For heavy-duty cleaning, use an alkali solution of TSP (tri-sodium phosphate) to clean brick: start with 1 tablespoon TSP to 1 gallon (4 liters) of warm water. Scrub the brick surface with a stiff-bristled brush, then rinse the brick well with clean water. TSP is very strong, so use care to avoid skin exposure, and do not spill on carpet or fabrics.

Granite

While strong and durable, this natural stone product needs special care to maintain its characteristic high-gloss finish.

Prevention is key with granite countertops. Mop up spills as soon as possible, before they can penetrate the surface. Use coasters under beverages, since acids common in soft drinks and fruit juices can etch and dull granite surfaces.

Clean granite with a solution of warm water and a few drops of liquid dishwashing detergent. Use a wrung-out cleaning cloth to clean the surface, then rinse with a cleaning cloth soaked in clear water. Avoid cleaning products containing acid, such as white vinegar, since they can etch or dull the surface.

How to clean windows

When it comes to cleaning windows, nothing beats the professional cleaner's tool of choice: the squeegee. You'll also need a squeegee wet cover (or a cleaning cloth attached with rubber bands) and dry cleaning cloths. Have your preferred window-cleaning solution ready in a large bucket.

1 Dunk the squeegee with the wet cover or attached cleaning cloth into the bucket, then smear the cleaning solution over the entire surface of the window. Don't worry about drips; we'll catch up with them at the end.

2 Remove the wet cover or cleaning cloth from the squeegee. Working from top to bottom, draw the squeegee across the window, skimming the cleaning solution and dirt from the glass. Curve the squeegee downward at the end of each stroke.

3 Wipe the squeegee dry after each pass across the window with a fresh cleaning cloth; remember to work from the top moving to the bottom of the window. A dry squeegee avoids drips and keeps unsightly streaks from forming.

4 Finished with the squeegee? Run the cleaning cloth along the "wet" side of the window to dry the drips left behind. Move to the window sill and soak up any puddled cleaning solution. Polish the sill dry with a fresh cleaning cloth—and let the light shine.

A timer Stopping clutter, like acquiring it, is a long-term process of short steps. Too often, the initial excitement of attacking the clutter problem causes people to bite off more than they can chew—or decide, store, or put away in a single session. Result: torn-up drawers, stacks of "I-dunno" items and a sense that the job is never finished.

Using a timer to keep STOP clutter sessions short and complete keeps the declutter momentum going, and prevents burnout. You'll use your timer to start—and stop—each session so that you can finish the put-away step and leave the newly decluttered area clean and ready for use.

Three boxes The put away, storage, and sell/donate boxes lie at the heart of the STOP clutter method. Labeled "Put Away," "Storage," and "Sell/Donate," they're the decision-making engine that drives the declutter process.

Use sturdy, good-sized boxes, preferably with handles and lids. Look for records boxes (sold in office supply stores), or scour supermarkets for lidded produce boxes. Handles make it easy to circle the house at the end of each STOP clutter session, emptying the Put Away box. Lids help you stack the Storage and Sell/Donate boxes as you gather out-of-season items or set aside boxes for donation or a yard sale. Lids also help to cut the temptation to peep inside and return decluttered items to their old haunting grounds. Out of sight is out of mind!

A garbage bag An opaque garbage bag or garbage can is star player in a STOP clutter session. Here's where you'll entrust all the true trash, the quicker, the better. Black garbage bags prevent the declutterer (or family members) from having a change of heart. If it can't be seen, it won't be returned to the scene.

Taking it a step at a time

To harness the power of the STOP clutter method, assemble your boxes and garbage bag and set the timer for 15 minutes. The timer's bell will tell you when it's time to stop deciding and start putting away. Working in 15-minute increments (plus another 5 minutes to return put-away items and stow the tools), you stay fresh and motivated to do the job.

1 Sort Turning to the day's chosen clutter cache—the area around the telephone, for example—take the first step and sort the items being decluttered. Quickly move through the pile of clutter that surrounds the phone, making a quick decision about each item: should I keep this here, put it away, sell it, or throw it away?

If the item belongs in the area being decluttered, sort it into a pile of like items: pens with pens, paper clips with paper clips, and notepads with sticky notes. If the item is an intruder that must be put away in another location, such as a pair of socks, consign it

organize ▲   **put away** ▲

to the Put Away box. Surplus items that can be donated to charity or sold are tossed into the Sell/Donate box, the proper place for the plastic flower pen and the clunky grocery list holder. Items that more appropriately belong in household storage areas—such as light bulbs left over from December's holiday decorations—are tucked into the Storage box.

2 Toss As you sort, toss trash straight into the garbage bag. Expired coupons, supermarket receipts, scribbled bits of paper, non-working pens all go straight into the garbage bag.

3 Organize When the entire area has been sorted and the trash tossed, it's time to organize. Take a good look at the newly decluttered area, and find ways to organize the items that belong there. Stand pens on end in an interesting coffee mug. Run an extension cord to power phone chargers or

tablets. Consider ways to organize the area for best use; can you replace messy message slips with a hanging write-on/wipe-off white board?

4 Put away When the timer rings, or the area is cleared, it's time to put away any out-of-place items identified during the STOP clutter session. Take the Put Away box and circle the house, returning items to their proper places. Toss the garbage bag into the garbage can, and return the timer and boxes to a closet or shelf, where they'll await the next STOP clutter session. As the storage boxes fill, add them to a storage area and begin a new box. Decide when you'll attack the household's next clutter magnet and note it on your calender (*see Planning Your Home, pages 72–87*). Finally, admire your new, organized telephone area. Using the STOP clutter method, you've created a working center for phone calls and messages.

STOP clutter step by step: the junk drawer

All homes have at least one of these: a drawer for small, often-needed items. The contents of this catchall arena seem to expand like bread dough, multiplying at will whenever the drawer is closed. When the mess reaches the rim of the drawer, it's time to STOP clutter.

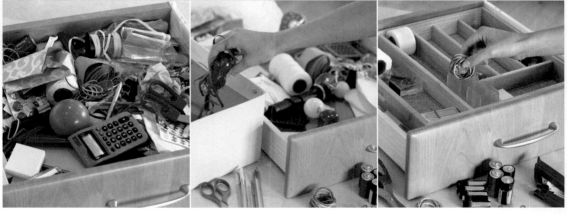

1 Sort. Assemble your tools: timer, boxes, and garbage bag. Set the timer for 15 minutes. Open the junk drawer, and begin the sort step. Sort items that belong in the drawer into like piles, and keep sorting until the timer's bell rings or the drawer is cleared.

2 Toss. Throw any trash, broken, or valueless items into the garbage bag. Place items that belong elsewhere in the Put Away box, and tuck any items for storage in the Storage box. Surplus items that are still useful go to Sell/Donate.

3 Organize. Once the drawer is empty, organize the survivors in the cleared space. Use drawer dividers to separate batteries from postage stamps, pens from store coupons. Bundle or bag small items to make them easy to find.

An Action File makes quick work of daily paper management. When it's time to handle weekly deskwork, you'll find it all in the Action File.

- **Use a small tabletop file** and add to it hanging folders labeled "To Pay," "To Do," and "To File."
- **Include separate folders** in each one for every member of your family, and for religious, sports, or school activities.
- **Sort and drop** incoming paperwork each day into the appropriate file.
- **Bills go into** the "To Pay" folder, while medical insurance papers and other important paperwork should be assigned to the "To File" folder.
- **File things** that need doing, such as permission slips that have to be signed, correspondence that requires a reply, and reminders to schedule the children's dental check-ups, in the "To Do" folder.

Free yourself
from paper clutter

Despite our best efforts, paper mounts up around the house. Stacks of bills breed in corners, while the week's mail spills across the kitchen table. Leave paper free to migrate, and each session of bill-paying will take twice as long. Keep paper in its place! Try the following tips to cut down on paper clutter.

Decide to decide

What force lies at the bottom of paper pile-ups? Like all clutter problems, the culprit is deferred decision-making. It's fun to flip through the day's mail at the kitchen table, but if it's left there to molder, it'll have to be sorted again later. Chances are, important items will go missing.

Instead, decide what to do with each piece of paper the first time you handle it. Ask yourself, "Will this item need to be paid, answered, or filed?" then drop the paper into the appropriate folder of your Action File. An immediate sort-and-stow operation heads off paper clutter at the source.

Keep it or toss it?

Desktop efficiency experts tell us that the 20/80 Rule is alive, well, and running amok amongst the filing cabinets. Specifically, we'll need only 20 percent of the papers that are entrusted to any filing system; the remaining 80 percent are never seen, consulted, or handled again.

When adding to your household files, always keep the 20/80 Rule in mind in order to cut down on clutter in the filing cabinet. Resolve to limit the contents of your filing cabinet to that important 20 percent; discard any item that won't be needed again.

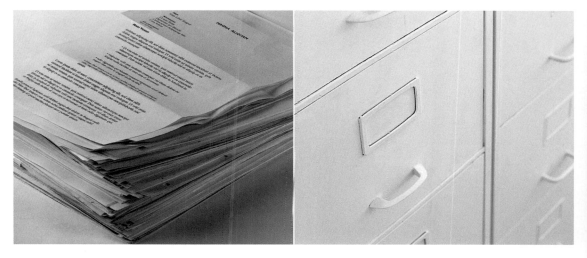

▲ **Day to day.** Establish a home for incoming paper, and use it daily to contain the incoming tide. You'll always know where to find the week's bills, mail, and announcements.

▲ **Store it away.** Don't consign completed paperwork to the messy mountain known as "To File." Filing records promptly means you'll always be able to find the information you need quickly.

Take back your space with these simple tips to pull the plug on paper clutter:

■ **Children's artwork.** When you can't see the refrigerator, it's time to triage the flow of children's artwork. Sort each day's papers into an "artwork" folder in the Action File (*see page 225*). Each week, select the best work to display as "Refrigerator Art of the Week," and consign last week's entry to a basic file marked with the child's name. At the end of the year, tuck the collection of the year's best works into a large envelope, mark it with the year, and add it to the household's classic files. Share extra art projects by writing letters to family members on the reverse side.

■ **Calendars, menus, and phone lists.** Save telephone time by putting calendars, schedules, take-out menus, and phone lists into clear page protectors in the Household Notebook (*see pages 84–87*). Flip through the Household Notebook to quickly check meeting dates or find phone numbers.

■ **Cards and correspondence.** Birthdays, celebrations, and events are a regular part of life —so why dash to the card store for each occasion? Once a year, purchase an assortment of greeting cards, sympathy notes, and stationery items. Stored together with stamps and pens, they'll handle social correspondence without stress.

■ **Daily mail.** Sort each day's mail over the recycling bin to make quick work of unwanted catalogs, coupons, or ad circulars. For safety, shred or destroy credit card applications and financial solicitations before recycling.

■ **Junk mail.** Bar the door to junk mail, depositing it straight into the trash. Where it can't be avoided, as when it's enclosed in bill envelopes, put the problem where it belongs: remove any identifying information from the application and mail it back to the offending company inside the postage-paid envelope with a quick note saying, "No, thanks!" You'll support the postal service and help discourage junk mailers.

■ **Manuals and warranties.** Three-ring binders and a supply of clear plastic page protectors make it easy to file and find product manuals and appliance warranties. Once a year or so, flip through the binder and remove any paperwork concerning items you no longer own.

■ **Newspapers and magazines.** Forget placing fanned-out magazines or neatly stacked newspapers on table surfaces. Low-sided baskets or trays use the principle of "controlled clutter" to display readable items without permitting them to overrun the family room at will.

■ **Receipts.** When business expenses or tax considerations require that you save receipts, drop paper copies into a hanging file folder in the Action File—or make use of scanning apps and online receipts to cut paper.

Clutter-busting tips

▲ see also pages 210–211, 212-213

Set up a
household filing system

Create a household filing system as easy as 1, 2, 3. What's the purpose of a household filing system? It's the place where we store papers against the time we'll need them again. Set up properly, a household filing system will allow users to find documents easily, and maintain and retrieve important papers in the future.

Efficient paper management can be as easy as 1, 2, 3. Simply incorporate the following three key elements into your household filing system:

1 An Action File.
A tabletop file used for daily, short-term filing chores. Use your Action File to hold bills for payment, to set aside correspondence and other papers that require response, and to provide short-term storage paperwork and other information that must be filed (*see also pages 225 and 226–227*).

2 Basic Files.
These are a household's working file system. Kept in a file cart, cabinet, or desk drawer, your basic files should hold medical insurance records, credit card statements, rent receipts, and bank statements. Use your basic files for routine activities such as paying bills, tax files, medical information, and home maintenance.

3 Classic Files.
Archive files used for papers that need to be stored for the long term. What files belong in classic files? Most families save copies of income tax returns, cancelled checks, real estate documents and receipts, insurance policies, automobile documents and warranties, and credit card statements. Use file cabinets or records boxes to protect these items for long-term storage. Note: original documents such as insurance policies, legal documents, or tax records should be stored in secure facilities such as safe deposit boxes.

"Efficient paper management can be as easy as 1, 2, 3."

File it right: setting up a filing system
To set up your own household filing system according to the 1, 2, 3 plan, follow these three steps.

Step 1 Gather paperwork and records. To set up your filing system, scour the house and collect the family paperwork. Look for these types of documents and files:

■ **Automobile:** Car titles, automobile insurance policies, car repair records, tire warranties, owners' manuals, and car loan documents.
■ **Banking:** Bank statements, cancelled checks, check registers, safe deposit box numbers and keys, money market accounts, and certificates of deposit.
■ **Bills and loans:** Credit card statements, receipts from utilities, cable and phone companies, bank debit cards, loan documents, furniture loans and department store accounts.
■ **Health and healthcare:** Medical records, doctor and dentist information, prescription receipts, medical bills, health insurance policies, insurance handbooks and insurance cards.

▶ **Smart storage.** Away with boring beige and olive drab! Paperwork files and storage containers can be decorative as well as organized. Look for new colors and design options.

RETENTION SCHEDULE

Document	How long to keep it
Bank statements	6 years
Birth certificates	Forever
Canceled checks	6 years
Contracts	Until updated
Credit card account numbers	Until updated
Divorce Papers	Forever
Home purchase and improvement records	As long as you own the property or are rolling over profits from it into new property
Household inventory	Until updated
Insurance, life	Forever
Insurance, car, home, or property	Until updated
Investment Records	6 years after tax deadline for year of sale
Investment certificates, stocks and bonds	Until cashed or sold
Loan agreements	Until updated
Military service records	Forever
Real estate deeds	As long as you own the property
Receipts for large purchases	Until the item is sold or discarded
Service contracts and warranties	Until the item is sold or discarded
Social Security card	Forever
Tax returns	6 years from filing date
Vehicle titles	Until sold or disposed of
Will	Until updated

Source: United States Federal Citizen Information Center

Housing: Mortgage statements or rent receipts, house title, property appraisals, floor plans, deeds, home inspections, land surveys, title insurance policies, and property tax assessments.

Insurance: Insurance policies, policy amendments, and declarations sheets.

Legal: Marriage certificates, birth certificates and adoption papers, estate files and wills, powers of attorney, medical powers of attorney (living wills), military service and discharge papers, passport and proofs of citizenship, and Social Security cards.

Retirement: Pension documents, Individual Retirement Accounts, Social Security information and annuities.

Valuables: Appraisals, inventories and photographs of art, antiques, jewelry, rare books, silver, china, or crystal.

Step 2 Give each record a home. Good filing systems are like snowflakes: each family's system is unique. While prefab filing schemes (which often require filing documents according to numbers or numero-alphabetic codes) seem as though they might be easy to use, a filing system won't work for your family unless your family understands what's in it and where every record belongs. Make your filing system make sense—to you. Label file folders in everyday language, using terms that will help you remember what's inside each file folder. If more than one family member handles household paperwork, make sure everyone agrees on file headings. What's "bills" to one partner may be "payments" to another, so come to terms. Commonly used options for file labels include:

- **Automobile:** Label files for automotive records descriptively, such as Auto, Car, or by car model.
- **Banking:** Use folder names like Bank, Checking, Savings, or bank name.
- **Bills and loans:** File by name of payee, or by type of bill (Utilities, Telephone, Long Distance).
- **Health and healthcare:** Include files for Medical Bills, Insurance Records, Prescription Drugs, and by family member's name (Michael—medical records).
- **Housing:** File labels can include House, Mortgage, Repairs, or can be listed by address (3310 Threadneedle Road).
- **Insurance:** Set up files by insurer or by policy type: Homeowners, Life, and Automobile.
- **Legal:** Sort family members' personal records in separate files (John, Mary, Alice), and set aside folders for specific legal issues (Grandma's Estate, 2004 Auto Accident)
- **Retirement:** Label file folders descriptively, such as Internal Revenue Service, Social Security, Pension.
- **Valuables:** Choose folder labels that make it easy to find information: Art, Books, Jewelry, and Antiques.

As you set up folders and sort paperwork into them, set aside original documents that must be stored away from the home. Legal documents, birth and marriage certificates, titles to automobiles and deeds to real property, stocks and financial instruments all should be stored off-site, in a bank safe deposit box or in the case of wills, filed with the family attorney for safekeeping.

Don't forget to add photo negatives—or archived copies of digital photo files—to the safe deposit box. Memories are valuable, too!

"Good filing systems are like snowflakes: each family's system is unique."

▶ **Flip and file.** "Vertical beats horizontal" is never more true than when handling paperwork. Hanging file folders allow you to locate paperwork with a quick peep.

Step 3 Create a retention schedule. Everyone has a friend or relative who will never part with paperwork—ever. Over the years, their household files become so bloated and cumbersome that it's impossible to find anything again.

Knowing what to keep and how long to keep it is the key to an efficient file system. Professional records managers call this list a retention schedule. Develop one for your organized home; it'll provide guidelines that will help you keep filing systems lean and mean. You'll need to check with legal and financial advisors for specific recommendations for your household, but use the list on page 230 as a general guide to how long to keep household files. A simple list—tax records (keep 7 years); credit card receipts (4 years); house documents (forever)—makes it easy to prune stale files.

Resources

Unclutterer
https://unclutterer.com
A comprehensive site to fight clutter of all kinds, UnClutterer is the brainchild of blogger Erin Doland. Get the how, and the when to cut the clutter.

Direct Marketing Association
http://www.dmaconsumers.org/index.html
To reduce junk mail, request that your name be removed from marketing mailing lists. Send a notice, including your name and address, to:

Mail Preference Service, Direct Marketing Association, PO Box 643, Carmel, NY 10512

Canadian Marketing Association
www.the-cma.org
This private trade organization provides a "Do Not Contact" service for consumers to reduce the number of marketing offers received by mail, phone, and fax.

Dress for Success
http://dressforsuccess.org/
This nonprofit organization accepts donations of interview suits for low-income women entering or re-entering the workforce. Clean out your closet and give a sister a leg up!

Freecycle
http://freecycle.org/
An international grass-roots organization devoted to reducing the amount of waste in our landfills. Recycle unneeded items with others in your local area through the Freecycle network.

I'm An Organizing Junkie
http://orgjunkie.com
Articles, and tips for home organization.

MSN House and Home
http://houseandhome.msn.com
Check the "Decor and Home Living" area for storage and organization solutions for every room.

Clean
Consumers Answer Line
http://www.extension.iastate.edu/answerline/
A service of the Iowa State University Cooperative Extension Agency, check this web resource for tips and articles on household cleaning, food safety, home management, and laundry.

National Soap and Detergent Association
http://cleaning101.com
This site from an association of cleaning product manufacturers offers guidance on laundry, household cleaning, dishwashing, and using cleaning products. Don't miss their annual survey of cleaning attitudes— it's always a good read!

The Clean Team
http://thecleanteam.com/
Jeff Campbell's professional cleaners can clean a two-bedroom apartment in 43 minutes. His books, products, articles, and advice will speed cleaning in any home. Be sure to check out the rules for speed cleaning and clutter control.

Plan
Getting Things Done by David Allen
http://davidco.com/
Productivity expert David Allen provides a road map through time chaos with principles for Getting Things Done. Discover the secret of 43 folders and clear the "stuff" from your life.

Reminder services

Remember The Milk
http://rememberthemilk.com
Outsource to-do lists and reminders with this online reminder site. Includes applications for smart phone users.

Jott
http://jott.com
A voice-activated online reminder service. You can use Jott from any US phone. Spoken reminders are translated into text, and there are options for e-mail and appointments.

Follow up then
https://www.followupthen.com
Highly recommended email reminder service sends e-mails to your inbox or smartphone.

Green living

Big Green Purse
http://www.biggreenpurse.com
A site aimed at changing women's shopping habits, identifying environmentally safe, socially responsible products and services at affordable prices.

Green Home
http://www.greenhome.com
Comprehensive online resource for making your home or business greener, supplying environmentally friendly products and offering advice and information.

The Green Guide
http://www.thegreenguide.com
Get the information you need to live green at home with articles and resources from National Geographic. Use the Home and Garden guide to make green choices for every room in your home.

More good stuff

Consumers Union
http://consumersunion.org/
Publisher of Consumer Reports, this non-profit organization provides valuable tips and advice on topics ranging from health care to financial matters to cleaning products.

eHow: Homemaking
http://www.ehow.com/list_1096.html
Short and sweet, this homemaking resource offers how-to advice for myriad homemaking issues.

USDA Food Safety Information
http://www.foodsafety.gov/
From freezer cooking to pantry storage, get tips on safe cooking and food storage practices.

Canadian Food Inspection Agency
www.inspection.gc.ca
This site provides food safety facts and tips, information on food labelling, and food recalls.

OrganizedChristmas.Com
http://organizedchristmas.com
OrganizedChristmas.com offers holiday organizing tips, free printable holiday planner forms, easy craft gifts, recipes, and gift ideas. Get organized for a great holiday season!

Craigslist
http://www.craigslist.org
Craigslist is the grand-daddy of online classified ad sites. Drill down to your local Craigslist listings to find values for donated items or to advertise de-cluttered items for sale.

Consumer Council of Canada
www.consumercouncil.com
Provides consumers with financial service information, including credit reports and consumer-protection issues.

Index

A

abrasive cleaner 53, 65

abrasive scrubbing pads 62

Action Files (paper management) 225, 226, 228

activity centers 34, 40, 41, 43
  see also individual centers

address books 75, 85

ads 93

aerosols 67

all-purpose cleaner 52
  homemade recipe for 55

allergens, control of (bedroom) 171

ammonia, non-sudsing 55

appliances, small kitchen 103
  see also electrical appliances

aprons, for cleaning 57, 63

archives 228

arts and crafts 34, 214–215

arts and crafts activity center 41

artwork 209, 227

B

bags, reusing 10

baking soda 54, 55

Banishment Candidates 216

Basic Files (paper management) 228

basic skills 12

bath bundles 193

bathrooms
  cleaning 62, 188–189
  decluttering 184–185
  STOP clutter 185
  storage in 186–187

bathroom cleaners 52, 53, 57, 62

bedding 192

bedding bundles 193
  control of allergens 171
  decluttering 190

bedrooms 34
  cleaning 197
  control of allergens in 171
  decluttering 196–197
  organizing 198–199
  STOP clutter 196–197

beds 170–1

beginner's pantry 118, 119

bills 222, 223, 225

books, storing/organizing 45, 212–213

boxes, for decluttering 21

breakfast requirements, keeping together 106

brick, care of 158

brooms 59

C

calendar 73, 75, 86, 87

carpets
  caring for 163–164
  deep-cleaning 164

catalogs 34, 213

centers 34, 40, 41, 43
  see also individual centers

ceramic tiles 164
  care of 158

change/changing 34
  behavior 14, 15, 28
  gradual, and children 70
  habits 83

chaos 10, 39

charity 28

checklists (daily, monthly, seasonal, weekly) 73, 74, 76–7
  household systems 75

child-friendly solutions 206

children
  artwork by 209, 227
  book storage 45
  and chores 70, 71
  clothing archive 135
  clothing needs 124
  teaching to clean 70–1

children's rooms 206–207
  decluttering 204–205

choice, and cleaning 51

Chuck-it Bucket (paper handling) 223

circuit box 174

Classic Files (archive papers) 228

classified ads 28

clean enough, standards 49, 50–51

Clean Extreme 51

Clean Sweep declutter method 24

Clean Up Time, weekly 70

cleaning 13, 41, 49, 65, 68–9
  clothing to wear while 57, 63, 64
  kitchen 108–111
  schedules 68
  special surfaces 158
  teaching children how to 70–71
  top tips from the pros 64–5
  walls 156–157
  see also individual entries

cleaning cloths 57, 145

cleaning products 52–3
  the Big Four 65
  homemade/green 54–5, 67, 108, 110, 188
  ones to avoid 67
  saving money on 53, 54

cleaning tools 57, 145
  choosing 58–9

dusting 60–61
wet cleaning 62–3
cleaning totes 57, 62
closets 215
decluttering 128–131
organizing 130
clothes closet
decluttering 128–131
organizing 130–133
planning 124–125
STOP clutter 128–129
clothes moths 135
clothing 13, 123
buying quality 126–127
care labels 146
care and maintenance 136–139
decluttering/STOP clutter
128–133
dry-cleaning 137
inventories 124
mending clothes 41, 138–139
planning 124–125
recycling 145
saving money on 127
storage of 130–131, 133
swapping 29, 127
see also seasonal storage
clutter 10, 19, 180–181
causes of 19
clearing 20–23
clutter-busting tips 227
reducing paper 222–223
selling 28, 32, 213
stopping it coming
back 28–9
whole house 24
clutter consultants 34, 35
clutter magnet areas 130

clutter personalities 14, 30–31, 34–5,
133, 197
see also individual personalities
collections, and clutter 32
compact fluorescent light bulbs
(CFLs) 175
composting 102
computer games 29
consignment stores 28, 127
cooking activity center 104–105, 107
cooking for the freezer 95
correspondence basket 41
cosmetics 184, 186, 187
crafts 34, 214–215
cutting boards 111
cycles of home keeping 12, 13

D
daily cleaning checklist (sample) 68
Daily Do-Its 76
sample Morning/Evening
checklists 76
daily to-do lists 81
dander 171
decision-making 21
declutter buddy 15
decluttering 12, 24
see also individual entries
deferred decision-making 20, 226
deferrer personalities 30, 133
defrosting do's and don'ts 114–115
degreaser 52, 62, 65
deodorizers 102
detergent 143, 149
dinners, planning menus 92
direct marketing preference services 213
dirt 10
Dirt Dodger 51

disaster plan 176–177
dishwashers 173
disorder 10
disposable wipes 53, 189
dividers
drawer 46, 133
Family Notebook 84, 85, 86–7
document shredders 220
documents, how long to
keep 230
Drawer-a-Day declutter
method 24
drawers 46, 133
dressers 133, 206
dry-cleaning clothes 137
dry-room cleaning 60–61
dry suds 170
drying laundry 143, 149
dust mites 171
dusting 60–61
fine wood furniture 166, 169
using the vacuum for 59, 164
dust cloths 60
duvets, putting on cover
200–201

E
electric blankets 203
electrical appliances 174–175
electrostatic dry cleaning
cloths 61
emergency information 85
emotions 31
energy costs, reducing 175
entertainment systems 41
entryway, decluttering 183
Evening Do-It Checklist 76, 77
Evening Pick-up/Sweep 27, 207

F

fabric care 146–147
    washing/drying guidelines 147
fabric protection 167
fabric softener 54, 55, 143
    green 149
    and sheets 193
family
    and cleaning plans 65
    clutter, dealing with 34–5
    and household organization 40
    put-away time 27
    teamwork 34, 49, 50, 65
    see also Launch Pads
family calendar 73, 75, 86, 87
family disaster plan 176–177
family information center 73, 75, 86, 87
    see also Household Notebook
family organizer see Household
    Notebook
family room
    decluttering 210
    STOP clutter 210
farmers' markets 97
fear of letting go 32
feather dusters 61
files/filing 45
    paperwork 222, 223, 225, 226
setting up household systems 228–231
financial issues and clutter 32
fine wood furniture 166–167, 169
first aid center 187
first aid kit 177
first steps 14
fix-it desk activity center 41
flexibility 35
flip-files 45, 207
floor care 161, 163–164
    shoes-off policy 161, 164
floor cleaners 58–9

folding techniques 143, 193, 194–195
food
    back-up products 118, 119
    shopping for 93, 96–7, 118
    storage guidelines for 98–9, 117,
        120–121
    see also menu planning
food ads 93
food preparation surfaces 111
freezer 95, 101, 115–116
    cleaning 115
    cooking for the 95
    decluttering 114–117
    food storage guidelines 95, 117
    inventories 116
    STOP clutter 115
freezer bags 95, 115
fridges 112–113
Front Door Forward declutter
    method 24
frozen pipes 172–173
furniture care 166–167, 169

G

garage sales 28, 127
garbage bags, for clutter 21
garbage cans 104
GFCIs 174
glass 52, 55, 62
    cleaning 159
glass cleaner 65
    homemade recipe for 55
good enough 70
granite, care of 158
green cleaners 54–5, 108, 110, 188
greeting cards 227
groceries see food
grooming 41, 184, 187
grout, cleaning 62
gum, gunk, and goo remover 53

H

habit buddy 83
habits 12, 28, 74, 82–3, 94
    where to start? 82
hangers 46, 131, 134, 206
hanging files 45
hard-surface floors 164
hardwood floors 164
health center 187
heating systems 175
heirloom clutter 32–3
hoarders 30, 186
hobbies 34, 214–215
home library 212–213
homeless household items 28
homework activity center 41
hooks 46
household filing system 228–231
Household Notebook 75, 84–7
    dividers in 84, 85, 86–7
household storage plan
    216–217

I

identity clutter 33
infant clothing 29
information center/resource 73, 75,
    86, 87
    see also Household Notebook
Information Central (paper
    handling) 220
inherited clutter 32–3
ironing 146, 147
    how to avoid 153
    top tips for 152–153
ironing boards 152

J

junk drawer 22, 34
junk mail 10, 222, 227

K
keepsakes 31
kitchens
    activity centers/organizing 43,
        104–107
    cleaning 52, 62, 108–111
    storage 102–103
    tools/equipment 43, 107
L
labeler, electronic 223
labels 44, 45
    in the clothes closet 133
    on frozen food 95, 115
    graphic, for children 207
    paperwork file folders 230–231
lambswool dusters 60
Launch Pads 28, 183
laundry 142–143, 149, 187
    activity center 41, 140–141
    product storage 140
    schedules 140
    see also fabric care
laundry baskets 140
leaks 172
least-used items 44
leather furniture 166
leftovers 101, 113
lemon juice 54, 55
library 212–213
lighting 175, 200
lime and scale remover 53, 63
linen closet 44, 194–195
    decluttering 192–193
linoleum floors 164
little and often 68

M
magazines 34, 45, 46, 213, 227
Magic Minimum 69
mail 226, 227

maintenance routines 69, 175, 207
makeup 186, 187
manuals, product 227
marble, care of 158
Master To-Do lists 74, 80–81
maternity clothing 29
mats 161
mattresses 170–171
meal centers, in refrigerator 113
meal planning *see* menu planning
meal preparation 77, 95
mementos 31
memories 31, 33
mending clothes 41, 138–139
menu planning 91, 92–5
    basics/tips 93–4
    flexibility 94
    routine 94
microwave oven 110
mind clutter 74
mini-vac 59
mirrors 52, 55, 62
Moderate Mopper 51
mops 58–9
Morning Do-It Checklist 76–7
morning habits 82, 207
most-used items 44
multi-surface cleaner 65

N
neat, keeping things 44
newspapers 28, 227
No-Buy-It Diet 28–9

O
one-in, one-out 28
one step at a time 21, 24
online
    auctions 28, 32, 127, 212, 213
    bill-paying 223

mailing options 228
    planning systems 79
oosouji 29
organic bedding 203
Organize clutter 20, 22
organized function 39
organizing 12, 39, 44–5
    products for 46
    rules of 40
    other people's clutter 34–5
    out-of-place belongings 27
outdoor clothing activity center 41
ovens 108, 175

P
packaging 10
paint 203
panic clutter 190
pantry 118–119
    building, on a budget 121
    storage guidelines 119, 120–121
paper handling/paperwork 13, 45, 75,
        85, 209
    Action File (daily) 225, 228
    activity center 41, 220
    dealing with clutter 226–227
    document types 228, 230–231
    speedy 222–223
    storage of 220
paper towels 61
party equipment 29
pegs 46
Penicillin declutter method 24
perfectionist personalities 31, 133
personal care centers 187
personal planner 75, 84–7
    dividers in 84, 85, 86–7
personal solutions 14
photograph surplus clutter 31
Pick-up Time 70, 207

place for everything 28, 40
planning an organized home
     13, 73
   activity centers 41
   four tools for 74–5
planning family menus 91, 92–5
plumbing systems 172–173
polish 167
possessions no longer used 33
power strips 175
press cloths 153
price books (grocery) 97
psychological feelings, about clutter and
     stuff 24, 32–3
Put away clutter 20, 21, 22, 81

Q
quizzes 51, 181

R
reading activity center 41
reading materials, decluttering 213
rebel personality 31, 133, 197
receipts 222, 223, 227
recycling 10, 102
   centers for 41
   clothes 147
refrigerator/fridges
   decluttering 112–113
   weekly clean-outs 113
   see also freezer
repetition, and habit 82
retention schedule, documents
     230, 231
right way 70
routine chores 76, 77
rubber gloves 57
rubbing (isopropyl) alcohol 55
running to-do list 81
rust remover 53, 63

S
safety supplies, basic 200
safety tips, electrical 174–175
sanitation 110
sanitizing cleaner 62, 63, 111
scarcity thinking 32
scheduling 41, 80
scouring powder 53
scrapbooking 31
scrapers 57, 62
scrubbing sponges 57, 63
seasonal cleaning 68
seasonal storage 44
   clothing 134–135
second-hand clothing 127
seeing a benefit 35
self-care 76, 82
self-knowledge 14
selling/donating clutter 21, 28, 32
sentiment 32
sentimentalist personality 31, 197
sewer valves 174
sewing 34
   see also mending clothes
sharing change 15
sheets
   folding 192, 193–194
   mitring 198–199
shelf units 46
shoe storage 131
shopping lists, food 93–94
   see also food
showers 55, 173, 188–189
shut-off valves 174
sinks 52, 53, 55, 62, 110, 138
skill sets 12–13
Sort clutter 20, 21
specialty cleaners 53
specialty surfaces, cleaning 158
specified areas for activities 40

speed cleaning 64
spills, on carpets 163
sponge mops 58
sports equipment 29
spot-remover, carpet 163
spray bottles 57
spray cleaners 52
   homemade recipe for 55
spring-cleaning 68
squeegees 57, 159
squirt bottles 57
stainless steel, cleaning 53, 110
stains 150–151
   on carpets 163
   on clothes 137
   common problems with 148
   emergency kit for 151
   on mattresses 170
stale energy 20
stamps-by-mail service 222
standards of cleaning 50, 65
STOP clutter 20–23
   decluttering strategies 24
   see also individual entries
storage 45, 46, 216–217
   assessment/inventory of storage areas
        216, 217
   children's 206–207
   clearing 217
   clothing 130–131
   crafts and hobbies 214–215
   food 98–9, 117, 120–121
   outsourcing 217
stoves 108, 110
stuff 12, 19
   dealing with 32–3, 216
   pile-ups of 180
support groups/networks 15, 83
surfaces 13
   cleaning 158–159

swap parties 127
sweeping 59, 164
sweeps 210
symbols, instead of clutter 33
symptoms of clutter 19
systems 13

T
tabletop files 45, 225
tag sales 28
take-out menus 40, 41, 75
tax chores 222, 223
teamwork *see* family
telephone activity center 41
Telephone Directory 85
thermostats 172, 173
thrift stores 127
tidy isn't organized 39
tile floors 164
tiles 164
    brushes for 53, 57, 63
    care of 158
    cleaner 52, 53, 57
    cleaning 62
time-saving tips for every
        day 81
timers, for STOP clutter sessions 21, 22
to-do lists 76–7, 80–81
toilets 53, 55, 62, 63, 173, 189
tools
    for cleaning 57, 58–9, 60–1, 62–3, 65
    for mending/sewing 138–139
    kitchen 105
    paper handling 220
Toss clutter 20, 22
totes, cleaning 57, 62, 65
towels 40, 190, 192, 193, 194–195
toys 204, 206, 207
TSP (tri–sodium phosphate) 158
tubs 53, 63, 188

U
under-bed areas 198
under-sink
    cleaning 110–111
    storage 104
unit prices (grocery shopping) 97
upholstered furniture 167
utility rooms 62

V
vacation stain kit 151
vacuum cleaner 59
vacuuming 163, 164, 167
vertical storage 45
videos 29
vinyl floors 164
volatile organic compounds
        (VOCs) 203

W
walls, cleaning 156–157
wardrobes *see* clothes closet
warranties, appliance 227
washing machines 140, 143, 149
washing-up gloves 57
water softeners 173
water spots, removing 111
water usage, reducing 173
wax polish 164, 167
weekly cleaning checklist
        (sample) 68
wet-room cleaning 58, 62–3, 164
where do I start? 14
white cotton cleaning cloths 57, 60
white vinegar 54, 55
whole house STOP clutter methods 24
windows
    cleaning 52, 55, 159
    wire hangers 134, 136
wrap and mail activity center 41

Y
yard sales 28, 127
you 14–15, 34

Acknowledgments

Author's acknowledgments

Behind this book stands an entire community: the members who gather at OrganizedHome.Com to encourage one another to clean house and get organized at home. The heart and soul of the OH membership is a bright light in a world of chaos, and I am grateful for their friendship, inspiration, and example.

I send special thanks to members of the OH Mod Squad. These dedicated friends hold the unsung and uncompensated job of managing a large online community—and they were the sounding board and cheerleaders I relied upon throughout this project.

I offer honor and respect to my grandmother, Helen Betty Townley, for the homemaking heritage she embodies. She guided my first embroidery stitches, taught me to block a sweater, and has been a life-long role model on my journey to a clean and organized home.

I offer grateful kudos to super-cleaner Denise Davis, from Merry Maids. Always generous with her technical expertise and on-the-job know-how, she kept our home clean while I was too busy writing about cleaning to do any!

Last (first and always), I send love and acknowledgment to my husband, Dr. Steve Ewer. Without his unflagging encouragement and support, there would be no writer—and without his patient tolerance of my unending writerly megrims, there would have been no book. Every writer should be so blessed

Publisher's acknowledgments

Dorling Kindersley would like to thank photographer Howard Shooter and his assistant, Michael Hart; models Alex Farrell, Jennifer Matter, Frances Wingate, Max Jones, and Luke Shooter; Karen Shooter, for her patience; stylist Bo Chapman; Shanron Beatty and Hilary Mandleberg for editorial assistance; Lynn Bresler for the index; Clara Latham for assisting on the photography shoot; and Sonia Charbonnier for all her DTP support.

All photographs by Howard Shooter except for the following: Peter Anderson: 5, 38; Carolyn Barber: 12; Andy Crawford and Steve Gorton: 20, 126, 142r; Vanessa Davies: 18, 45, 176, 184, 215; Steve Gorton: 226l; Gary Ombler: 181; William Reavell: 115; Russell Sadur: 7, 54, 96, 111, 119, 148, 152, 167; Pia Tryde 1, 196, 214, 226r, 227; Matthew Ward: 133. All images © DK Images. For further information see www.dk.images.com

About the author

Since 1990, Cynthia Townley Ewer has been writing online about home organization and management. As editor of OrganizedHome.com, Cynthia brings encouragement, information, and support to today's home managers. She has been widely quoted in print and in online media, including interviews on simplifying life at home in *Modern Maturity* magazine, *Working Woman* magazine, and the *New York Times*. She has appeared twice on the daytime TV show ABC's *The View* (awarded the Emmy for Outstanding Talk Show in 2003). OrganizedHome.com has received numerous web awards since its debut in 1998, including the coveted *USA Today* HotSite and *USA Weekend* "Best of the Web" awards.

Cynthia started her working life as a freelance legal writer while bringing up two children as a single mother, which required the highest level of home and personal organization. This provided an apprenticeship in the principles of home management that she teaches today. She now lives with her husband, cardiologist Dr. Stephen Ewer, in Richland, Washington.

Cynthia's juggling act of publishing web sites, writing projects, volunteer work, speaking engagements, and travel continues to require a high level of organization. "I'd still rather play than do laundry," she says.

Life, love, and cleaning the refrigerator. It's all in a day's work for Cynthia.

Floor care is like weeding: a little work at the right time prevents a jungle of problems. Daily floor-care routines remove dirt and soil quickly, before it bonds with the floor—but passive resistance can play a role, too. Preserve your flooring investment with these tips to keep floors clean without trying:

■ **Mats matter.** Placed both inside and outside household doors, entrance mats remove 80–85 percent of the dirt coming into the home. Look for mats with a raised, ridged surface that cannot be compressed easily and has non-slip backing.

■ **Shoes off—but socks rule.** Worn outside, shoes become covered with tiny bits of grit and dirt that grind into flooring with each step. Spike heels can dimple hardwoods, puncture vinyl flooring, and pierce carpet backing. Even bare feet leave a film of body oils that attract dirt. Be kind to your flooring and wear socks or soft-soled house slippers.

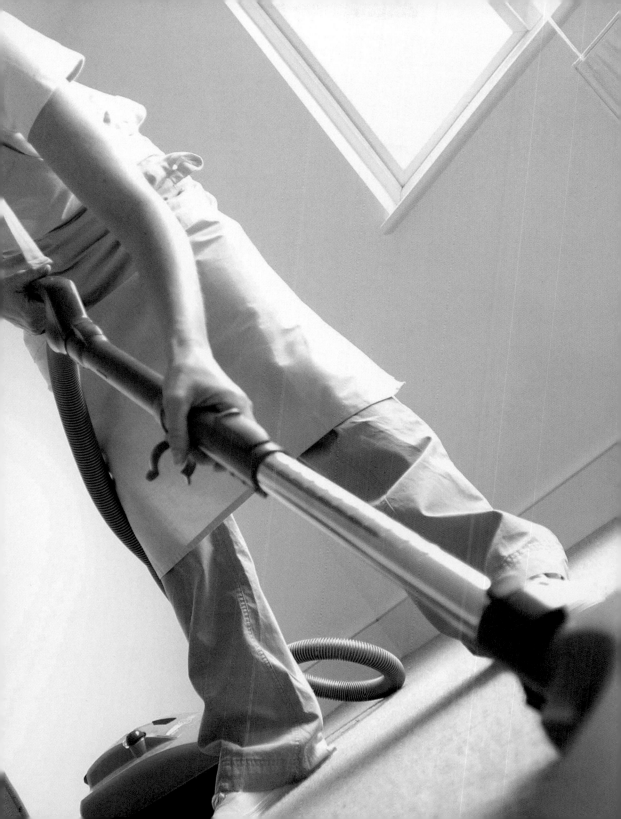

Fresh underfoot:
caring for floors

Dirt on the floor isn't just unsightly; it's the prime cause of premature wear on floor materials. Dust and grit scratch smooth floor finishes, remove wax and protective coatings, and crush carpet fibers and backings. The solution: simple daily care routines that keep them clean—and avoid the need for elbow grease down the road.

Caring for carpets

The three keys for clean and healthy carpets? Vacuum regularly, treat spills and stains promptly, and have carpets deep cleaned once a year. First rule of carpet care: vacuum regularly, even if the carpet doesn't look dirty. The vacuum delivers a one-two punch: combining suction, which pulls free dust inside the vacuum bag or dirt cup, with agitation from a beater bar, which fans carpet fibers, raising them and releasing dirt and soil. For high-traffic living areas, daily vacuuming keeps carpet dirt under control; less-used rooms, such as guest rooms, still need weekly or bi-weekly attention. Here's how to vacuum carpet for best results:

■ **Inspect the area to be vacuumed.** Remove any small objects that could be sucked into the vacuum.
■ **Check the vacuum.** Straighten kinked hoses, and empty the dirt cup or vacuum bag if needed.
■ **Plug in the vacuum, and go to it!** To save your back, vacuum in short strokes, moving forward across the room. Overlap strokes for even coverage of the carpet.
■ **Work in alternating directions.** For best cleaning and to raise carpet nap, make passes across the room in alternating directions. After covering the carpet, turn 90-degrees and vacuum again in a perpendicular direction.
■ **Finish with baseboards and wall edges.** Use an extension wand and crevice tool to clean dust from these areas.

◀ **Household carpets** are a major investment. Regular vacuuming extends their useful life—and enhances their beauty—by removing dust and grit that damage carpet fibers and backing.

Treating spills and stains

Speed is of the essence when removing spills and stains from carpeting. The longer stains stand, the more chance that the substance will soak through the carpet backing and pool up in the carpet pad beneath.

To treat liquid spills and stains:
■ **Blot up as much of a liquid spill** as possible. Use clean white cleaning cloths or white paper towels to avoid dye transfer. Continue to blot gently, using fresh cloths, until no more liquid can be absorbed.
■ **Don't scrub** or brush the stain.
■ **Apply an appropriate carpet spot-remover.** Spot-test the product in an inconspicuous place before using.

For solid or semi-solid spills:
■ **Use a spoon or spatula** to scrape up as much of the spilled material as possible. Don't use a knife, even a blunt one, as it can harm carpet fibers.
■ **Allow the spill to dry,** then brush gently to release it from carpet fibers. Vacuum up as much of the spilled material as possible.
■ **Treat any remaining stain** with an appropriate spot-remover.

Do-it-yourself carpet cleaning. Carpets keep their beauty longest if deep cleaned at least once a year. This job is one where it pays to bring in the pros, as they have muscle, methods, and machinery not usually available to home carpet cleaners.

If your budget won't stretch to professional carpet cleaning, there are do-it-yourself alternatives that make a respectable—if sweaty—job of home carpet cleaning, as long as you work carefully, use the right equipment, and observe these cautions:

■ **Know your carpet.** Be sure you understand the type of cleaning method recommended by your carpet's manufacturers.

■ **Stick to steamers, not shampooers.** When you buy or rent a carpet cleaner, choose a carpet steamer. Older "carpet shampoo" units use rotary agitators to apply detergent solution and may overwet carpets. The shampoo film can be difficult to remove, causing resoiling.

■ **Vacuum first.** Dirt plus water equals mud, which is almost impossible to remove. Before cleaning the carpet, vacuum thoroughly to remove as much loose dirt as possible.

■ **Buy the right cleaners.** Stick with cleaning products designed specifically for home carpet cleaning, and follow package directions to mix cleaning solutions.

■ **Pretreat.** Use a traffic-lane cleaner or pre-spray to treat areas of high soil before cleaning.

■ **Keep it dry.** Over-saturated carpets aren't cleaner, just wetter. After extracting, make a second dry pass over the carpet to remove as much moisture as possible. Keep traffic off freshly cleaned carpeting until it is dry.

Hard-surface floors

As with carpets, routine cleaning is the best way to maintain the beauty of hard-surface flooring. Daily sweeping, vacuuming, or dust-mopping removes abrasive grit and dust from the floor. Establishing a "shoes-off" policy and using entrance mats helps prevent street soil from entering the home and being tracked onto floors.

When it's time to clean, clean with a light hand. Hard-surface floors look best when clean and clear, but detergent use or cleaner build-up can create a hazy film that dulls floors—and attracts and holds more dirt. Rely on these cleaning tips to keep hard-surface floors looking clean and beautiful:

Laminate, vinyl, and linoleum floors To care for vinyl, linoleum, and laminated flooring, sweep, vacuum, or dust-mop daily to remove surface grit. Damp-mop with clear water to remove dirt and restore shine. For more heavily soiled floors, vacuum first, then damp-mop floors using a very light solution of about 1–2 teaspoons liquid dishwashing detergent per gallon (4 liters) of warm water. Rinse the floor with clean water before drying it with white cleaning cloths. If there are depressions in the floor, use a scrubbing pad to loosen any soil in these areas as you clean, then rinse with fresh clear water.

Hardwood floors These floors are susceptible to abrasion, are easily dented, and can be damaged by moisture or incorrect cleaning methods. Remove dust and surface soil from hardwoods daily, preferably with a large-headed microfiber dust mop. Alternately, hardwood floors may be vacuumed, but be sure to turn the beater bars off to avoid scratching the floor. When necessary, damp-mop with plain water to pick up dirt, using a barely-wet mop. Avoid any drips or standing water; the mop head or terry mop cover should be wrung till nearly dry before it touches the floor. A solution of white vinegar and water will up the cleaning ante, so try it for stubborn dirt.

More intense cleaning will require a cleaning product formulated for the floor's specific finish. Do not use oil soap on hardwood floors; it will create a dirt-trapping sticky film and it can interfere with recoating or refinishing floors later on.

Ceramic tile floors Keep ceramic tile floors looking their best with daily sweeping or vacuuming to remove surface grit. If using a vacuum, set the beater bar to the off position to vacuum. Every week or so, damp-mop with a solution of 2 tablespoons liquid dishwashing detergent to 1 gallon (4 liters) of warm water. Use a cleaning toothbrush to scrub stained or dirty grout. Rinse with clear water. Buff the tile with a clean, dry towel to remove any water spots. Never apply wax to ceramic tile floors; it can be difficult to remove, can cause slip-and-fall injuries, and may interfere with resealing grout. For advice on cleaning heavily stained grout, see pages 188–189.

▶ **Ceramic tile floors** are tough—if brittle—and are easy to keep clean with a daily sweep plus a damp-mop once a week.

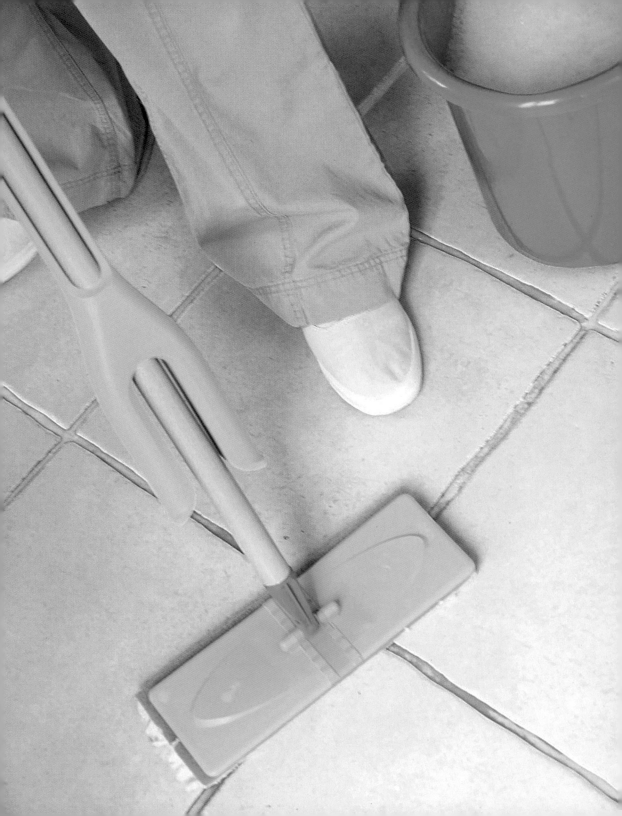

Sitting pretty:
caring for furniture

Fine wood furniture is a treasured possession in any home, and with good care, it can last for generations. Upholstered furniture provides us with comfort, color, and texture. Who doesn't love sinking into the cushioned softness of a favorite sofa?

Caring for leather furniture

Leather upholstery can last for many years if looked after correctly. Follow these tips to take good care of leather furnishings:

■ **Keep away from heat and light.** Leather furniture is very sensitive to heat and sun damage. Position it away from windows, and from heat sources such as fireplaces, radiators, and central heating vents.

■ **Uncoated leathers.** Furniture made from uncoated leathers should be dusted frequently. An art gum eraser may remove some stains or deposits safely, but do not use leather creams, conditioners, or saddle soap on uncoated leather, since these products can change the color or appearance of the leather.

■ **Coated leathers.** Check with the manufacturer for recommended cleaning methods. Vacuum regularly to remove surface soil. Commonly, leather creams or conditioners may be used to clean coated leather once or twice or year. Test leather cleaners in an inconspicuous spot before using.

■ **Avoid unsuitable products.** Never use oil, furniture polish, dusting sprays, or ordinary stain removers on leather furniture.

Fine wood furniture

Care for fine furniture with these recommendations:

■ **Avoid heat and light.** In a natural state, wood contains a surprising amount of moisture. Preserving appropriate moisture levels is key to the preservation of fine furniture. Accordingly, position fine wood furniture away from heating vents, fireplaces, or radiators. Don't store fine furniture in attics, where temperature and humidity levels vary widely from summer to winter, day and night. Avoid placing furniture in areas where it will sit in direct sunlight, which can fade fine furniture; use drapes, sheers, or protective window films to guard against the sun's rays.

■ **Protect from damage.** Everyday life can be hard on wood furniture. Moisture from sweating beverage glasses leaves round rings in the finish, while the heat from a hot dish can ruin the wood finish beneath. Provide cork- or felt-bottomed coasters if you will set glasses or mugs on fine wood, and always use trivets to support hot serving dishes. Place mats, tablecloths, or padded table covers protect dining-room tables from spills or scrapes.

■ **Clean safely.** Dust frequently (see page 169). Occasionally, wood furniture will require heavier cleaning. To remove greasy soil or the film from cigarette smoke, mix a solution of oil soap and water as instructed on the oil soap package. Using a natural sponge, moisten it with oil soap and wring out most of the water. Gently stroke the furniture to loosen soil. Rinse the residue from the wood with a sponge wrung out in clear water, and then dry the piece with fresh cleaning cloths.

Note: Seek professional advice before cleaning if the wood is in poor condition or the item of furniture is an antique.

Polish or wax? Both wax and furniture polish are applied to fine wood furniture to protect the surface—but you'll need to pick one or the other. Don't try to combine these products or you'll create a gummy mess. Make sure that you have selected the appropriate treatment for the piece's finish. Check with the manufacturer for recommended polish or wax options.

Which to choose? Wax is a semi-solid product; it requires elbow grease to apply, but it creates a long-lasting coat. Furniture polish is easier to apply than wax; it is made using petroleum distillates (a solvent), and evaporates fairly quickly. Most people overuse polish to restore a fresh finish. Layers of polish build-up, combined with body oils and dirt, create a sticky, dull film over the surface. If you use polish, use it with restraint.

The same applies to furniture sprays. They contain silicone oil, which is inert and which does not evaporate like furniture polish. Use them sparingly, and buff the sprayed area well with a clean cloth. Buff it again to raise the shine.

Apply wax or polish to furniture that has been freshly cleaned with oil soap (*see Clean safely, opposite*), and allowed to dry thoroughly. Follow package directions, and have plenty of clean white cleaning cloths available.

Note: Seek professional advice for the care of antique furniture, or if the wood is in poor condition.

Upholstered furniture

Dust and dirt act like sandpaper on furniture fabric, so remove it frequently. Vacuum upholstered furniture weekly; lift cushions, and use the crevice tool to remove hidden crumbs beneath. Keep upholstered furniture looking new with these tips:

■ **Flip, swap, and rearrange.** Being territorial creatures, most humans gravitate to their favorite places—but when it's the same seat on a long sofa day after day, that preference will start to show. Flip loose cushions regularly, and rotate them on a multi-cushion unit. Similarly, rearrange upholstered furniture once or twice a year to distribute wear more evenly. Switch the position of a love seat and a sofa, or swap the positions of a set of chairs as the seasons change.

■ **Arm caps.** Places where bare skin or hair come to rest— armrests, chair backs, seat cushions—are subjected to higher levels of soil and abrasion. Protect high-contact areas of

▲ **Wax adds shine** and provides the best protection against scratches and damage. It'll remain on the piece longer than furniture polish, and needs less frequent maintenance.

upholstered furniture with arm caps tailored to fit snugly over chair and sofa arms. Made from the same upholstery fabric, they're all but indistinguishable as they protect fabric from wear.

■ **Slipcovers.** In areas with hot summer weather, consider washable slip covers. Traditionally applied to furniture during the warm season, slipcovers protect against sweat, suntan oil, and other summer hazards.

■ **Fabric protection.** Spray-on fabric protectors coat fibers and protect upholstery from spills and stains. Fabric protectors can be applied at the mill as the fabric is processed, by the furniture retailer, or at home using commercial spray products. If you apply fabric protection yourself, read the product instructions and observe safety procedures carefully.

Dust is everywhere, but no one wants to see it film fine furniture. Keep your cherished pieces glowing with these dusting tips:

■ **Clean safely.** Dust fine furniture often with a lambswool duster or barely damp white cotton cleaning cloth. Microfiber cloths do a good job of attracting and removing fine blown-in soil. Avoid using a feather duster, as a broken quill can scratch and damage delicate finishes.

■ **Dust damp.** Dusting with a dry cloth can scratch, so lightly spritz your cleaning cloth with water, a spray dusting agent, or wood polish. Never spray furniture directly, as overspray can leave a difficult-to-remove film. Follow the grain of the wood as you dust to avoid cross-grain scratches.

■ **Dust often.** Frequent dusting removes dirt before it has a chance to settle in and make itself at home. Dusting often keeps an oily build-up from forming on wood furniture.

Getting the most from
beds and mattresses

A good night's sleep starts with a good bed. How does yours stack up? Since we spend one-third of our lives in them, beds and mattresses deserve proper care. They'll repay us with a clean, healthy place to sleep. Whether heaped with pillows or minimally spare, beds and bedding will stay in top shape with these tips.

The Pea Princess' guide to mattress care

While the fairy tale "The Princess and the Pea" was meant to show the delicacy of the true princess, in reality, it showed up her future mother-in-law's housekeeping habits. Keep your castle's bedding in top shape with these tips for mattress care:

■ **Frame it right.** Just as our bodies need the support of a good mattress, so mattresses need a proper place to rest. Purchase mattress and box springs as a set to make sure that the two pieces will work together harmoniously. Check the bed frame; larger mattress sizes—queen- or king-sized beds —require center support or full-width slats to span the wider width.

■ **Take a seasonal spin.** Unless the manufacturer advises otherwise, rotate mattresses from heel to toe when the seasons change. To rotate, revolve the end of the mattress nearest the headboard toward the foot of the bed, then nudge the mattress back into place on the box springs. Rotating mattresses helps prevent the formation of sleeping "wallows," caused by the same body in the same spot every night.

■ **Flip it.** Some mattresses should also be flipped when the seasons change. While pillow-top mattresses should not be flipped, other mattresses wear more evenly when the bottom surface nearest the box spring is flipped over to the top of the bed during a seasonal rotation. Check with your manufacturer for specific recommendations for your model.

■ **Ban bouncing.** Kids enjoy bouncing on the bed, but the poor mattresses loathe the practice. Discourage these child gymnasts. Jumping on beds can damage mattresses and box springs, and fracture bed frames.

■ **Use protection.** Sweet dreams are the goal, but accidents happen. Protect mattresses from messy mishaps with mattress pads. They'll absorb moisture and spills before they soak through to the mattress.

■ **Suck it up.** Regular vacuuming will keep mattresses clean and fresh. Remove all bedding from the mattress, then use the upholstery brush to vacuum the top surface and sides of the mattress. Vacuuming removes dust, skin flakes, and the dust mites that feed upon body waste. Vacuum mattresses thoroughly when rotating them seasonally.

■ **Clean stains safely.** If a stain does occur, use an upholstery shampoo as directed to remove it. An alternative cleaner, recommended by manufacturers for use on mattresses, is called "dry suds." Create them by placing about ¼ cup (125ml) of liquid dishwashing detergent in a small mixer bowl. Turn the

"Protect the planet—regular cleaning and care extends the useful life of your mattress."

mixer on, and add a few teaspoons of water, a teaspoon at a time. Stand back! The bowl will quickly fill with foam. Scrape the top layer of foam into a small bowl, and take it to the mattress. Rub the stained area gently with the foam, using a sponge or a soft brush, being sure not to wet the padding beneath. Leave the mattress exposed until it is thoroughly dry before replacing the bedding.

Controlling allergens in the bedroom

We share our sleeping quarters with more than family pets or beloved teddy bears. Carpet, window treatments, and mattresses collect dust and dander and provide a happy playground for dust mites. Found anywhere there are humans, humidity, and warm temperatures, dust mites are a major cause of allergic symptoms in the home. More correctly, it's their feces and dead body parts that cause allergic reactions—and their food source is us! Dust mites feed on discarded skin flakes, making bedding and bedrooms prime dust-mite real estate.

Over the years, they'll multiply inside mattresses to the point where it's estimated that 50 percent of the weight of a 10-year-old mattress is caused by dust mites and their leavings. If family members wake each morning with puffy eyes and sneezing noses, it's time to control allergens in the bedroom. Fight back against dust mites, dander, dust, and pollen with these tips:

■ **Cover mattresses.** Use vinyl covers designed to form a barrier between mites and the mattress.

■ **Replace down products.** Pillows, comforters, and other items should be made from synthetic fibers. Encase pillows in vinyl covers for added protection.

■ **Clean well and often.** Regular cleaning is the best defense against allergens and dust mites.

■ **Send Duff to other quarters.** Bed down household pets in an area outside the bedroom if allergies are a problem. Pet dander is an allergen for many, and pets shed fur and skin cells, too, promoting dust mite populations. Banish Duff from the bedroom at night, and make it up to him with extra walkies in the morning—after a good night's sleep.

■ **Keep humidity levels low.** Dust mites die back when there's insufficient moisture in the air. In humid climates, use a portable or whole-house dehumidifier to reduce in-house humidity levels to between 30 percent and 50 percent.

■ **Keep cool.** Mites thrive in warm weather, so keep household temperatures on the low side in the bedroom.

▶ **Sleep sustainable.** Retired mattresses present big problems at disposal sites. Protect your investment—and the planet—with regular cleaning, weekly clean bedding, and care to extend the useful life of your mattress.

■ **Fight back with spring-cleaning.** Because mites grow best in warm, humid weather, take advantage of early spring to clean the house. Vacuuming and dusting will remove the mites who've wintered over before they can run riot in spring.

■ **Kiss Teddy good-bye.** Stuffed toys are a comfort for children of all ages, but harbor dust mites just as mattresses do. Replace the teddy bear with a plastic model for a healthier night's sleep.

■ **Wash bedding often, in hot water.** Temperatures of 130°F (54°C) are required to kill mites; mites can survive cold-water washing. Wash sheets and pillowcases weekly, and give pillows, comforters, and blankets a trip to the washer every month to six weeks.

■ **Pitch the houseplants.** They are lovely to look at, but plants bring pollen, insects, dust, and microbes into the bedroom. For best rest, restrict them to other rooms.

Plumb perfect: maintenance tips
for plumbing systems

Plumbing. It's been with us since Roman times, but today's homes have a lavish supply of hot and cold water on demand, thanks to modern plumbing systems. The principles are simple—pressure and valves—but if they fail, the household may be faced with a soggy mess. When this happens, act quickly to avert major problems.

Smart householders know how to spot and resolve small plumbing problems before they become major issues at home. Help your plumbing stay dry and happy with these tips:

■ **Keep an eye out for trouble.** When it comes to plumbing, little leaks can lead to big problems. Be alert to signs of impending plumbing failures; leaking faucets, damp cabinets, rocking toilets, or dripping refrigerators all signal problems that need prompt attention.

■ **Repair problems early.** A leaking faucet isn't just annoying; the moisture it releases puts wear on sink fixtures and can encourage the growth of mold and mildew. Stay on top of problems to keep the household clean and dry.

■ **Know where to go when trouble happens.** Should plumbing fail, will you know how to stop the flood? Locate the main shut-off valve for the home water supply. If it's in a dark, hidden, or hard-to-reach place, gather any tools you'll need for a quick shut-off, and store them nearby. There's nothing like the frustration of a missing flashlight or a misplaced shut-off key when water's pouring down the stairs from a broken pipe.

■ **Shutting off appliances.** Similarly, know how to shut off water to sinks, toilets, washing machines, and water-using appliances like the refrigerator's icemaker. Should they misbehave, knowing the location of the shut-off valve will save the day—and a lot of wet clean up.

■ **Spot the sewer valve.** Finally, hunt down the location of the household's main sewer valve. It's there to provide access to correct a clogged sewer line; don't make the Ready Rooter man spend pricey labor time looking for it when the toilets overflow.

■ **Learn how to tackle small problems.** With a few tools and a little knowledge, most of us can handle small plumbing emergencies. With a plunger, a pipe wrench, and a sewer snake in your tool kit, you'll be able to take care of small problems like clogged drains, blocked toilets, stuck valves, and dripping faucets. How-to books, home improvement stores, and adult education classes can pay for themselves when it's time to call the plumber.

Cold snap: keep plumbing safe in cold weather

In hard-winter climates, freezing pipes can create a sudden household emergency. Frozen water expands, cracking pipes; when the area thaws, the cracks vent a flood. Plumbing help can be hard to find in a weather crisis, so try these tips:

■ **Prevent frozen pipes before they start.** Best defense: insulation. Insulate exposed pipes in a crawl space or in the garage with easy-to-install plastic insulation. It's a peel-and-stick solution. Before winter comes, remove exterior hoses, and apply insulating caps to outdoor fixtures, as a frozen exterior spigot can damage interior pipes. Households with automatic sprinkler systems can clear standing water with compressed air; public service groups like the Boy Scouts offer this service each fall at reasonable rates—much cheaper than replacing split pipes come spring.

■ **When cold weather strikes, go into action.** Open the cabinets beneath sinks and bathroom fixtures; warmer household air will help prevent the pipes inside from freezing. Opening taps to a bare trickle keeps water flowing and avoids a frozen blockage.

■ **If pipes do freeze, don't panic.** First, shut off the water supply to the house, then open a faucet near the blocked area to vent vapors from the frozen water. If you suspect that pipes in the hot water system are frozen, turn off the hot water heater. Use a hair dryer to warm the frozen pipe (never use an open flame to thaw a pipe), starting at the end of the pipe nearest to the tap. (Don't use a hair dryer in areas of standing water.) You'll know the pipe has begun to thaw when water begins to trickle from the open faucet. When the flow is restored, check the plumbing carefully for cracks or leaks.

Call a licensed plumber if your efforts are unsuccessful.

Maintaining water conditioning systems

In hard-water areas, water softeners condition water to remove unwanted minerals. Softened water uses less soap, prevents mineral build-in pipes, and extends the life of appliances and hot water heaters.

Keep them on the job with proper maintenance. Most models use a salt-exchange method that depends on a supply of salt pellets or nuggets. Use the type of salt recommended by your manufacturer for best results. Check the brine tank regularly to be sure salt levels are adequate. The salt should sit above the water line. "Salt bridging" occurs when a crust of salt forms over the top of the water in the brine tank; break it up by adding hot water to the tank or by poking the crust with a broomstick if it occurs.

After a period of use, water softeners will need to regenerate or recharge: the unit will flush collection areas of accumulated mineral particles pulled from hard water. If your unit offers an automatic regeneration scheduling, use it—you'll have soft water automatically. If your unit requires manual recharging, stick carefully to the manufacturer's recommended time intervals.

▲ **Be brave—and save.** Plumbing systems are fairly simple; don't be intimidated by small repairs. Invest in basic tools and plumbing supplies to keep the water flowing.

Reduce household water usage

A more sustainable and cost-efficient household means conserving water, but green living doesn't have to be dusty and dry. Try these strategies to cut water use at home:

■ **Load up the dishwasher.** Hand-washing dishes may feel authentic, but it's wasteful; automatic dishwashers use less hot water and energy than washing by hand. No need to rinse, either; most modern dishwashers are designed to remove food without need for pre-rinsing.

■ **Go with the (low) flow.** Household toilets can be water hogs; replace older models with low-flow alternatives.

■ **Save in the shower.** Keep showers short and sweet to stay sustainable. You can also save water—and money—by installing a low-flow shower head, which use up to fifty percent less water than older models.

Power play:
electrical safety at home

It's a true miracle: the electrical power that infuses your home. Your electrical system keeps the lights on and the household humming, and illuminates every aspect of life. Power has its price, however. Treat your electrical system with respect: learn these simple safety routines and schedule maintenance chores.

Follow these guidelines to maintain your home's electrical system and keep the lights on and the power flowing:

■ **Be alert for problems.** Keep a careful eye out for electrical hazards at home. A flickering lamp or crimped extension cord could cause a short—or worse, a fire. Be on the lookout for frayed or bent wires, or a shock or tingling when you touch an appliance.

■ **Repair quickly.** If an appliance appears to have an electrical problem, take it out of active use until it is repaired. Don't pass the trouble on to others by donating or selling the item. Have the appliance repaired if possible; if not, dispose of it to keep every home safe.

■ **Know your circuit box.** Most homes have a central circuit box or breaker panel. This service box controls delivery of power to different areas of the home. At the circuit box, you can cut power to any—or all—areas of the home.

■ **Take time to get familiar with your circuit box.** If your circuit box uses fuses, lay in a supply of extra fuses for emergencies. Work as a team with another family member to label each circuit; labels will make it easier to cut the power in the right place if an emergency arises.

■ **Test GFCIs monthly.** Ground fault circuit interrupters, known as GFCIs, are special outlets used in kitchens, bathrooms, and utility areas—anywhere water is present. GFCIs have a sensor that detects fluctuations in electrical current; when current surges, they shut down to protect against shock.

GFCIs have small colored buttons that permit you to reset a tripped circuit. The red "test" button allows you to test the GFCI.

Test GFCIs monthly, and after any thunderstorms, to be sure their protective function continues to work. Replace them if they no longer trip when the "test" button is pressed.

Note: do not plug refrigerators or freezers into outlets with GFCI protection. In the event the circuit is tripped without your knowledge, the appliances will shut down, spoiling the food inside.

Use electricity safely

Prevent shock hazards and system outages by observing these safety rules:

■ **Use hair dryers safely.** Keep hair dryers away from water in sinks and bathtubs.

■ **Take the right precautions.** Unplug appliances before you clean them, and never carry a small appliance by the cord.

■ **Avoid overloading.** Don't overload outlets with multiple cords, or try to force a plug into an outlet where it won't fit. Avoid the use of "cube taps," and if a tap or cord feels warm, unplug it immediately.

■ **Avoid extension cord hazards.** Don't run extension cords beneath rugs, under carpets, or across doorways.

■ **Childproof electrical outlets.** Install childproof outlet caps on electrical outlets in households with young children.

■ **Check light bulbs.** Make sure that light bulbs have the correct wattage for the lamp in which they'll be used. Don't use bulbs with a higher wattage than that specified by the fixture. This can overheat the bulb, and may cause a fire. Tighten light bulbs securely; loose bulbs can also overheat.

Checklist for household systems

Household systems work hard to keep us comfortable and safe. Keep them running smoothly with this maintenance list:

Every month:
■ Check bathrooms, kitchens, and utility rooms for leaking faucets or signs of water damage. If the refrigerator has an ice dispenser, include it in the inspection.
■ Change the filters on the central heating and air systems. Clean air filtration devices as recommended by the manufacturer.
■ Test smoke detectors.
■ Test remote alarm systems according to the instructions of the monitoring service.

Every 3 months:
■ Make an inventory of first aid supplies. Replace any missing items. (Print a free first aid kit inventory checklist at Organized Home.com; see also page 177.)
■ Hold a family fire drill, and review the family disaster plan with all household residents.

Every 6 months:
■ Drain sediment from the bottom of hot water heaters (if sediment is allowed to accumulate, it can affect the efficiency of the heating element).
■ Replace batteries in smoke and carbon monoxide detectors.
■ Check fire extinguishers to make sure they're charged and ready for use.
■ Clean the ashes from the fireplace or a wood-burning stove, and empty the ash pit.
■ Check the hoses installed on washing machines, and replace them if they show signs of wear, or every two years.
■ Vacuum refrigerator coils to remove dust.
■ Check refrigerator gaskets with the "dollar-bill" test: insert a dollar bill between the door and the refrigerator. If you can pull it out easily, the refrigerator gaskets are loose and they should be replaced.
■ Remove and clean kitchen exhaust fan filters. Most can be washed in the dishwasher to remove grease build-up. Alternately, spray the fan filters with a degreaser and then rinse. Dry them before replacing.

Reduce energy costs

In these days of rising prices, opening the power bill can be a shocking experience. Save money and lower your household's energy use with these ideas:

■ **Light it right.** Home lighting is a major player when it comes to energy use. Reign in unneeded lighting with low-tech practices such as turning off lights when you leave the room, together with high-tech methods like motion-sensitive light switches.
■ **Light it well with CFLs.** Compact fluorescent light bulbs use one-third the energy of their conventional counterparts—and they last 8 to 12 times longer. To help cushion higher up-front costs, look for governmental rebates that assist with the transition to CFLs.
■ **Harness the power of power strips.** Even when not in use, computer equipment, televisions, and home electronic devices continue to draw power. Cut them off at the source with by using a power strip to turn these devices on and off. Look for new "smart power strips" that will power down printers and peripherals automatically when the computer is turned off.
■ **Bundle up the hot water heater.** Adding an insulating jacket to the hot water heater lowers energy costs for hot water. Don't miss any exposed hot water pipes; plastic pipe insulation is inexpensive and easy to apply.
■ **Double up in the oven.** When you turn the oven on, make its energy use count. Slide side dishes in next to the Sunday roast for a whole-meal solution. When baking potatoes, add extras, for making potato salad later in the week.

Be prepared with a
family disaster plan

Life happens—and so does fire, flood, and natural disaster. Will your family know what to do if disaster strikes? Just as schoolchildren practice fire drills, family members need to prepare for the unexpected. A family disaster plan teaches everyone what to do and where to go when an emergency arises.

Make a family disaster plan

Does your family know what to do in the event of fire, earthquake, or severe weather? A simple family disaster plan will help all family members deal with natural disasters on the home front. To create a family disaster plan, follow these steps from the "Family Disaster Plan" developed by the US Federal Emergency Management Agency and the American Red Cross:

Four steps to safety

1 Find out what could happen to you:

■ Contact your local Red Cross chapter or emergency management office before a disaster occurs—be prepared to take notes.

■ Ask what types of disasters are most likely to happen. Request information on how to prepare for each.

■ Learn about your community's warning signals: what they sound like and what you should do when you hear them.

■ Ask about animal care after a disaster. Animals are not allowed inside emergency shelters because of health regulations.

■ Find out how to help elderly or disabled persons, if needed.

■ Find out about the disaster plans at your workplace, your children's school or day-care center, and other places where your family spends time.

2 Create a Disaster Plan:

■ Meet with your family and discuss why you need to prepare for disaster. Explain the dangers of fire, severe weather, and earthquakes to children. Plan to share responsibilities and work together as a team.

■ Discuss the types of disasters that are most likely to happen. Explain what to do in each case.

■ Pick two places to meet:

✳ Right outside your home in case of a sudden emergency, like a fire.

✳ Outside your neighborhood in case you can't return home. Everyone must know the address and phone number.

■ Ask an out-of-state friend to be your "family contact." After a disaster, it's often easier to call long distance. Other family members should call this person and tell them where they are. Everyone must know your contact's phone number.

■ Discuss what to do in an evacuation. Plan how to take care of your pets.

3 Complete this checklist:

■ Post emergency telephone numbers by the phones (fire, police, ambulance, etc.).

■ Teach children how and when to call 9-1-1 or your local Emergency Medical Services number for emergency help.

■ Show each family member how and when to turn off the utilities (water, gas, and electricity) at the main switches.

■ Check if you have adequate insurance coverage.

■ Get training from the fire department for each family member on how to use the fire extinguisher (ABC type), and show him or her where it's kept.

■ Install smoke detectors on each level of your home, especially near bedrooms.

■ Conduct a home-hazard hunt.

■ Stock emergency supplies and assemble a Disaster Supplies Kit.

- Take a Red Cross first aid and CPR class.
- Determine the best escape routes from your home. Find two ways out of each room.
- Find the safe places in your home for each type of disaster.

4 Practice and maintain your plan
- Quiz your kids every six months or so.
- Conduct fire and emergency evacuations.
- Replace stored water and stored food every six months.
- Test and recharge your fire extinguisher(s) according to the manufacturer's instructions.
- Test your smoke detectors monthly and change the batteries at least once a year.
- Check and update emergency numbers on phone lists, cellphones, and PDAs.

The first aid kit

The following list covers the contents of a basic first aid  kit. In addition, you may want to include a first aid manual and a flashlight and extra batteries for emergency use. Keep the kit out of reach of children.

- Antiseptic wipes
- Tweezers
- Antiseptic ointment
- Antiseptic solution
- Assorted plasters
- Sterile gauze
- Adhesive tape
- Selection of bandages
- Sharp scissors
- Safety pins
- Plastic gloves
- Painkillers (acetaminophen and ibuprofen)
- Diarrhea medication
- Insect repellant
- Thermometer
- Instant cold packs

Earthquake, fire, or weather disaster can happen any time, anywhere. When the unexpected disrupts life at home, keep these points in mind to stay safe:

- Remain calm and patient. Put your plan into action.
- Check for injuries.
- Give first aid and get help for seriously injured people.
- Listen to your battery-powered radio for news and instructions.

Check for damage in your home
- Use flashlights. Do not light matches or turn on electrical switches, if you suspect damage.
- Sniff for gas leaks, starting at the water heater. If you smell gas or suspect a leak, turn off the main gas valve, open windows, and get everyone outside quickly.
- Shut off any other damaged utilities. (You will need a professional to turn gas back on.)
- Clean up spilled medicines, bleaches, gasoline, and other flammable liquids immediately.

Remember to ...
- Confine or secure your pets.
- Call your family contact—do not use the telephone again unless it is a life-threatening emergency.
- Check on your neighbors, especially elderly or disabled persons.
- Make sure you have an adequate water supply in case the service is cut off.
- Stay away from downed power lines.

If disaster **strikes**

Room by room around the house, clutter can stage a seemingly never-ending battle for space and place. While the principles for clearing clutter and regaining calm remain the same, specific tactics are needed for the distinct types of clutter challenges posed by the rooms in your home.

Private areas, such as bedrooms and bathrooms, may suffer from function overload, expected to do too many jobs in the same space. Public areas are afflicted with "too many generals" issues; in these shared spaces, fighting chaos is a team effort, and requires coordination with, and cooperation from, all members of the household.

In this section, we'll move through each area of the home to cut clutter, get organized, and clean house. We'll apply the STOP clutter methods to fight disorder, from the master bedroom to children's play spaces, entry hall to family room. We'll declutter books and magazines, entertainment areas, and create order among the arts and crafts supplies.

Room to live
cut clutter, organize, clean

Fighting clutter room by room:
where does the shoe pinch?

Room by room, clutter and chaos take hold, complicating even simple everyday actions—but not all clutter is created equal. Where does your clutter shoe pinch? Pile-ups of "stuff" give valuable clues to where life isn't working. Let the clutter lead the way, and solve the biggest problems first.

Observe clutter clues A heaped-up dining room table, covered with mail and paperwork, signals a need for a household paper management center (*see pages 220–221*). Piles of backpacks, shoes, school projects, and jackets at the back door indicate an informal—and messy—attempt to create a family Launch Pad (*see pages 182–183*). Bathroom countertops heaped with tangled hair dryers, cosmetics bottles, and grooming products tell you that better organization—and a morning schedule—are needed to cut clutter in the bathroom.

Keep clutter magnets clear In every home, some "clutter magnet" areas attract clutter faster than black trousers attract lint. A convenient countertop or a table near the front door can't seem to shake off a constant influx of mail, newspapers, car keys, discarded toys, and loose change.

Because clutter breeds faster than rabbits, identify the clutter magnets, and build time into each day's schedule to clear them. A daily sort will prevent them from mushrooming into clutter mountains when your back is turned.

▲ **Clean.** Around the house, each area presents different challenges. Kitchens and bathrooms require more cleaning.

▲ **Declutter.** Shared living areas tend to inherit clutter from every family member. Children can help, too.

▲ **Organize.** Storage areas, such as linen closets or shelves, must be organized to make good use of space.

Clutter, like beauty, is in the eye of the beholder. A level of clutter that's cozy to one person will seem sterile and bare to someone with a higher tolerance level. Find your tolerance level with this quiz, and shape solutions that are right for you.

1   There are monthly bills to pay. How do you tackle the job?

A   I shove aside the breakfast dishes, dig out the grocery sack holding the bills, and write the checks —who cares about a few toast crumbs?

B   I turn on the TV, pull up a lap desk, and tear into the envelopes during commercial breaks. Hey, it's good exercise to get up and go hunt for the bills!

C   I stack the bills neatly on the desktop, get out the calculator, and arrange the pens in the pen can before I begin.

2   Time for bed. What's your routine?

A   I remove the cat from the pillow, sweep a few crumpled tissues onto the floor, and plop down amidst the magazines—it's been a long day!

B   I shake out the sheets (it was a busy morning!), plump the pillow, and move a few things to make a spot for my water glass on the bedside table.

C   I turn down the fresh bedding and frown at the wrinkle that developed in the pillowcase during the day. I arrange my water glass, bedtime book, reading glasses, and emergency flashlight neatly on the bedside table.

3   Stand on the front porch or entryway to your home. Based on what you see— decorations, shoes, and clothing—what season is it?

A   Christmas. Actually, it's Christmas two years ago, if you really want to know—but I think it would be wonderful if every day were Christmas. Also, I see a few Halloween decorations in the corner, over there, next to the swim fins from last week's trip to the lake.

B   Gosh, I've been meaning to take down the sign from John's birthday party last month; think I'll do it right now, thanks for reminding me.

C   Aside from the holiday season, I don't believe in decorating the front door. Even then, I think a simple evergreen wreath makes just the right statement, don't you?

4   First thing in the morning, you enjoy reading the newspapers. What does the table look like afterward?

A   Table? What table? I read the papers catch-as-catch-can ... I think the local section is still in the bathroom, and last I saw, the children had the comics in the family room.

B   OK, I admit it: I just toss them in a pile on top of the table and hope the Newspaper Elves come and put them in the recycling bin.

C   I read the newspapers front to back, and when I'm finished with them, I fold them neatly for the next person. Doesn't everyone?

If you answered mostly A, congratulations! You have a high tolerance for daily clutter. You'll get the job done even in disorganized surroundings—but you do admit that life would improve if you didn't spend so much time looking for lost items.

If you answered mostly B, you're a happy medium. You tolerate some clutter in your life, but take active steps to keep the clutter level down. Since you become stressed when life gets too chaotic, focus on building daily routines that bring life back to center.

If you answered mostly C, why are you reading this book? You have a very low tolerance for visual clutter, and know that life runs most smoothly—and you are happiest— when you keep possessions under control and disorder at bay.

Decluttering
the entryway

It's the portal of passage between home and the outer world: the entryway. For the family, it's the place from which they launch themselves each day and hit the road; for guests and visitors, it's the place where they form their first impression of the house or apartment that lies behind that front door.

A clutter-free, organized entryway makes life easier on all fronts—and creates a beautiful entrance to your family's home. Try these tips to organize door areas and entryways:

- **Focus on floors.** In the entryway, the outside meets the inside—and brings plenty of mud and moisture with it. Place entrance mats on both sides of the door to trap tracked-in dirt and rainwater before it hits your clean house.
- **Clear clutter regularly.** Family comings and goings tend to deposit mail, paperwork, newspapers, magazines, library books, broken items, and extra clothing at the door. Schedule regular STOP clutter sessions in the entryway.
- **Climb the walls.** Make the most of wall space for storage. Hang a key rack near the door for easy access. Pegs and hooks hold rain gear, jackets, and summer hats.
- **Use the door.** Hang or attach a shoe organizer on the back of the door. Roomy pockets hold mittens and scarves, sunglasses and suntan oil, pet leashes, and garden gloves and shoes where they're accessible but not in the way.
- **Contain it.** Provide a mix of open and closed storage to house entryway contents: cubbies or shelf units for baskets or dishpans used as family Launch Pads (*see right*). Add a low storage bench for seating when changing shoes or donning galoshes. Label containers to help family members remember to use them.

◀ **Transition zone.** The entryway brings the outside in—along with boots, umbrellas, and overcoats. Plan storage for outerwear and foul weather gear near the front door for an organized home.

Mission Control: family Launch Pads

Just as a spaceship must have a dedicated structure to support liftoff, so family members need a Launch Pad to stabilize them as they blast out the door in the morning. What is a Launch Pad? It's a dedicated space—perhaps on a bookcase shelf—to contain all the "out-the-door" essentials for each person.

"Handbags, car keys, and return videos—or homework and lunchboxes—can all live in personal Launch Pads."

- **First principle: corral, corral, corral.** So you've cleared a shelf on that bookcase? Give each family member a different-colored plastic dishpan for their Launch Pad, and nobody's field trip permission slip will walk to school with the wrong sibling—or disappear behind the shelf.
- **Second principle: make putting away easy.** Child comes home from school, tosses homework and lunch menus in her dishpan. Dad comes home and tosses paycheck, keys, billfold, receipts, and pocket change into his. There things stay, safe and segregated, until they are needed next morning.
- **Third principle: think creatively.** A Launch Pad need not be a space on shelf or table. In one family, each child has a backpack that lives on the back of its owner's dining chair. Lunches, papers, and gym clothes go directly to the packs.

Decluttering
a bathroom

The scene: a master bathroom in any suburban location. It's home to grooming rituals and heir to all sorts of oddments and obsessions. To cut the clutter here can be a journey into the heart of darkness.

Bathrooms are dedicated areas set aside for grooming, health, and hygiene, but have an unacknowledged purpose, too—as a repository for inner hopes, dreams, and insecurities. Follow these tips to loosen the ties that bind you to bathroom clutter:

■ **If you don't use it, lose it.** In any bathroom cabinet, you'll find products that Simply Don't Work. The "rotary hair straightener" built around a power screwdriver—that pulled your hair straight out from the roots. The brush-on nail treatment, guaranteed to grow long, strong nails in just seven days, that peeled like sun-damaged skin. Wonder products are sold on the basis of hope; if there's no hope for those in your cabinet, take their message to the landfill.

■ **If you won't lose it, use it!** Pricey salons know when we're ripe for a sale; tantalized by the lovely new look in the mirror, we can be suckers for expensive cosmetics. Once home, these products migrate to the recesses of the medicine chest, but memories of the high price tag keeps us from decluttering them. Fine—you may keep the luxury shower gel—but on one condition: that you use it.

■ **Knock down the number.** Every bathroom-dweller has a secret grooming product obsession; they buy multiples of their fetish item. When faced with more than three of anything in the bathroom, invoke the Law of Numbers: keep two favorites, declutter the rest.

■ **Time to toss it.** Let cosmetics languish too long, and bacterial growth can pose a danger to health. Call on safety concerns to toss those that are past safe storage intervals.

before decluttering ▲

STOP clutter in the bathroom

In an average bathroom, expect to devote two to three STOP clutter sessions to the task. Start at the bathroom sink area, and then move to nearby cabinets or drawers. Finish with the shower/bathtub area. Assemble your tools: timer, Put Away box, Storage box, Sell/Donate box and a black plastic garbage bag. Set the timer for 15 minutes.

1 Sort
Starting at the bathroom sink, sort items that belong into like piles. Place items that belong elsewhere in the Put Away box, and tuck any items for storage in the Storage box. Surplus items that are still useful go to Sell/Donate.

2 Toss
Toss any trash, broken, or valueless items into the garbage bag. This being a bathroom, you'll find lots of the following: dried strings of dental floss, crumpled tissues, grimy makeup applicators, dried-out bars of soap. Let dust be your guide: any bottle with a dusty coating goes straight to the trash! Ditto for broken items: combs with missing teeth, fraying toothbrushes, the perfume mister that's missing the spray bulb. Out!

3 Organize
Once the sink is cleared, organize the survivors in the cleared space. Shallow baskets, cosmetics organizer trays or bathroom totes bring order to countertops. Then move on to the rest of the room.

4 Put away
When the timer bell rings, stop the session and put away the items in the Put Away box. Store the timer and boxes for the next STOP clutter session. Toss the garbage bag in the trash.

after decluttering ▲

The rules of
bathroom storage

Spartan or spacious, all bathrooms have one thing in common: there's never enough storage space. Plumbing fixtures take center stage, leaving precious little room for lotions and potions. Factor in turf wars between family members competing for the same sink-and-mirror space, and you've got an organizational challenge.

Savings or safety?
Cutting bathroom clutter

For many families, bathroom storage areas are a magpie's nest of scent bottles, sample packets, and throwaway cosmetics—but given the high prices for health and beauty products, it's hard to know when to keep, when to toss perfumes, cosmetics, or grooming products. Keep more than money in mind when cutting bathroom clutter: using outdated or stale products can be harmful to your health. To help cut ties to the cosmetics pile-up, take to heart these issues of health and safety—and get decluttering!

■ **Perfume loses** its potency after 3 years.
■ **Liquids** can support bacterial growth. Liquid and cream foundations are fine to use for between 6 and 12 months, then throw them away.
■ **Using stale eye-makeup** or mascara can cause serious eye infections. Once opened, never keep mascara for longer than 3 months. Liquid eyeliner lasts for about 6 months; powder eyeshadow is usually fine for between 14 months and 2 years.
■ **Wax-based products** such as lipstick and lip balm harden and crumble if kept too long. Throw them away after a year.

Bathrooms, like other activity-intensive rooms such as kitchens, need a refined, systematic plan for storage. It's not enough just to stuff it all in there somewhere. Organize them according to the rules of bathroom storage, to make best use of that scarce domestic real estate.

1 **"A" is for every day.**
Active, accessible, and meant for daily use—that's the definition of "A" storage areas. In a bathroom, the "A" areas get the toothbrush and the hairdryer, the shampoo bottle and the razor.
"A" storage areas should be user-friendly. They should welcome the groping hand with no hidden hazards, even before the poor, blind shower-taker has inserted his or her contact lenses or found his or her glasses. The vanity countertops, the top drawer, a chrome mesh bucket, or hanging organizer in the shower area are all "A" storage areas.

2 **"B" is for occasional.**
Items that are used weekly to monthly should be given homes in the "B" storage areas. The box of nifty, pore-unclogging strips, the collection of hair scrunchies for exercise-class ponytails, nail care equipment, and the battery-operated beard trimmer are all consigned to "B" areas.
"B" areas aren't so easy to reach. You'll stretch or bend to reach the middle drawer, the under-sink spaces, and the toilet-top storage cupboard. "B" also stands for "box;" candidates for "B" storage can often be accommodated in labeled boxes underneath or behind their more popular "A" companions.

3 "C" is for seldom.

Storage areas that are designated "C"s are those that require excessive bending, stretching, or standing on tiptoe—and home to those items that are seldom used. They're where you stash the gold-flecked makeup for fancy nights out, the foot-massage machine, and the upper-lip mustache wax cooker. If you use an item less than once a month but more than twice a year, it belongs in the lowly "C" category, so put it where the sun doesn't shine.

Personal care centers

One creative solution to bathroom gridlock is to create "centers" for personal care items that will make it easier to outsource bathroom storage. Assign each member of the family a different-colored plastic organizer or basket to hold cosmetics and toiletries. Each person's "center" should hold it all—their toothbrush and toothpaste, shampoo and conditioner, shower gel or soap, and any other essential or often-used products—and be stored in that person's bedroom when not in use.

Hang lighted makeup mirrors in bedrooms belonging to teenage girls. Assigning each daughter her own makeup center reduces early-morning squabbling and frees up space in the bathroom. Cosmetics benefit, too, because they stay fresh longer away from heat and steam.

Similarly, set up a health and first aid center in an accessible area away from the bathroom. Storing prescription medicines, over-the-counter remedies, and vitamins elsewhere also protects them against the bathroom's harmful heat and moisture. Consider relocating heating pads, hot water bottles, feminine hygiene products, and the first aid kit in a cool, dry storage location outside the bathroom. Laundry, too, can be outsourced in collection areas outside the bathroom. Dirty laundry can be collected in the laundry activity center (*see pages 140–141*), or in individual hampers in family bedrooms.

▼ **Shower tote.** Sharing bathrooms comes more easily if the room's users don't have to work around one another's gear. Handled plastic baskets make it easy to tote personal-care products.

Bathroom
cleaning challenges

Considering what we put them through each day, sinks, showers, tubs, and toilets deserve special cleaning attention. Thankfully, modern plumbing fixtures are designed to make the job of bathroom cleaning as easy as possible. Keep your bathroom fixtures bright with these cleaning tips.

Sink

From toothpaste dribbles to overspray from hair products, the lowly sink endures a daily barrage of dirt and grime. Keep it sparkling back at you with regular cleaning.

> "Put the job off and deposits harden and ossify, and mildew and mold take up residence in dark corners."

■ **Right for the job.** Use all-purpose bathroom cleaner to remove light soil and film. For more hardened deposits, abrasive or soft-scrub cleaners may be used: they will be easy to rinse from ceramic (vitreous china) surface. Cleaners formulated with bleach will remove toothpaste dribbles and sanitize surfaces, too. Keep bathroom cleaning green by using homemade cleaners (see page 54). They'll make your bathroom sparkle and shine without harsh chemicals—or a harsh price tag.

■ **On the edge.** Clean the rim and fixtures with a disinfecting spray glass cleaner or all-purpose bathroom cleaner. Buff fixtures shiny and dry with a fresh cleaning cloth.

Shower and tub

Soap scum, bath oil, hair products, and body soil combine forces to assault the shining surface of the shower and tub, while tub rims, fixtures, and faucets provide hiding places for moisture,

mold, and mildew. Put the job off and deposits harden and ossify, and mildew and mold take up residence in dark corners. Harness time and cleaning power to make short work of cleaning the shower and tub.

■ **Spray and stand.** Before cleaning the rest of the bathroom, spray the tub area with a generous layer of all-purpose bathroom cleaner, and allow the product to stand while you clean elsewhere. The standing time helps the cleanser to dissolve oils and soap scum, so you'll need less elbow grease to remove it.

■ **Get scrubbing.** Use abrasive scrubbing pads to remove bathtub rings or deposits on shower floors. Tile brushes scrub tile grout and reach into cracks and corners, while the handle protects knuckles from accidental contact with the tub. A cleaning toothbrush does a quick job of removing build-up deposits around tub fixtures or faucet.

■ **Rinse clean.** A detachable showerhead allows you to rinse off cleaner quickly and cleanly. If you don't have one, stock your cleaning tote with a removable rubber showerhead that attaches to the bathtub tap. Commonly used for shampooing hair or bathing pets, they're inexpensive and make it easier to rinse tub and shower walls after you clean.

Fiberglass showers and glass doors

These surfaces need special treatment. Clean them with a non-abrasive cleaner such as an all-purpose bathroom cleaner, pine oil, or baking soda. Avoid abrasive cleansers or scrubbing pads because they may scratch or dull the finish.

Cloudy glass shower doors may be cleaned with full-strength white vinegar or a commercial lime and scale remover. Use good ventilation and protect skin and clothing when using these products.

Toilet

Cleaning the toilet isn't most people's idea of a good time, but where would we be without it? I'll tell you: back in the outhouse. Try these ideas to keep it clean and inviting:

■ **Take your time.** Place granulated or liquid toilet bowl cleaner into the bowl, and let the cleaner go to work. Standing time is necessary to dissolve deposits and kill germs, so don't cut the time short.

■ **Brush up.** A good bowl brush is a must. If yours is flattened or mashed, replace it; you need those bristles bristling to do a good job. Curved bowl brushes reach up-and-under the toilet rim to scour away hidden deposits.

■ **Scrub up.** If the toilet develops a stubborn ring that regular cleaning won't cure, bring on the pumice stone! This natural stone is porous and crumbles. Rub the stone directly on the ring to remove the deposit.

■ **Disinfect.** Use a disinfecting spray cleaner or all-purpose bathroom cleaner to spray toilet rims, seat and lid, tank and bowl exterior. Be sure to check the label for the recommended standing time; antibacterial cleaning products require a certain amount of wet exposure in order to kill germs. Wipe clean and dry with fresh cleaning cloths.

■ **Drips and dribbles.** These are a predictable hazard in a home containing boys—of any age—and can cause odor problems and floor damage if urine is allowed to stand at the base of the toilet. Use disinfecting cleaner and the cleaning toothbrush to rout out stray dribbles—or assign the job to the manly offenders.

▶ **Fresh and frugal.** Bathroom cleaning products need time to soften dried-on soil (*top*). Allow them to stand for a few minutes before scrubbing to avoid over-applying.

▶ **Dump the disposables.** Disposable bathroom cleaning products are costlier than reusable cloths (*bottom*). Take a pass on throwaway cleaners to save money—and the environment.

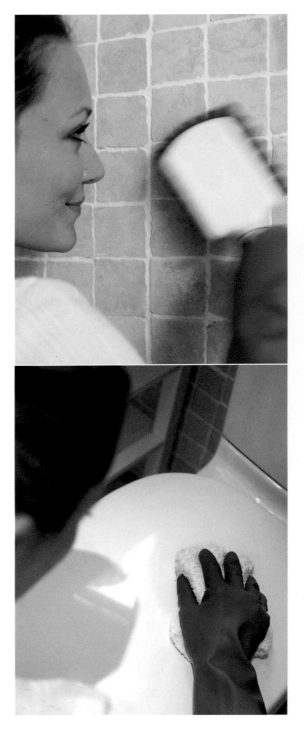

Decluttering the
linen closet

What is the state of your linen closet? Is it crammed with clutter or neat and tidy? While it's tempting to use linen storage areas as a stash-all for homeless items, resist the temptation!

Tossing broken appliances, seasonal decor items, or everyday clutter among the sheets and towels in the linen closet can introduce unwelcome dirt, insects, and odors into the family's linens. An organized linen closet extends the life of expensive bedding and towels. Properly folded and stored, linens are protected and ready for use—and far less likely to be appropriated for misadventures, such as washing the car or wiping down a muddy pet. Most of all, an organized linen closet is a delight for the eye—and for the nose! Honor your family's linens with a proper place to live.

Attention panic clutter

Cluttered linen closets can be found in the tidiest homes. Why? They're the natural place to store panic clutter. "Panic clutter" is born when the doorbell rings unexpectedly. Fearing drop-in guests, family members sweep up out-of-place items and look wildly for a door, any door that will shut them away from view. Enter the linen closet—the storage area most accessible and most amenable to depositing panic clutter.

As a result, expect that STOP clutter sessions in the linen closet will require about twice the normal time for the "put-away" step. You'll also find many more storage items than you would expect. Swept up into the linen closet, lost items find snug hiding spots among the jumbled towels.

Save-your-back tip: set up a portable table or clean another surface nearby when decluttering the linen closet. There will be a good deal of refolding to do, so make the process easier on your lower back with a good work area.

before decluttering ▲

STOP clutter in the linen closet

Pick a cool day—or turn up the air conditioning—to begin linen closet decluttering; it's more pleasant to handle blankets and thick towels when you're fresh and cool. Ready to STOP clutter in the linen closet?

1 **Sort**
Set the timer for 20 minutes, grab your sorting boxes, and turn your attention to a single shelf, area, or drawer. Remove everything from the shelf—sheets, towels, lost toys—and sort into like piles. Linens to be returned to the closet can be placed on the portable table for refolding; out-of-place items are delivered to the appropriate boxes (Put Away, Sell/Donate, Storage).

2 **Toss**
Assess your linens while you toss trash. Ripped sheets, ragged towels, and stained tablecloths deserve an honorable retirement, offering new life if repurposed. Worn pillowcases, a hole snipped for a hanger, serve as dust covers for stored clothing; the household's car washer will prize shredded sheets for polishing chrome bumpers.

3 **Organize**
Once the space is clear, use spray cleaner to remove dust and dirt. Turn to the stacked linens on the temporary table. Refolding is probably a must, but fold smart (*for folding tips, see pages 193, 194–195*).

4 **Put away**
When the shelf is replaced or the timer rings, grab the Put Away box and circle the house, restoring items to their proper home. Tuck away the Storage and Sell/Donate boxes, and toss the trash.

after decluttering ▲

Top tips for
the linen closet

Crisp sheets, fluffy towels, and colorful tablecloths represent gracious living and a happy home—and deserve proper storage to maintain your investment. Whether your household includes a formal linen closet, or you store linens in a cupboard or chest of drawers, these tips will keep household fabrics looking their best.

▲ **Make your bed work.** Tuck an extra set of pillowcases and sheets between the mattress and base of every bed. The weight of the mattress will keep linens smooth, and they'll be close at hand.

1 **Store clean and dry.**
Keep the linen closet fresh and preserve pretty fabrics by storing only clean, dry linens. Even if a tablecloth looks clean, any hidden stains will harden and discolor during storage. Body odors trapped in blankets can cause musty odors, while moisture encourages mildew.

2 **Keep cool, dark, and dry.**
The watchwords for proper linen storage: cool, dark, and dry. In humid areas, packaged de-humidifying granules will help keep the linen closet free from moisture and mildew.

3 **Take turns.**
For best wear, ensure that you rotate linens. Place freshly washed towels at the bottom of the stack, or draw clean sheets from the bottom of the pile to use all your linens in rotation.

4 **Refold.**
If linens aren't in active use, refold them once or twice a year. This will prevent creases becoming fixed and avoid fiber damage along the creases.

5 **Avoid cardboard.**
They may seem a practical storage option, but don't store linens in cardboard boxes. Acids in the

cardboard transfer to the fabric, causing yellowing and damage, while the glue between the layers is attractive to pests—and when they're finished with the cardboard, they'll often start feeding on the fabrics.

6 Store sweet and fresh.
Tuck fabric softener sheets into the linen closet or the linen storage areas—and your bedding and towels will come out smelling sweet and fresh.

7 Make bedding bundles.
If you use sheets in sets, store them that way, in a "bedding bundle." Fold both sheets, and all but one pillowcase. Tuck the folded linens inside the remaining pillowcase and fold the "case" down around the linens into a tidy packet.

8 Use the shelf system.
Sorting through different-sized bed sheets can be an exercise in frustration—just ask any parent who has had to change a sick child's bedding in the middle of the night. If space permits, store sheets on different shelves in the linen closet, or label closet shelves with sheet sizes.

9 Introduce a family color strategy.
Make it easy to get the right sheets on the right beds by designating a color, pattern, or style of sheet for each size of bed: plain white sheets for the infant crib, patterned sheets for children's beds, and solid colors for the parental double bed. That way, you will know at a glance which sheet belongs to which bed.

10 Make bath bundles.
For easy storage and instant access, make bath bundles: sets each containing a bath towel, hand towel, and washcloth. Place the folded hand towel and washcloth in the center of the folded bath towel, and roll the three towels together from the short end. Store the rolled bath bundles on their side in the closet, stacking them as needed.

The word "shambles" must have been invented to describe linen shelves after a late-night rummage for a warmer blanket. Carelessly folded linens invite the risk of an avalanche; they tumble and fall to the floor at the slightest provocation. Keep stored linens easy to find and easy to store with proper folding techniques. Think of it this way: better to fold the linens right just once, than to refold them poorly once each time you visit the shelf for a fresh towel.

■ **Flat sheets.** Fold in half lengthwise, quarter them, and then fold in half again. Depending on the size of the sheet, flip the remaining rectangle into halves or thirds to make a smooth fabric packet.

■ **Pillowcases.** These look prettiest (and sleep best) when you avoid creating sharp center creases as you fold. To fold, grab the pillowcase by the top corners and shake it smooth. Fold in half lengthwise, then in half again. You'll have a long, slender strip of pillowcase; fold gently in half, then in quarters to store.

■ **Hand towels and washcloths.** Folding in quarters makes sense for hand towels and washcloths, as they're used more often—and more quickly—throughout the day. To fold a hand towel, hold the two upper corners of the towel's short side in your hands. Bring your hands together, being sure the right side of the towel is on the outside of the fold. Tuck the folded edge between chin and chest as you grasp the towel halfway down the length. Drop the top half over the bottom. Hang the towel or washcloth, or set aside for the linen closet.

Housework hacks: folding linen

Folding a fitted sheet

Hospital nurses, military recruits, and my 97-year-old grandmother can make a taut bed using only flat sheets, but the rest of us are grateful for the invention of fitted bottom sheets.

1 Fitted sheets are great on the bed, but can be tricky to fold. Here's how. Hold up the sheet, inside-out, and slip your hands inside the top two corners. The wrong side of the fabric should be facing you and the right side should be touching your hands.

2 Carefully lay the sheet down on a large, flat surface—such as a table, or the top of a bed—so it is spread out smoothly . Fold the sheet right side together, slipping the top corners gently inside the two bottom corners. Arrange the corners neatly.

3 Fold the sheet edges to the inside. The flaps of fabric that hug the mattress should be neatly folded down in line with the corners, making a large rectangle with all loose edges tucked in smoothly.

Folding a bath towel

Large towels should be folded in thirds, lengthwise, and hung over a towel rack from the center. This ensures that they will dry more quickly after use.

1 To fold a large bath towel, pick it up so that the front is facing you. Grasping it by the two upper corners, hold the towel up at shoulder height and stretch it out sideways so that it is smooth and flat.

2 Bring one corner toward the other to a point roughly two-thirds of the width of the towel. Hold it there as you fold the second corner of the towel over toward the first, creating three layers.

3 Pinch the folds between your fingers and shake the towel gently to distribute the folds. Tuck the towel between your chin and your chest to pin it down.

"If linens aren't in active use, refold them once or twice a year to avoid fiber damage along the creases."

4 Fold the sheet in half, stacking all four corners on top of one another and encasing the folded sheet sides. The curved edges should be tucked down to create a (more-or-less) smooth rectangle

5 Fold the sheet in half again to create a long, narrow strip. The tighter and smoother the folds, the less likely it is that the sheet will become wrinkled—or balloon to an enormous size in the linen storage area.

6 Fold the strip in half, then (depending on the sheet size) in half or in thirds to make a compact—and wrinkle-free—rectangle. Match the fitted sheet with its flat partner (and any pillowcases), and tuck away neatly in the linen closet or linen storage area.

"For best wear, ensure that you rotate linens. Place freshly washed towels on the bottom of the stack."

4 Grasp the towel midpoint down its length, then lift your chin to allow the top half of the towel to drop down over the bottom half.

5 Lay the towel on a flat surface and fold it again in the middle to form a neat bundle, and store it in the linen closet. If the towel is to be used right way, it doesn't need as many folds; just flip it over a towel rack.

6 Having a different-colored towel for each family member makes it easy for people to find the right fresh towel when needed. Let children pick the color of their towel and they'll happily cooperate.

Sweet dreams in the **organized bedroom**

Marriage counselors and doctors who treat sleep disorders tell us that clean, uncluttered bedrooms make for happy homes and a good night's rest—but you wouldn't know it, judging by the clutter in a typical master bedroom, which for many families becomes a second-level storage area.

The theory seems to be that since the eyes are closed while sleeping, the mind won't notice the disorder. Tumbled laundry spills over fitness equipment, books and crafts projects compete for floor space, a motley gang of dirty dishes sends colonies of water glasses to new settlements under the bed and atop the bureau, and the bedroom television wears a rakish cap of piled mail and unpaid bills.

A chaotic bedroom makes you feel wired and tired. If you want sweet (organized) dreams, it's time to get organized—but be prepared to devote several declutter sessions to rout out chaos in the bedroom.

Get it tidy

Gather your declutter tools—timer, boxes, and garbage bags—for a STOP clutter session in the bedroom. Because so many unauthorized items wander into the bedroom (or are thrust there, unwilling, at the sound of the doorbell), the Put Away box will do extra duty during a bedroom declutter.

■ **Sort.** Set the timer for 20 minutes, and start by tackling the bed area. Drag everything out from beneath it, and behind and inside the nightstand. Sort each item into one of the boxes: Put Away, for items that belong in other rooms; Sell/Donate for no-longer-needed items that are still in good repair; Storage, for items that belong in storage areas. Using the same

◄ **Calm oasis.** A bedroom is the home's most personal space. Time spent there should be devoted to rest and renewal. Clean and decluttered, the bedroom can be an oasis of calm and order.

strategy, move on to dressers and bureaus, and any clutter littering the floor. Work systematically around the space and, little by little, you'll reclaim the bedroom as the sanctuary it's intended to be.

■ **Toss.** As you sort, consign broken items and litter straight to the garbage bag.

■ **Organize.** The smart declutterer notes where the clutter is coming from, and then looks for ways to prevent the build-up in the future. As you declutter, pay attention to the cause of the problem. Scattered piles of dirty clothes signal a need for a laundry basket in a nearby spot. Linty piles of pocket change, subway tickets, and crumpled receipts can be kept under control with a pretty copper bowl or wooden box designated for pocket-emptying at day's end. Stacks of unopened moving boxes, resident along the wall since you moved in, indicate a need for a household storage plan.

■ **Put away.** When the timer bell rings, stop the session. Circle the house with the Put Away box, put Sell/Donate items in the car trunk for delivery to charity. Add Storage items to attic, basement or garage storage areas.

Keep it clean

If the bedroom is to be a calm and peaceful haven, it's not enough for it to be tidy—it must be clean, too. To achieve this, include it in the household cleaning schedule. The primary goal: to reduce and remove dust, dander, and other irritants.

Weekly vacuuming and dusting is a must in the bedroom. Pay particular attention to window treatments; vacuuming drapes and dusting shades will help to keep air quality high. Baseboards, too, need regular attention to keep dust build-up away. If the room contains a television, computer, or entertainment center, use an electrostatic dry cleaning cloth to collect dust weekly, as electronic equipment attracts dust.

Wash windows seasonally, and wipe down sills and window fittings to remove dust and dirt. A lambswool duster picks up any dusty residue on walls and snags cobwebs on ceilings or in corners; when necessary, wash the walls to remove smudges and stains. Seasonal cleaning should also include lampshades and the light-diffusing bowls from overhead fixtures; you'll see clearly and cut the dust with clean lighting. Allergy sufferers may want to add a portable air filtration unit to improve air quality.

Tips for bedroom clutter personalities

Our bedrooms reveal more about us than our taste in bed linens; they offer bedrock evidence of clutter personality type. Expressing personal taste in the bedroom is one thing, but try to rein in clutter personality excess with these tips:

■ **Sentimentalist.** Visiting the sentimentalist's bedroom is like a trip in a time capsule. Too often, the room sports so many cherished symbols of the past that there's no room to move. Childhood teddies nestle next to sports equipment, the walls are papered with posters and portraits tracking earlier enthusiasms, and bureaus sprout a forest of athletic trophies.

If you're a bedroom sentimentalist, learn to celebrate the now! Cut the ties to sentimental clutter by saving a symbol and releasing the surplus. Deforest the bureau of a trophy collection, for example, by choosing the most memorable award. Photograph it, and then write a brief description of the memory it provokes. Tuck photo and journal entry into a scrapbook—then donate the trophy collection to a youth organization for recycling.

■ **Rebel.** The bedroom can be the last refuge of a rebel clutter personality. While he or she may present a self-controlled face in the rest of the house, the riotous bedroom remains, strewn knee-deep in rumpled clothing and half-eaten sandwiches.

If you're a rebel, remind yourself that you're a big kid now! Big kids have better things to do in their bedrooms than relive a childhood power struggle. Give yourself permission to pursue your adult side, and create an atmosphere of relaxation, not rebellion, in this most intimate of all rooms.

Top tips for organizing
the bedroom

Clutter conquered, it's time to get organized in the bedroom and stop clutter from creeping back. The bedroom is our most private and personal home sanctuary. Focus on the room's function—rest, relaxation, and renewal—with these ideas to arrange and organize bedrooms.

1 Light up your life!
Given the bedroom's function as a haven for rest and relaxation, harsh overhead lights have to go. Reading lamps and indirect lighting will enhance comfort and induce a sense of calm.

2 Furnish right.
Arrange furnishings to support the activities you'll conduct. Add a row of hooks next to the treadmill to hold exercise clothing, pulse monitor, and towel. Set up a restful reading spot on the bookworm's side of the bed, with reading lamp, extra pillows, a basket for books and magazines and, on the nightstand, a coaster for his or her mug. Use hanging pegs and desktop organizers to create a cosmetics center on top of a bureau; hang jewelry, scarves, and hair accessories for a neat and pretty touch.

3 Avoid "suite syndrome."
Often, bedroom furniture is purchased as a suite of multiple pieces—and you'll find every blessed one of them crammed into many bedrooms, space notwithstanding. Pare down bedroom furniture and release living space by dispensing with the idea that a furniture suite cannot be separated. The extra tallboy or spare bureau can do good service in the entryway or hall, where it won't cramp your style—or your night's sleep. "Mix and match" works as well in the bedroom as in the closet.

4 Tap under-bed areas.
Commercial organizing products are available to slide neatly in the space beneath the bed, or check the restaurant supply store for sturdy, inexpensive bus trays. Use them to store handbags, out-of-season clothing, bulky sweaters, or gift-wrap.

5 Safety counts!
Be sure the bedroom includes basic safety supplies: a nearby smoke detector, flashlight and batteries, and for upper-storey bedrooms, an escape ladder. Tuck safety supplies beneath the bed to avoid stumbling around in the dark next time there's a power outage. A tip from earthquake country: never retire for the night without placing robe and slippers near the bed.

6 Go for dual-duty.
When selecting bedroom furnishings, look for double-duty solutions that will add storage space to the bedroom. A bed headboard that doubles as a bookcase keeps a bedtime reader's books close at hand. Toss a long cushion over a cedar chest, and you'll create a seating area and storage in one. Add a fabric skirt to a dressing table to conceal a small rolling drawer organizer.

▶ **Hidden storage.** Incorporate organizing products under the bed, beneath upholstered chairs, or supporting a night table to increase storage options in the bedroom.

Mitring a sheet

Taking a tip from woodworkers, who join wood pieces at a 45-degree angle, mitring a sheet bottom keeps it snug and sharp beneath the bed covers.

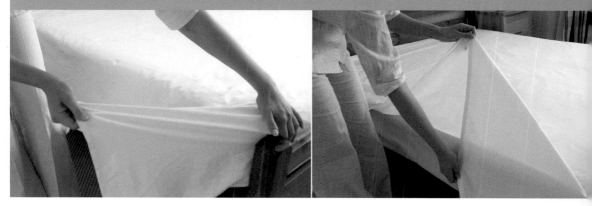

1 Center the flat sheet on the bed, and tuck the bottom of the sheet underneath the mattress. Grab the trailing edge of the sheet, about 2ft (60cm) from the corner of the sheet, to make a 45-degree angle away from the mattress corner and pull toward you.

2 Still holding on to the sheet, pull it up vertically to form a triangle (the sheet should fold at a 45-degree angle).

Putting on a duvet cover

This method of putting on a duvet cover beats crawling inside the cover while attempting to stuff the duvet in—and you won't feel as if you've been in a three-way wrestling match!

1 Try this method for putting on a duvet cover that I learned from a Swiss hotel maid. Standing, grab the top two corners of the duvet cover, fabric right side out, holding one corner in each hand.

2 Holding tightly to the corners, toss the duvet cover up and inside out, allowing it to fall over your arms. The upper corners of the duvet (with your hands inside them) should be visible.

3 Grab the corresponding corners of the duvet through the corners of the cover. Make sure you've got the duvet aligned properly, matching short and long sides.

"Designate a color, pattern, or style of sheet for each bed, and you'll know at a glance which belongs to which."

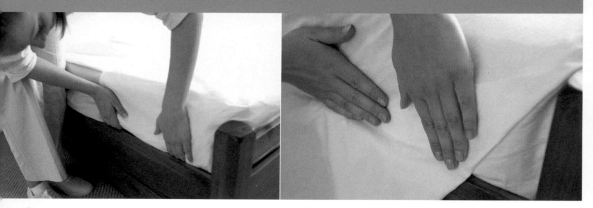

3 Lay the triangle of sheet onto the bed, then tuck the bottom part of the sheet under the mattress. Building in this tucked fabric is the secret to a well-mitred, taut-fitting sheet.

4 Drop the triangle of sheet down toward the floor, then tuck it under the mattress to form a mitred corner. Smooth the hanging sheet bottom underneath the mattress, all the way to head of the bed. Repeat on the other side of the bed.

"Tuck fabric softener sheets into the linen closet—and your bedding will come out smelling sweet and fresh."

4 Hold on tight to the duvet-cover combo, and shake. As you shimmy, the duvet cover will fall right side out, down and over the duvet itself.

5 Flip the newly covered, freshly fluffed duvet up and over the bed, and turn your attention to the cover's bottom. Some covers have sewn-in pockets; if so, tuck the duvet's remaining corners into place.

6 Fasten the bottom of the duvet cover; some makes have snaps, others have buttons or ties. When you've finished fastening, give the duvet a final shake to distribute the down or filling. Bed made!

Reach for sweet, sustainable dreams in the bedroom with these ideas to cut energy use and improve sleep quality:

■ **Warm it up.** Add an electric blanket or down comforter to the bed to replace standard blankets, then lower the thermostat in winter to save on heating costs.

■ **Chill out.** In summer, a bedroom ceiling fan circulates air for comfortable sleep—and lowers the need for air conditioning.

■ **Buy organic.** Sleeping in your bed for eight hours each night can mean maximum exposure to the chemicals and resins found in synthetic materials. When buying sheets or mattresses, go for organic fibers to lower exposure to toxins.

■ **Pick the right paint.** Even when dry, standard paints continue to emit VOCs, or volatile organic compounds. Preserve a clean environment in the bedroom by using low- or no-VOC paint on bedroom walls.

Decluttering a
child's room

"Clean your room!" It's the battle cry of millions of parents. Try these strategies to calm clutter and bring order to children's rooms.

Special challenge

It's a conundrum. Children's rooms are usually small, often shared, and may lack built-in storage. Yet these rooms are host to out-of-season and outgrown clothing, surplus toys, and even household overflow from other rooms. Children can't stay organized when the clothes closet is crammed, the drawers are stuffed, and playthings are strewn across the whole carpet area.

The solution: use the STOP clutter method to sort, store, and simplify children's belongings. Long sessions of "clean your room" are an ordeal for all concerned, but by working for a limited time with a defined method, kids and parents can come to terms with clutter.

Skills for life

For all but the youngest toddlers, resist the urge to wade into the mess alone, garbage bags flying. Instead, look at the decluttering process as a learning activity, and put the focus on the child. In your role as organizational consultant, survey what's working, what's not, what's important to the child, what's causing the problems, and why the child wants to get organized. If they're involved in the effort, children are better able to understand the organizational logic and maintain the new, organized room.

It will take a number of STOP clutter sessions to clear a crowded child's room. Boost your patience with the process by remembering that you're not just clearing out the stuff—you're building skills that will stand the small fry in good stead for life.

Let's play the STOP clutter game

In addition to the usual STOP clutter tools—timer, boxes, and garbage bag—you'll need a good selection of lidded plastic shoeboxes or other stackable containers and a few floor level open containers. Set the timer, and show the child how to play the STOP clutter game.

1 Sort
Start with a small section of the little person's domain: a single shelf, a small area of floor, or one drawer. Grab each object and ask the question: is this something we want to keep, to put away, to give away, or to throw away? Nope, we can't put it down! We've got Magic Clutter Sticky on our hands, and we can't put it down until we make a decision!

2 Organize
STOP clutter for 15 minutes, and then begin to sort the keepers. Here's where the lidded storage containers earn their star billing. Toss small items such as all connecting blocks into one bin, dolly's clothing into another, tiny trucks and cars into a third. Playing "match the toy" is a good identification-and-labeling game for young children, and teaches them organizing skills.

Warning from an Old Mom: there will be resistance to the Give Away and Throw Away options. Try tactics like Choose Three to break through the block: "Yes, you may keep the space hideouts—but only three. Which are the most exciting?"

3 Toss and put away
Finally, when the timer bell rings, toss the trash and return Put Away items to their homes in other rooms. Deliver Sell/Donate and Storage items to their storage locations, and stack and store the newly sorted kids' toys.

before decluttering ▲

after decluttering ▲

Top tips for organizing
children's rooms

Decluttering achieved, it's time to bring order to children's rooms and play areas. The trick is to take a child's eye view. Look at the space, storage, furniture, and possessions from his or her vantage point—and tailor organizing strategies to suit.

1 Think child-friendly.

To organize a child's room, solutions must fit the child. Adult furniture and organizing systems don't translate well to children's needs. Sticky dresser drawers are hard for small hands to manage. Folding closet doors pinch fingers and jump their rails when pushed from the bottom. Closet hanging rods are out of reach, while traditional toy boxes house a jumble of mixed and scattered toy parts.

For younger children, remove closet doors entirely. Lower clothing rods and invest in child-sized hangers —adult versions don't fit children's clothing. Use floor-level open containers to hold toys, and open plastic baskets to store socks and underwear.

▼ **The smaller the child,** the lower you go. Organize children's rooms according to their eye level. For the smallest children, that means floor level. Open bins allow toddlers to play "put away" easily.

2 Hard to get out, easy to put away.

The premier rule for efficient children's storage? Make it easier to put something away than it is to get it out. For example, store picture books as a flip-file, standing upright in a plastic dishpan. The child flips through the books, makes his or her selection, and tosses the book in the front of the dishpan when he or she's done. It sure beats a traditional bookcase, where little fingers can pull down a whole shelf faster than they can replace one book.

3 Organize bottom to top.

Befitting a child's shorter stature, start the organizing process from the bottom of the room, and work to the top. Most-used toys and belongings should live on lower shelves, in lower drawers, or on the floor. Higher levels are designated for less-frequently-used possessions.

4 Label, label, label.

Use a computer printer to make simple graphic labels for young children. Pictures of socks, shirts, dolls, or blocks help remind the child where these items belong. Enhance reading skills for older children by using large-type word labels. Slap labels everywhere: inside and outside of drawers, on shelf edges, on boxes and bookcases and filing cubes. Playing "match the label" can be fun—and turns toy pick-up into a game.

5 Build a maintenance routine.

The usual peaks-and-valleys approach to keeping a room in order can vex and frustrate children. Their room is clean and tidy, they play, and suddenly their room is back to messy normal. Help children stop the cycle by building maintenance routines into the family's day. "Morning Pick-up" straightens the comforter, returns the pillow to the bed, and gets yesterday's clothing to the laundry hamper. Before dressing for bed, "Evening Pick-up" involves putting away the day's toys.

Reduce, reuse, recycle: children's toys

Like children's clothing, toys are outgrown early and often. Shoddy construction and easy-to-lose pieces cause toys to lose play value quickly; inadequate storage options mean toys are easily damaged or scattered. Result: the household boasts a wealth of toys—but nothing fit to play with.

Go green in the playroom with these strategies to reduce, reuse, and recycle children's toys:

■ **Buy good once.** Sure, it's fun to dream about buying out the toy store—and take it from a Nana who knows, nearly impossible to restrain doting grandparents with the same idea—but sustainability starts when shopping. Take a pass on the latest plastic fad items in favor of well-made classic toys. They'll stand the test of time—and the toy box.

■ **Store smart.** Most playthings lack viable storage off the shelf, so provide a proper home for toys and games to protect their play value. Lidded plastic storage containers keep game parts together, garage small cars, and serve as closets for dolls and their clothing.

■ **Seek to share.** Good-quality toys are often outgrown before they're outworn; one family's old toys will be another family's treasure. Share the wealth by shopping yard sales for children's toys; allow children to sell items at a yearly garage sale. Community toy libraries allow children to check out toys, and families to donate unneeded playthings. At year's end, contributing to holiday toy drives helps pare down children's possessions before the Christmas season.

The paper tide begins with a toddler's first crayoned scrawls, and grows to a school age high by primary school: children's artwork. Displaying a child's artistic creations brings bright affirmation to their creative efforts.

Be equally creative when displaying, sharing, and storing art projects. Lightweight, inexpensive laundry lines—designed to take a traveler's drip-dries on the road—offer a great way to display the week's artistic triumphs. Mount these short lengths of laundry cord behind a desk, and use the clips to hang paintings and papers. Alternatively, use clear acrylic frames to display artworks—they make it easy to swap out projects on an ongoing basis.

Share the wealth with others in your child's life. A monthly mailing to Grandma not only celebrates family ties, but also gives her bragging rights at the bingo game or exercise class. Best of all, sharing children's artwork in this way helps introduce them to the delights of correspondence.

Family room
declutter

The family room: it's the center of family life—and in too many homes, the cluster of activities we do there leads to an explosion of clutter.

Divide and conquer

Clutter is like chickenpox: it spreads from person to person with only casual contact. One person's ongoing craft project becomes authorization for the next guy to spread his stuff out, too. How to control family room clutter? With a family STOP clutter session. The communal nature of the room means that any clutter solution will require everyone's cooperation. By agreeing to divide and conquer, a STOP clutter session can attack problem areas simultaneously.

Tips to organize family rooms

Try these tips to make the most of storage space in shared spaces and family rooms:

■ **Contain clutter.** Practice containment policies to keep clutter under control. Store the week's newspapers in a low-sided metal tray; a knitting project in a wicker basket.
■ **Practice "cart and carry."** Establish a policy that, while family members are welcome to do homework, work on crafts, or play with toys in the family room, their supplies must be carted and carried. Plastic laundry baskets, shopping bags, or flat-bottomed dishpans can be used to bring out the playthings—and collect them at the close of the evening, for return to the bedroom.
■ **Sweep it clean!** Take time during the day for a "sweep." During a pause in a television program, announce that it's time for a sweep, and ask all family members to pick up out-of-place items and put them away. Quick! The show will be back on the air in just minutes!

STOP clutter in the family room

Gather your tools: timer, STOP declutter boxes (marked Put Away, Sell/Donate, and Storage), garbage bags for trash. Set the timer for 20 minutes. To make it easier to do a group declutter, double or triple the number of boxes used for Put Away. Limit the STOP clutter session to 20 minutes to shortcut the potential for argument.

1 **Sort**
Start sorting. Assign each family member a small area to clear—a shelf, table, or corner—and a tight timeline to declutter it to make the job specific and short. Key targets: the choked video storage rack, the stacks of old magazines, the scattering of toys all over the carpet. Give the kids a Put Away box for far-flung toys, the family crafter another box to collect his or her paints for return to the craft corner.

2 **Toss**
Disagreement is a potential hazard when diving into a group STOP clutter session. Mom may be perfectly happy to send a stack of old motocross magazines to recycling, but a teenage son objects. Limit potential disagreements by assigning the interested parties—the motocross enthusiast himself—to sort and decide. A second tactic: use black plastic garbage bags to collect trash. If the clutterers across the room can't see the contents, they're less likely to put up a fuss about the discards.

3 **Organize and put away**
When the timer bell rings, toss the trash and return Put Away items to their homes in other rooms. Organize the remaining family-room residents— DVDs, videos, and game equipment—into flat-bottomed open containers for easy access.

Organizing
books and magazines

Every household is rich if it is home to books, but for some of us, there's such a thing as "too rich." When household reading materials have swelled past the point where they can reasonably be termed a library, it's time to prune the literary collection with a STOP clutter session.

STOP clutter in the library

Depending on the number of books you have, expect to devote two to three STOP clutter sessions to the task. Gather your tools: a timer and a STOP clutter box marked Sell/Donate (you may need more than one Sell/Donate box!). Set the timer for 20 minutes. To help focus the STOP clutter decision-making process in the library, ask yourself these questions:

- When was the last time I read this book?
- Will I read it again?
- If a reference book, is it current? If so, have I consulted it in the last year?
- If it's a cookbook, do I use it? Hint: the presence of food stains indicates a keeper.
- Is this a textbook from my old school days?
- Is the book a classic?
- Does the book have intrinsic value—is it a signed copy, first or collectible edition?
- Is the book out-of-print or hard to replace?
- Is this a book I've borrowed and need to return?

The answers to the above will point you to a decision. Books that have never been read don't belong in an active library; release virgin books so that another reader may love them. Similarly, you should pass along any read-it-once titles; there's nothing so stale as reopening a whodunit when you already know who did.

Cookbooks and reference works are the gym rats of any library, and should be kept only if they are exercised regularly.

Similarly, old school textbooks are dead weight on household bookshelves; find a more endearing souvenir of university days to cherish, and free space on the shelves for titles that don't bring the agony of calculus to mind.

> "Cookbooks and reference works are the gym rats of any library, and should be kept only if they are exercised regularly."

Be cautious in your approach to classic works; far too many families spend literal generations dusting old matched sets of "great books" for their imagined cachet. If you read the classics for enjoyment, hold on to them—but dead paper does nothing to promote knowledge or culture if it is simply sitting there as a status symbol. Pass unwanted classics on to a library or school, where the great minds can reach out and touch a rising generation.

Finally, don't focus too closely on value when deciding whether to keep a book. A signed copy of a friend's cookbook is a keeper, but a "first edition" of a widely distributed "Sex Among The Cavemen" bodice-ripper has negligible intrinsic value. Online auction sites are a great way to get a quick valuation of most books and can help you decide whether to keep so-called "valuable" titles.

Organizing a home library

Even pared down, the household library needs to be organized so that you can find the book you want when you need it. Think like a library, and sort your books by collection.

Children's titles belong in the children's room or on a low bookshelf in a family room where they're convenient and accessible for little readers (*see also page 207*). Computer users or work-at-home professionals need their reference works shelved close at hand. Don't make the household's computer geek go too far from the keyboard to find his or her guide to Linux operating systems, and shelve work titles in the home office area. Keep cookbooks on a handy kitchen shelf where everyone knows where to find them.

Just as a library has a reference section, it's best to group dictionaries, encyclopedias, and reference works together. If you house them on shelves in a family area, they'll be easy to consult for questions over homework or arguments over the Scrabble board.

Separate novels and non-fiction titles to make it easier to find a good read on a rainy night. The library shelves novels alphabetically by author, and while that treatment causes those of the decorating persuasion to shudder, you'll get a hearty thumbs-up from the literati among us if you follow this system.

Non-fiction titles work best grouped by subject matter. Sorting books into history, politics, biography, travels, and foreign language sections make it easy to prepare for a vacation trip or check your French spelling.

> "To find the book you want when you need it, think like a library, and sort your books by collection."

Shelving books according to size or color is a dead giveaway of books bought by-the-foot to accessorize a model home, but shelving limitations may require a separate section for oversized books. Stack them on their sides so that they fit more easily on bookshelves.

Right-size reading materials

Pare the library down with these ideas to declutter reading material:

■ **Assess magazine subscriptions.** Issues that are devoured within a day of hitting the mailbox are fine, but cancel subscriptions to periodicals that you don't really read.

■ **Set limits.** When a new catalog arrives, recycle any older offerings from the same firm. Store magazines in magazine holders. When the holder is full, recycle the oldest issue to make room for the newest one. A roomy (but not too roomy) basket provides active storage for current magazines. Place unread issues in the basket; when it's full, weed it of older editions.

■ **Store where useful.** Issues of "Threads" are most usefully housed in the sewing area, while "Popular Mechanics" can be assigned to the car repair area of the garage.

■ **Say no to catalogs.** In the US, register with the Direct Mail Marketing Association's Mail Preference Service to remove your address from mailing lists (for further information, visit http://dmaconsumers.org). In Canada, contact the Canadian Marketing Association at www.the-cma.org. Alternately, call the catalog company directly and ask to be removed from the mailing list.

■ **Borrow, not buy.** Reduce book clutter the old-fashioned way: borrow reading materials from the local library.

■ **Sell online.** Use online sales sites to recoup your investment in hot titles that you've already read—somebody out there will pay a respectable price to read that blockbuster, so sell it after you've read it!

Declutter
crafts and hobbies

Few collections of objects provide as much clutter potential as craft materials and hobby supplies. The quilter's fabric stash reproduces stealthily until closets and containers overflow. For the tole painter, model train builder, or scrapbook maker, supplies multiply like a population of rabbits. Add the tools required by each activity, and even the most organized home is overwhelmed.

Storage solutions

How do you meet the space-gobbling demands of all the materials and supplies, tools and gizmos involved in the family's craft activities and hobbies? The answer is to get creative: check out these pointers to keep the necessities under control and maximize storage in your crafting area.

Wallspace Look up and down the walls to find storage possibilities at the work area. Empty space above and below workstations can be tapped to store most-needed tools and equipment. Wall-mounted organizers keep tools and equipment close at hand. Thread racks, pegboards, and shelves inserted in the desk's kneehole area corral small items and store manuals and idea books for easy reference.

In the clear Clear-view organizers are a crafter's best friends. Their see-through property allows crafters to locate needed items quickly without opening the box. Use mid-sized storage towers with clear drawers to sort and store rubber stamps, embellishments, paints, and adhesives.

Because these larger units roll easily beneath tables or desks, they offer an added bonus: they provide handy access to much-used tools while crafting, then allow you to remove supplies from sight when you have finished with them.

◀ **Recycle craft supplies.** To control clutter in craft areas, recycle scraps for other purposes, rather than storing them away. Leftover fabrics are easy to stitch into totes or gift pouches.

Smaller clear storage containers may be used to house eyelets and brads, beads, and sequins. Because their contents are easily visible, the busy crafter can quickly pinpoint just the right tiny embellishment, tool, or fastener.

Off the peg They're an oldie but a goody: pegboards. Fabric and craft stores use pegboards to organize and display notions. So should you. Construct pegboards on top of 1in (2.5cm) wide spacers, and trim them with molding for a finished, built-in look. Prowl through the hardware store to find specialty hooks to add to the traditional selection of small, straight, and curved hooks.

Use pegboards to store scissors and tools, hang hanks of yarn, or keep quilting supplies in view. Hang instruction sheets from a document clip suspended from a spare hook to keep directions in front of your eyes but out of your way.

A tisket, a tasket Flat-bottomed plastic storage baskets have many uses in the crafts room. Use them to create flip-file pattern storage, in which items are stored upright for easy access. Organized by category, you can find that special blouse pattern in record time.

Covered plastic storage containers stack neatly beneath desks or tables. Load them up with works-in-progress. Pile them in unused corners or on closet floors; they're neat, light, and easy to locate.

Count on closets Make the most of closets to store crafts materials. Using commercial organizers, install shelf units to maximize usable space where clothing once hung.

Short or long, fabric lengths can be hung from clothing rods in the closet. So can rotary cutting mats, if you pinch the mat into a hanger designed for skirts or trousers.

Still more room on the clothing rod? Take some clean plastic grocery bags and slip both handles over the rod. The grocery bags will hold light, bulky items such as batting, pillow forms, or yarn.

Add rolling drawer towers to closets for maximum use of closet space. See-through drawers sort tools and notions. Stackable units let you squeeze out every cubic inch of crafting storage space.

Culling craft supplies

For many of us, love of our craft transmutes into an obsessive tendency to collect the materials it uses. Problem is, after a certain point, the clutter interferes with our ability to pursue our avocation. Consider these questions when deciding whether to declutter crafting supplies:

■ **Is the item high quality?** Is a fabric length a pure, natural fiber—or a stiff, low-quality blend or synthetic? Did that hank of yarn fray when used for plastic canvas? Crafting time is too precious to spend it frustrated with low-quality materials.

■ **Is the item dated?** Craft projects, like fashions, come in waves. One year, needlepoint is the crafter's choice, the next, knitting needles flash from every corner. Give dated craft kits and out-of-fashion materials to a crafter more in tune with retro styling.

■ **Is the skill level appropriate?** You're a beginner at cross-stitch? No matter how beautiful it is, find a new home for the kit marked "Advanced Stitchers Only." Attempting a crafts project outside your skill level can bring a new hobby to a quick end. Pass it along to the neighbor with the flashing needles, and find a simpler project.

■ **Do I love this item?** Last and best test for decluttering craft supplies: the love affair. Yes, when you bought it, every item in the crafts cache tugged at your heart in some way. But as with old lovers, has the magic moved on? Recycle everything that doesn't make your heart pound and your fingers itch to start crafting. Why waste precious time and energy working with something you don't absolutely love?

The rules
of household storage

In most homes, storing and retrieving household items involves a pitched battle. In one corner, we have family members who want only to find holiday decorations or seasonal clothing when they need it. In the opposite corner, crammed cabinets, cluttered basements, and inaccessible attics bursting with bags and boxes.

For most of us, an efficient household storage system seems like an impossible dream. The answer? A household storage plan. Follow this battle plan to conquer storage clutter:

- **Assess**
- **Banish and box**
- **Corral and control**

With a storage plan, you'll find the kids' summer clothes while it is yet summer. You'll save money by using stored goods, instead of buying new (because you are able to find that box of sprinkler-system parts you bought last year). You'll know what you have, where it is, and how to find it.

1 Assess.

Grab a notepad and pen and start with List One: Storage. Walk the house from attic to cellar, and list every potential storage area, large or small. The hard-to-reach top shelves in children's closet, the skinny space beneath the master bed, the attic, the storage shed in the back yard.

Now for the second part of your assessment: Stuff. Make a quick list of the items you need to retain. These will include: out-of-season clothing; seasonal décor; personal documents; keepsakes; tools and hardware; and original packaging for electronic equipment that is still under warranty.

The other half of your "stuff" list is stored clutter that may need to be banished. Good candidates for banishment include ugly knick-knacks, unused small appliances, and building and decorating leftovers. Look over your list and circle Banishment Candidates with a big red pen.

Within the Stuff List there's another category: the "let's negotiate" group. These are stored items that might appear to be worthy of banishment, but which belong to another family member. This tricky category includes: collections of LPs and a grown child's childhood possessions; sentimental overload, such as every school paper ever brought home by each child; and tool-o-holic indulgences—unused tools and sewing and craft supplies.

For "let's negotiate" items, a confab is in order with the interested party. Goal: eliminate, reduce, or accept the necessity of storing each class of item.

2 Banish and box.

This is the working phase of setting up efficient household storage. Shelf-by-shelf, room-by-room, rout out your storage areas. One at a time, pull out currently stored stuff, sort it out, banish the rejects, and box everything that belongs elsewhere. Only then put away the designated stored items. Banished items can be donated to charity, sold in a yard sale, or hauled to the dump.

3 Corral and control.

Now that your storage plan is largely in place, buy, scrounge, or make storage containers necessary to corral what's left. Last step? Take a brief inventory of your completed, corralled storage areas. As with your assessment lists, your Inventory Control list comes from a top-to-bottom walk through your home. This exercise should make you feel good—and provide your family a road map to stored items.

Easy storage guidelines

A storage plan is only the starting point; putting it into effect can seem daunting. Take the process step-by-step, and try these tips to make the changeover easier:

■ **Keep your assessment list in view.** Know exactly what items are assigned to the top-most shelf in your daughter's closet: boxes containing out-of-season clothing. With your plan in the forefront of your mind (and eyes), you won't be tempted to redistribute extra toys or bed linens to that space.

■ **Work one shelf at a time.** Never tear apart way more storage than can be reassembled in a single sorting session. Keep the effort small and sustained, and you'll win the storage battle. Spread your energies too thin and you'll merely muddle the battlefield.

■ **Box it, box it, box it**—unless you banish it. Say you're sorting out the top shelf in a utility room closet. You've decided that party supplies should live there, but right now, the shelf is a jumble of old floral vases, rejected knick-knacks, extra cleaning supplies, and board games. Drag the garbage can, a box marked "Donate" or "Yard Sale," and two or three extra boxes to the utility room. Item by item, pick it up and assign it to a box (or execute the sentence of Banishment). Cleaning supplies go in a box destined for the kitchen. Toss the vases into the "yard sale" box. Hubby insists on keeping his Mom's old china shepherdess, so wrap and place her into a box marked "U" for Ugly and Unwanted. Board games go into another box. Repeat until the shelf is empty.

■ **Shift boxes to their new storage site.** After you've cleared your shelf and wiped it down, deliver the contents of each surviving box to the new site according to your assessment list. Board games go to the family room shelves. Tuck the "U" box inside the attic, where you'll add to it when you clear the next shelf. Yard sale boxes live along a garage wall waiting for spring and your yard sale.

■ **Plan your put-away.** Like STOP clutter sessions, clearing storage is best done in little 20-minute bites. Clear storage into boxes until the timer rings, then spend the remaining time moving boxed items to their proper place. You'll never get caught with a clean shelf and a trashed house if you make put-away part of the process.

■ **Divide or conquer?** Only you can determine whether delegation and family involvement are appropriate as you put your storage plan into place. Struggling with a packrat spouse? It may be best to work alone and spare him the stress of boxing his treasures. Is a clean-freak husband cheering you on? Harness that energy with a family garage clean-out day. Weigh the benefits of family participation against the potential stress or distraction it may bring.

■ **Slow and steady wins the storage race.** Keep at it! When motivation flags, return to the spaces you've cleared and sorted. Admire them. Pat yourself on the back. Take the day off, but return to that hall closet the next day. Remember, your home didn't get into this state overnight, so you can't expect to undo it overnight, either.

■ **Consider outsourcing household storage.** Life changes can bring storage issues in their wake. An empty nest isn't quite so empty when the nestlings leave their childhood possessions behind. A parent's estate can bring a whole new generation of possessions to declutter and store. When sudden storage problems arise, consider outsourcing. Small storage lockers or units can be rented quickly to handle the overflow while you sort out a parent's belongings. To clear adult kid-clutter, next holiday season give the grown children notice that their stuff must be collected before the unit's lease expires.

Do you know where your tax records are? Chances are, they're swimming in a stack of paper … somewhere.

Rafts of paper flood into the average home each day. The mailbox discharges letters and bills and bank statements. Briefcases explode with professional journals, pay stubs, and calendars. School backpacks unload the children's artwork, meeting notices, and sports schedules.

Paper clutter costs money and time, and causes stress. A missing permission slip derails the entire family on the way out the door. Hide-and-seek bills lead to late payment fees. Lose the team roster, and it's back to the telephone directory each time you need to contact the soccer car pool.

Without a plan for paper management, a household can drown in a rising tide of paper. In this section, we'll establish a center for household paper handling, cut paper clutter, learn the 1–2–3s of household files, and create a home inventory.

Information Central:
create a center for paper

No business would ask a secretary or a bookkeeper to handle paperwork tasks without an appropriate workspace. Just as in an office, every home needs a center for paper handling: Information Central, a designated location for mail handling, paying bills, clipping coupons, filing chores, business, and social correspondence.

Information Central's focus is all aspects of your household paper handling: bills to budgets, grocery lists to tax preparation. The specified location of Information Central will vary according to your family's needs, but all home information centers need to have access to:

- Telephone
- Household Notebook (*see pages 84–7*)
- Address book
- Calendar
- Calculator
- Rolling file cart or file drawers
- Action file or in-and-out tray

A designated desk is ideal; it provides appropriate workspace and storage for the jobs handled at Information Central. If the family owns a computer, add it to the center or locate it in a nearby spot. A document shredder is a smart addition. Use it to shred bank records, junk mail, and credit card applications to help protect against financial loss and identity theft.

In tight quarters, one end of a kitchen table can serve as Information Central, with supplies stored in a nearby drawer and paperwork kept in a rolling file cart beneath the table.

> ## "Just as in an office, every home needs a center for paper handling."

Finally, Information Central requires these tools and supplies for quick and easy paper handling:

- Supply of extra file folders
- Extra hanging files
- Stapler
- Cellophane tape
- Paper clips
- Sticky notes
- Pens
- Highlighters
- Stationery or letterhead
- Greeting cards
- Stamps
- Mailing supplies
- Scissors

Use Information Central to handle all your paperwork at home. Clip and file coupons. Balance the checkbook. Pay the bills. File your tax information and insurance forms. Answer your correspondence and send greeting cards. Mail a letter. Information Central is the one-stop location to tackle paper chores, filing, and financial tasks.

Finally, make it comfortable. A supportive chair and good lighting make Information Central a pleasant place to work.

▶ **Bright ideas.** Colorful storage options for paper and desk supplies brighten any office area. Who says office supplies have to be dull? Fill your office space with color and style.

Save time, save money:
tips for paper handling

Paying the bills, filing tax returns, and dealing with correspondence all take time—and time is money! Digging documents you need out from stacks, piles, and paper sacks stowed deep within closets slows the pace of household paper handling. Try these tips to speed and organize paper chores. Get the job done fast!

1 Do it now.
Throughout the day, paper-handling chores pop up regularly. If the job can be completed in two minutes or less, you should do it now! Clip coupons from Sunday's newspaper, dash off a thank-you note to a friend, or file a receipt for tax purposes as soon as the newspaper, gift, or receipt comes into your hands. Since it takes at least two minutes to retrieve postponed items, doing short jobs on the fly makes sense—and it saves you time.

2 Put paperwork in its place.
Information Central features an in-and-out tray or action file, so use it! Whenever paperwork comes to hand—whether it's upon returning from work or when you're bringing in the mail—put the paperwork in its place. This way, you'll always know exactly where to find the bills when it's time to pay them.

3 Toss the trash.
Dispose of any unneeded paper immediately. Ditch junk mail and unwanted catalogs as you sort through the day's mail, toss supermarket flyers and unneeded receipts as you remove them from a handbag, and get rid of extra memos as you empty a briefcase. The sooner stray paper hits the bottom of the trash can, the better. Remember to shred any mail that is information sensitive, such as unsolicited credit card applications with your name and address ready printed.

4 Tag it.
Sticky notes light the way when paper-related issues can't be resolved right away. If a catalog company sends a broken item, use a sticky note to track phone calls to the company and other actions taken to resolve the matter. The sticky note reminds you of the current status as you work out the problem.

5 File it fast, file it right.
A "To File" folder is an invitation to chaos; week-by-week, its contents swell out of all proportion, leading to a long, weary session of catch-up filing. Stay on top of filing chores and file receipts, paycheck stubs, insurance paperwork, and tax records the first time you handle them. The extra second won't be noticed at that end, and will prevent filing gridlock.

6 Stay stocked up on mailing supplies.
New technology makes it easier to keep the household supplied with stamps—because nothing is more frustrating that having to end a bill-paying session with an unplanned trip to the post office. Investigate stamps-by-mail service from the United States Postal Service or Canada Post. The United States Postal Service, for example, will deliver stamps and mailing supplies to your mailbox, and online mailing options now include buying and printing postage labels from your home computer, and scheduled pick-up for packages and parcels.

7 **Schedule paper-handling chores regularly.**
Schedule banking, bill paying, and tax chores to keep them from overwhelming you—or costing money in the form of late payment charges. Set aside a weekend day early in the year to assemble tax information and prepare tax forms. Waiting until the last minute costs money, time, and stress.

8 **Create a Chuck-it Bucket.**
A quick and dirty way to help with filing paperwork is to create a Chuck-it Bucket. Designate a single cardboard box for records to receive any paper that you know should be thrown out, but which gives your hoarding anxiety meter a good shove. Dump all of the above into the Chuck-it Bucket as you file. Six weeks from now, dump the contents of the box into the trash bin. No looking, no sorting, no peeking. If you haven't needed that catalog in a month or so, you'll never need it again—so toss the whole mess out.

9 **Buy an electronic labeler.**
For a quick way to label files, invest in an electronic labeler. These small keyboard-driven machines print neat, perfect labels one at a time, and they're a boon to anyone who wants to have easy-to-find files. Make a mistake on a file label? Easy—just print a new one. Need to re-label a file? It's as simple as type, print, and stick.

10 **Make friends with your files.**
Filing is the bedraggled stepchild of home office chores—yet doing it promptly pays off a hundred-fold when it comes time to find Duff's vet records or a receipt for a returned gift. Bulging "To File" folders are the enemies of an organized home office, so complete each session of paper chores with a brief filing session. Tuck receipts, pay stubs, utility bills, and credit card statements into their respective file folders. Filing "to the back," placing each new paper behind previous ones, makes it easy to drop new items into their proper place.

Lean and green:
the paperless home

Household papers: you can stack them, sort them, and store them, but why not do without them entirely? Electronic options abound for paper-free bill-paying and record-keeping, while "going paperless" saves time, money, and storage space. Try these ideas to encourage paper-free information handling in your organized home:

■ **Bank on your bank.** Today's bank portals and apps offer a full range of safe, sophisticated money-management tools. Using smartphone apps and online tools, families can download statements, transfer funds, pay bills, and reconcile accounts—without touching pencil to paper. Contact your bank to learn about paperless options for household financial transactions.

■ **Do it online, not in line.** Check websites for credit cards, utilities, and local governments: chances are, you can handle most day-to-day transactions and bill paying online. Signing up for e-mail billing cuts the daily mail volume and provides a built-in reminder service. Renewing car plates/tags or driver's licenses over the Internet means no more time in line at the motor vehicle office!

■ **Yes, you scan!** Scanners and smartphones can turn a bulging pile of papers into streamlined digital content. Scan must-keep information into the computer for safekeeping, then shred or recycle the unwanted paper.

■ **Become a whiteboard whiz.** Sticky notes, scribbled reminders, and to-do lists are a refrigerator fixture in many households. Replace the scraps and scrawls with a family whiteboard. Track the calendar, assign chores, keep a shopping list—and share love notes—using erasable markers. No more paper clutter!